Edexcel Chinese for AS

Acknowledgements

The authors would like to thank the following people: So-Shan Au, our editor at Hodder Education, for her unwavering encouragement and practical guidance throughout; Pauline Lam, the copyeditor, for her patience and flexibility; Chris Tate for support, insight, and technical jiggery-pokery with text analysis and the glossaries.

Chapter 1 written by Linying Liu
Chapter 2 written by Linying Liu
Chapter 3 written by Xiuping Li
Chapter 4 written by Lisa Wang
Revision 1 written by Michelle Tate
Chapter 5 written by Nancy Yang
Chapter 6 written by Xiaoming Zhu
Chapter 7 written by Jiahua Liu
Chapter 8 written by Rebekah X. Zhao
Revision 2 written by Michelle Tate
Grammar Reference, Glossary and Character Look-up Dictionary written by Michelle Tate

The Publishers would like to thank the following for permission to reproduce copyright material:

Photo credits

p. 1 © Bob Krist/Corbis; **p. 3** © Chen Xiaogen/Xinhua Press/Corbis; **p. 8** © Yang Liu/Corbis; **p. 13** © So-Shan Au; **p. 14** © So-Shan Au, with thanks to Wai-Hong Au for his teapot collection; **p. 17** © Yadid Levy/Alamy; **p. 18** © Kelly-Mooney Photography/Corbis; **p. 20** © Lisa Wang; **p. 23** © Ian Dagnall/Alamy; **p. 28** © So-Shan Au; **p. 29** © Jiahua Liu; **p. 32** © Lisa Wang; **p. 34** © Henry Westheim Photography/Alamy; **p. 36** © Xiuping Li; **p. 41** © Jiahua Liu; **p. 44** © Professor Huang Guoying; **p. 46** © Michael S. Yamashita/Corbis; **p. 48** © So-Ha Au; **p. 50** (*top*) © Xu Yunhua/Xinhua Press/Corbis, (*bottom*) © Bruno Morandi/Robert Harding World Imagery/Corbis; **p. 53** © View Stock/China/Alamy; **p. 54** © So-Shan Au; **p. 57** © Beaconstox/Alamy; **p. 65** © Sean Yong /Reuters/Corbis; **p. 66** from *International Cuisine: China* by Christine Yau, Norman Fun and Deh-Ta Hsiung, published by Hodder and Stoughton 2004, photography by James Newell; **p. 68** © Peter Widmann/Alamy; **p. 70** © Adrian Bradshaw/epa/Corbis; **p. 77** © So-Shan Au; **p. 79** © McPHoto/WoodyStock/Alamy; **p. 81** © Bruce Connolly/Corbis; **p. 85** © Dave Oh; **p. 86** © Jiahua Liu; **p. 89** (*top left*) © Reuters/Corbis (*top right*) © PeerPoint/Alamy (*bottom*) © Richard Chung/Reuters/Corbis **p. 93** © Volker Dornberger/epa/Corbis; **p. 103** © Bobby Yip/Reuters/Corbis.

advancing learning, changing lives

Edexcel Chinese for AS

Student's Book

Series Editor: Michelle Tate

Xiuping Li

Jiahua Liu

Linying Liu

Michelle Tate

Lisa Wang

Nancy Yang

Rebekah X. Zhao

Xiaoming Zhu

HODDER
EDUCATION
PART OF HACHETTE LIVRE UK

Every effort has been made to trace all copyright holders, but if any have been inadvertently overlooked the Publishers will be pleased to make the necessary arrangements at the first opportunity.

Although every effort has been made to ensure that website addresses are correct at time of going to press, Hodder Education cannot be held responsible for the content of any website mentioned in this book. It is sometimes possible to find a relocated web page by typing in the address of the home page for a website in the URL window of your browser.

Hatchette's policy is to use papers that are natural, renewable and recyclable products and made from wood grown in sustainable forests. The logging and manufacturing processes are expected to conform to the environmental regulations of the country of origin.

Orders: please contact Bookpoint Ltd, 130 Milton Park, Abingdon, Oxon OX14 4SB. Telephone: (44) 01235 827720. Fax: (44) 01235 400454. Lines are open 9.00–5.00, Monday to Saturday, with a 24-hour message-answering service. Visit our website at www.hoddereducation.co.uk.

© Xiuping Li, Jiahua Liu, Linying Liu, Michelle Tate, Lisa Wang, Nancy Yang, Rebekah X. Zhao and Xiaoming Zhu 2008

First published in 2008 by Hodder Education,
part of Hachette Livre UK,
338 Euston Road,
London NW1 3BH

Impression number	5	4	3	2	1
Year	2012	2011	2010	2009	2008

Cover photo © Redlink/Corbis
Illustrations by Hart McLeod, www.hartmcleod.co.uk
Typeset in Minion, DFPHei, Song, Kai and Yuan by WorldAccent, www.worldaccent.com
Printed in Great Britain by Martins The Printers, Berwick-upon-Tweed

A catalogue record for this title is available from the British Library

ISBN: 978 0340 96784 3

目录

About the authors

Series Editor: Michelle Tate

Xiuping Li, Jiahua Liu, Linying Liu, Michelle Tate, Lisa Wang, Nancy Yang, Rebekah X. Zhao and **Xiaoming Zhu** are practising secondary school and higher level Mandarin Chinese teachers and are active in developing and promoting the Chinese language and culture in UK schools.

Xiuping Li, Monkseaton Community High School, Gosforth Community Education College and School of Modern Languages at Newcastle University.

Jiahua Liu, Sir John Deane's College and The Grange School.

Linying Liu, Head of Chinese, Kingsford Community School, SSAT Confucius Classroom and Chinese Network Coordinator for SSAT.

Michelle Tate, Head of Oriental Languages, Katharine Lady Berkeley's School, SSAT Confucius Classroom and Chinese Network Coordinator for SSAT.

Lisa Wang, Head of Chinese, Calday Grange Grammar School, SSAT Confucius Classroom and Chinese Network Coordinator for SSAT.

Nancy Yang, Withington Girls' School, Excel College, Confucius Institute at Manchester University and Asset Languages.

Rebekah X. Zhao, Ampleforth College.

Xiaoming Zhu, Djanogly City Academy, SSAT Confucius Classroom and Chinese Network Coordinator for SSAT.

引言

Edexcel Chinese for AS is the first part of an exciting two-part course designed to help you master the skills you will need for success in the latest Edexcel GCE A Level specification in Chinese.

Edexcel Chinese for AS provides a smooth transition from GCSE to AS level and *Edexcel Chinese for A2* completes the course through to A2 level, following the new three-unit exam specification.

This book is organised into eight chapters. Each chapter explores an aspect of the Edexcel topics, ensuring that you cover all the specification topics. Exam-style practice questions and activities give practice in the assessment areas of speaking, listening, reading and writing. Authentic text types and interesting topic areas will inspire and motivate you to engage with the language.

Features of the book

The four language skills

You will see the following symbols throughout the book to indicate the key language skill that you will be practising:

 speaking task   reading task

 listening task   writing task

Edexcel topics

Edexcel topics are indicated in the grey Chinese seals that appear on each chapter opening, giving you a clear indication of which Edexcel topic the chapter is relevant to. Two chapters are assigned to each topic to ensure that you cover a variety of themes and concepts, thus expanding your knowledge of Chinese culture and society.

Edexcel topics	in Chinese
Food, diet and health	食物、饮食和健康
Transport, travel and tourism	运输、旅行和旅游业
Education and employment	教育和就业
Leisure, youth interests and Chinese festivals	休闲、青年兴趣和中国节日

生词

New vocabulary is identified in the 生词 boxes accompanying each text and recording. By highlighting new vocabulary in context with the texts and recordings, your learning is supported, and it should mean less frustrating time thumbing through the dictionary for every other word new to you. You may want to make a habit of putting together a set of flashcards to go with each chapter as you work your way through the book. These will then be a useful revision resource for you at a later date, especially if you keep flashcards by topic. You could even colour-code the cards for easy reference.

复习

Two revision sections are provided to give you the opportunity to reflect on your learning, to practise the new vocabulary you have learned and to use some of the grammar structures which appear in the book. One of these revision sections appears half way through the book, offering a variety of exercises which focus on vocabulary and structures introduced in the first four chapters. The other revision section appears after Chapter 8 and acts as a summary of everything covered in the book. The exercises are designed to challenge you! They test your eye for slight differences between characters, for preciseness in manipulating characters and grammar, as well as developing translation skills both from and into Chinese.

Edexcel GCE in Chinese – The new three-unit specification

The Edexcel GCE Chinese specification has been redesigned in a new three-unit format, offering discrete testing of all four language skills – listening, speaking, reading and writing – at AS level.

At Advanced level, advanced research into the society and culture of Chinese speaking countries or communities is promoted and rewarded.

This course, *Edexcel Chinese for A Level*, follows the same format. *Edexcel Chinese for AS* covers Unit 1: Spoken Expression and Response in Chinese and Unit 2: Understanding and Written Response in Chinese, and *Edexcel Chinese for A2* completes the course with Unit 3: Understanding, Written Response and Research in Chinese.

Unit 1: Spoken Expression and Response in Chinese (AS)

You will be required to demonstrate your ability to speak Chinese for 5–6 minutes in response to a short English-language stimulus. You will be expected to refer to a series of questions printed on the stimulus so that you can communicate effectively in Chinese about the stimulus topic.

 Spoken expression and response

In this book, you are given two specific opportunities in each chapter to practise your speaking. Each chapter starts with a topic specific quiz. You are encouraged to think about the topic in depth, brainstorm and show the extent of your knowledge about the topic. It is an opportunity for sharing knowledge and to participate in lively discussions about what you already knew, what you learned and what surprised you.

The second speaking activity has been written to reflect the format and style of the new Edexcel AS exam. An English language stimulus, often accompanied by a visual stimulus, with bulleted discussion questions are offered so that you can prepare for and practice for the exam.

Unit 2: Understanding and Written Response in Chinese (AS)

You will be rewarded for your understanding of spoken and written Chinese, for your ability to transfer meaning from Chinese into English and for producing continuous writing in Chinese.

In this book, you are given the opportunity to acquire and develop the Chinese language with authentic text types and interesting topic areas which will inspire and motivate you to engage with the language. Exam-style practice questions and activities ensure exam success.

 Section A

In this book, you are given three specific opportunities in each chapter to practise your listening. You will be listening to a variety of text types, including: conversations, radio shows, announcements etc.

 Section B

A variety of text types have been used including newspaper and magazine articles, online articles, brochures, letters and emails.

 Section C

By the time you reach the writing sections of each chapter, you will have come across lots of new vocabulary which will be relevant to the chapter's topic, and specifically for the writing tasks. You are given the opportunity to produce written material that mirrors the text types that have appeared in the book so that you are able to see it in context and use the texts as models for your own writing. A variety of text types have been used including essays, articles, informal letters and emails, formal letters, diary entries and blogs, debates and argumentative essays.

Unit 3: Understanding and Written Response in Chinese (A2)

You will be rewarded for your ability to understand and respond in writing to written Chinese. This unit enables you to demonstrate your ability to produce extended writing in Chinese. It also promotes knowledge and understanding of Chinese culture and/or society through focused research.

Unit 3 is covered in the A2 component of the course, *Edexcel Chinese for A2.*

Student's Book 978 0340 96783 6

学习努力！祝你成功！

第一章 饮食与健康

中国餐桌礼仪

练习A 🗨 餐桌礼仪会因文化不同而有很大差异。你对中国的餐桌礼仪了解多少？

请阅读下面六个问题，选出你认为最佳的答案，然后进行双人或小组讨论。

一 吃饭时，你的筷子应该怎样放？

　　a) 竖插在饭碗里

　　b) 放在菜盘子上

　　c) 放在饭碗旁

二 倒茶时，应该先给谁倒？

　　a) 先给孩子倒，再给大人倒

　　b) 先给自己倒，再给别人倒

　　c) 先给年纪大的人或重要的客人倒

三 你和一位中国朋友在餐馆吃饭，你发现每次别人给你的朋友倒茶时，他都会用手指轻轻敲打桌子，你知道这是为什么吗？

　　a) 他是在表示："请再多倒点儿。"

　　b) 他是在表示谢意

　　c) 他是在说："不用了。"

四 你请中国朋友吃饭，事先说好由你付帐，但饭后你的朋友仍表示要付帐单，你应该

　　a) 让你的朋友付，既然他想付

　　b) 坚持由你来付账，因为你的朋友只是出于礼貌才表示要付账的

　　c) 感到生气，因为你的朋友很虚伪

五 在中国人家里做客吃饭时，你最好

　　a) 把你碗里的饭吃得干干净净

　　b) 碗里留一点儿饭，表示你已经吃饱了

　　c) 碗里留很多饭，表示你不饿

六 在餐馆吃饭时，你的中国朋友把茶壶盖子打开放在一边，这表示

　　a) 茶水太热了

　　b) 他想让服务员把茶壶拿走

　　c) 他想让服务员添茶水

生词

cān zhuō lǐ yí 餐桌礼仪 *table manners*	zhòng yào 重要 *important*
chā yì 差异 *difference*	fā xiàn 发现 *to discover*
liǎo jiě 了解 *to understand; to know*	qīng qīng 轻轻 *lightly; gently*
kuài zi 筷子 *chopsticks*	qiāo 敲 *to tap; to knock*
shù 竖 *vertical*	biǎo shì 表示 *to show; to express*
chā 插 *to stick into*	shì xiān 事先 *beforehand*
pán zi 盘子 *dish*	fù zhàng 付帐 *to pay the bill*
dào 倒 *to pour*	réng 仍 *still*

生词			
continued from page 1	xū wěi 虚伪 hypocritical	liú 留 to remain; to leave	dǎ kāi 打开 to open
jì rán 既然 since	zuò kè 做客 be a guest	chī bǎo 吃饱 full	fú wù yuán 服务员 waiter; waitress
jiān chí 坚持 to insist	gān gān jìng jìng 干干净净 cleanly; without leaving anything behind	chá hú 茶壶 teapot	tiān 添 to add
lǐ mào 礼貌 good manners		gài zi 盖子 lid	

Chinese New Year food

练习B 请阅读下面关于中国新年食物的文章。

生词	
qìng zhù 庆祝 celebration	jí xiáng 吉祥 auspicious
xiàngzhēng yì yì 象征意义 symbolic meaning	hǎo yùn 好运 good luck/ fortune
jiǎo zi 饺子 dumpling	

Chinese New Year is one of the most important festivals for Chinese people and food plays a crucial part in the celebrations.

Although the menu varies from region to region, most of the dishes served during the New Year feast have one thing in common; they all have the symbolic meaning of bringing fortune for the coming year.

Fish plays an important role in the New Year celebrations. The Chinese character for fish, 'yu', sounds like the character for abundance. So, on New Year's Eve, fish is served at the end of the evening meal, symbolizing a wish for abundance in the coming year.

In southern China, people eat a cake called 'niangao', which is made from glutinous rice flour. In Chinese the words sound like 'get higher/ better each year'.

In northern China, where rice was not easily accessible in the olden days, people usually eat dumplings made from wheat flour pastry, with meat and vegetable stuffing. The dumplings are shaped like shoe-shaped gold ingots from ancient China, symbolizing fortune in the New Year.

There are many other kinds of traditional food enjoyed during the Chinese New Year, each expressing an auspicious wish for good fortune.

词组 / 表达法

上 面 这 篇 文 章 是 关 于 …
The above article is about …

tā men chī   yīn wei tā xiàngzhēng
他 们 吃 … 因 为 它 象 征 …
They eat … because it symbolizes …

gǔ lǎo ròu
古 老 肉
sweet and sour pork

dàn chǎo fàn
蛋 炒 饭
egg fried rice

chǎo miàn
炒 面
fried noodles

chūn juǎn
春 卷
spring roll

wèi dào hǎo jí le
味 道 好 极 了
It's delicious!

hěn jiàn kāng
很 健 康
It's very healthy.

kǎo ròu
烤 肉
roast meat

zhá yú hé zhá tǔ dòu tiáo
炸 鱼 和 炸 土 豆 条
fish and chips

Please respond in Chinese to the bullet points below. You are *not* expected to refer to the full content of the above.

- State what the article is referring to (a full summary is *not* required).

- Explain why Chinese people choose to eat certain kinds of food during the New Year celebrations.

- Have you ever had any Chinese food? When and where? What do you think about it?

- Think of a festival you celebrate. What kind of food do you eat at the festival? Does any of the food have a symbolic meaning?

- Talk about one of your favourite foods.

西红柿炒鸡蛋

请阅读下面一篇介绍一道中国家常菜的文章和菜谱，然后用英文回答问题。

西红柿和鸡蛋

西红柿和鸡蛋，这种在有些人眼里看似奇怪的搭配，却可以做出一道许多中国人喜爱的家常美味——西红柿炒鸡蛋。

西红柿炒鸡蛋有多种吃法，比如拌上面条，就成了香喷喷的西红柿鸡蛋面。记得小时候，每当妈妈做了西红柿鸡蛋面，全家人就会胃口大开，就连平时不爱吃面的我，也会一连吃掉两大碗！

除了拌面，拿西红柿炒鸡蛋来下米饭，也是既营养又好吃的。

下面我们就来学习一下怎样做这道菜。

西红柿炒鸡蛋（二人份）

材料：

西红柿三个
鸡蛋两个
葱一根
蒜两瓣
盐
油
酱油少许

准备：

一　西红柿去皮，切成小块；
二　鸡蛋打匀，加少许盐；
三　葱切成小段；
四　蒜切碎。

做法：

一　锅中放一汤勺油加热；
二　倒入鸡蛋炒至金黄，盛出；
三　锅中放一茶勺油加热；
四　倒入葱、蒜、西红柿翻炒，加几滴酱油，
　　倒入鸡蛋一起炒一分钟，营养美味的
　　西红柿炒鸡蛋就做好了。

生词

xī hóng shì **西红柿** tomato	dā pèi **搭配** combination; to arrange in pairs or groups	měi dāng **每当** whenever	yíng yǎng **营养** nutritious	yán **盐** salt	qiē suì **切碎** to crush
chǎo **炒** to stir-fry	měi wèi **美味** delicious food; delicacy	wèi kǒu dà kāi **胃口大开** to have a good appetite	cái liào **材料** ingredient	yóu **油** oil	bù zhòu **步骤** procedure; step
jiā cháng **家常** homely	chī fǎ **吃法** way of eating	jiù lián **就连** even	cōng **葱** spring onion	jiàng yóu **酱油** soy sauce	guō **锅** pan; wok
cài **菜** dish	bàn shang **拌上** to mix with	píng shí **平时** normally	gēn **根** unit for long thin objects such as spring onions	zhǔn bèi **准备** preparation	chéng chū **盛出** to dish out food
cài pǔ **菜谱** recipe	xiāng pēn pēn **香喷喷** savoury; appetising	yī lián **一连** in a row	suàn **蒜** garlic	qù pí **去皮** to remove the skin	fān chǎo **翻炒** to mix and stir-fry
kàn sì qí guài **看似奇怪** to appear strange	jì de **记得** to remember	chī diào **吃掉** to eat up; to devour	bàn **瓣** clove of	yún **匀** evenly	dī **滴** a drop of
				qiē chéng **切成** to cut into …	

练习A 📖 **Answer the following questions in English.**

一 According to the author, what might some people's first impression be of a recipe for tomato with egg?

二 What does the author think about this dish? Identify the sentence in the text to support your answer.

三 What childhood memory does this dish remind the author of?

四 What can this dish be served with?

五 How many people does this recipe serve?

六 Which ingredients listed below are not ingredients for the recipe? Circle the correct letter.

a) Soy sauce, egg, garlic

b) Egg, garlic, tomato

c) Tomato, onion, noodles

d) Spring onion, egg, garlic

七 Put the following into the right order according to the recipe. Write 1–5.

☐ Stir-fry the tomato with spring onion and garlic.

☐ Add some soy sauce.

☐ Stir-fry the egg.

☐ Mix the tomato with the fried egg.

☐ Add some salt to the egg.

中国菜

请阅读下面关于中国菜的文章，然后用英文回答问题。

中国菜在世界上，和法国菜、意大利菜一样有名，深受各国人民喜爱。中国菜不但花样多，而且色、香、味、形俱佳。

由于中国很大，各地的物产、气候和生活习惯不同，人们的口味也各不相同。南方人爱吃清淡的食物、北方人口味重、四川人喜欢吃辣、山西人喜欢吃酸……因此，中国就形成了各具地方特色的菜系。其中山东、四川、江苏、广东、浙江、福建、湖南、安徽等地的菜最具代表性，统称为中国的"八大菜系"。下面我们来简单介绍一下这"八大菜系"的主要特点：

山东近海，所以山东菜中海鲜类较多，而且山东菜喜用葱；

四川菜的特点是麻、辣、酸；

江苏菜咸甜适中，吃起来很可口；

广东菜的最大特点是用料广泛，口味清爽不油腻。广东的点心深受各国人民的喜爱；

浙江菜的特点是鲜嫩软滑，清爽不油腻；

福建菜的特点是以海鲜为主要材料，色美味鲜；

湖南菜喜用辣椒。酸辣、鲜香是湖南菜的特点；

安徽菜的特点是保持原汁原味。

有人也许会问：北京有那么多名菜，怎么没有成为一大菜系呢？这大概是因为北京作为首都，融合了各大菜系的优点，成了"我中有你，你中有我"，难以归类了吧？

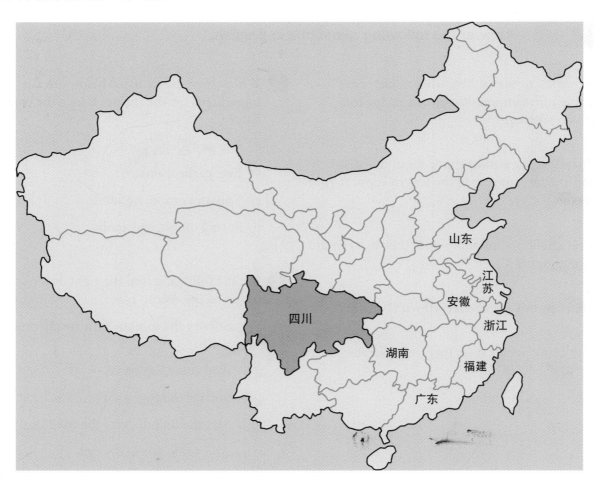

| yì dà lì 意大利 — Italy | yóu yú 由于 — because | là 辣 — hot; spicy | zhè jiāng 浙江 — Zhejiang Province | má 麻 — to numb | xiān 鲜 — fresh |

yì dà lì
意大利
Italy

yóu yú
由于
because

là
辣
hot; spicy

zhè jiāng
浙江
Zhejiang Province

má
麻
to numb

xiān
鲜
fresh

shēnshòu xǐ ài
深受…喜爱
well received by …

wù chǎn
物产(産)
product

shān xī
山西
Shanxi Province

fú jiàn
福建
Fujian Province

xián
咸
salty

là jiāo
辣椒
chilli

gè
各
every

qì hòu
气候
climate

suān
酸
sour

hú nán
湖南
Hunan Province

tián
甜
sweet

bǎo chí
保持
to maintain

bù dàn
不但…
ér qiě
而且
not only …
but also …

shēng huó xí guàn
生活习惯(習)
habits and customs

yīn cǐ
因此
therefore; so

ān huī
安徽
Anhui Province

shì zhōng
适中(適)
moderate; just
right

yuán zhī yuán wèi
原汁原味
original taste

huā yàng
花样(樣)
variety

kǒu wèi
口味
a person's taste

xíng chéng
形成
to form

děng
等
such; and so on;
etc.

kě kǒu
可口
tasty

dà gài
大概
probably; maybe;
about

xiāng
香
aroma;
pleasant smell

bù xiāng tóng
不相同
different

tè sè
特色
characteristic

dài biǎo xìng
代表性
representative

guǎng fàn
广泛(廣)
wide range

zuò wèi
作为(為)
as

wèi
味
taste

qīng dàn
清淡
not greasy or
strongly flavoured;
light

cài xì
菜系
cuisine

chēng wéi
称为(稱為)
to be called

qīng shuǎng
清爽
light and refreshing

shǒu dū
首都
capital

xíng
形
appearance

zhòng
重
heavy; heavily
seasoned

qí zhōng
其中
among which

jiǎn dān
简单(簡單)
briefly; simple

yóu nì
油腻
greasy; oily

róng hé
融合
to mix together;
to merge

jù jiā
俱佳
(things mentioned)
are all very good

sì chuān
四川
Sichuan Province

shān dōng
山东(東)
Shandong Province

jiāng sū
江苏(蘇)
Jiangsu Province

zhǔ yào
主要
major; main

lèi
类(類)
kind; type

xiān nèn
鲜嫩
delicious and
tender

ruǎn huá
软滑(軟)
soft and smooth

yōu diǎn
优点(優)
merit

guī lèi
归类(歸類)
to classify

练习B 📖 Answer the following questions in English.

一 What are the characteristics of Chinese cuisine?

二 What are the three reasons given in the article for the variations in Chinese cuisine?

三 Which two areas of China are famous for serving hot and spicy dishes?

四 Which two areas of China are famous for their seafood dishes?

五 What are the characteristics of Guangdong cuisine?

六 Why doesn't Beijing have its own cuisine?

七 In the phrase '我中有你，你中有我', what do '我' and '你' refer to?

八 Match the people to their preferred tastes. Write the correct letters in the boxes.

i) Northerners ☐   a) not strongly flavoured

ii) Southerners ☐   b) sour

iii) Sichuan people ☐   c) heavily seasoned

iv) Shanxi people ☐   d) hot and spicy

中国人的一日三餐

请阅读下面关于中国人饮食的文章，然后用英文回答问题。

中国人常说："早饭吃好，午饭吃饱，晚饭吃少"。这大概可以概括中国人一日三餐的饮食习惯，也可以反映中国人饮食习惯的科学性。

传统的中国早餐有馒头、包子、豆浆、油条、米粥、鸡蛋等等。由于现在中国人开始重视补钙，因此牛奶和酸奶也成了很多中国人的早餐。中国人喜欢吃热的早餐，就连牛奶也要加热后才喝。

午饭是很多中国人最主要的一餐，因为下午还有很长的时间要工作和学习，需要补充足够的能量，因此午饭一般都很丰盛。北方的午餐以面食为主，有各种面条、饺子、馒头、烧饼、肉类和炒菜；南方的午餐以米饭为主，配以各种肉类和青菜。过去中国人大多住在工作或学习的地方附近，而且中午休息的时间较长，所以可以回家吃午饭；现在很多大城市的人住得离工作或学习的地方很远，中午一般不回家，只在食堂或餐馆吃午饭。

晚饭一般是在六、七点钟吃的。因为晚上活动少，吃多了不容易消化，也容易发胖，所以中国人主张"晚上吃少"，一般以粥、馒头和比较清淡的炒菜为主。为了帮助消化，很多中国人还有晚饭后散步的习惯。中国人常说："饭后百步走，能活九十九"，可见中国人对健康的重视。

一 What saying do Chinese people recite when describing their three meals?

二 List four things mentioned in the article that Chinese people traditionally have for breakfast.

三 Why has milk become popular in the Chinese breakfast menu?

四 Which is the main meal of the day for Chinese people? Why?

五 What do people in Northern China have for lunch? How about people in Southern China?

六 In the past where did Chinese people have lunch? Where do they have lunch nowadays? Why?

七 Why do Chinese people eat little for dinner?

八 What do many Chinese people do after dinner? Why?

九 What does the sentence '饭后百步走，能活九十九' mean?

十 Put the following items under the correct columns in the table. Some items can appear in more than one column.

a) 面条　　　b) 牛奶　　　c) 烤鸭　　　d) 炒青菜

e) 炒鸡蛋　　f) 粥　　　　g) 炸鸡　　　h) 豆浆

早餐	午餐	晚餐

在餐馆里

练习 A 请听服务员和顾客在餐馆里的对话，然后根据对话内容，选出正确的答案。

生词

gù kè 顾客 customer	shēng jiāng 生姜 ginger
táng cù yú 糖醋鱼 sweet and sour fish	bái jiǔ 白酒 spirit distilled from sorghum or maize
gōng bǎo jī dīng 宫保鸡丁 Kungpao chicken	xiān zhà 鲜榨 freshly squeezed
yāo qiú 要求 to request	chéng zhī 橙汁 orange juice
bié fàng 别放 do not put ... in	yú xiāng ròu sī 鱼香肉丝 fish flavoured shredded pork
wèi jīng 味精 monosodium glutamate (MSG)	bīng zhèn 冰镇 refrigerated

一 女顾客想吃什么菜?

a) 糖醋鱼 ☐

b) 宫保鸡丁 ☐

c) 烤鸭 ☐

二 女顾客想要什么汤?

a) 三鲜汤 ☐

b) 酸辣汤 ☐

c) 鸡蛋汤 ☐

三 女顾客要求菜和汤里别放什么?

a) 味精 ☐

b) 辣椒 ☐

c) 生姜 ☐

四 女顾客想喝什么?

a) 茶 ☐

b) 果汁 ☐

c) 啤酒 ☐

五 女顾客对她的饮料有什么要求?

a) 一定要现做的 ☐

b) 一定要加冰块 ☐

c) 一定要加糖 ☐

六 男顾客没有点以下哪个菜?

a) 西红柿炒鸡蛋 ☐

b) 米饭 ☐

c) 红烧鱼 ☐

七 男顾客想喝点什么?

a) 茶 ☐

b) 白酒 ☐

c) 啤酒 ☐

去哪儿吃？

生词

hǎo jiǔ 好久 *long time*	jiāo 交 *to hand in*
jìn xíng 进行 *to take place*	máng de yào sǐ 忙得要死 *very busy*
lùn wén 论文 *dissertation*	dǎ suàn 打算 *to plan*
yuán yīn 原因 *reason*	hé lǐ 合理 *reasonable*
jià qian 价钱 *price*	bā zhé 八折 *20 percent off*
gǎn 赶 *to rush*	yōu huì 优惠 *discount*

一 这段对话是什么时间进行的？
a) 早上 ☐
b) 中午 ☐
c) 晚上 ☐

二 小王和汤姆是做什么的？
a) 学生 ☐
b) 老师 ☐
c) 商人 ☐

三 汤姆最近忙些什么？
a) 写毕业论文 ☐
b) 准备考试 ☐
c) 找工作 ☐

四 小王这两天在干什么？
a) 学习 ☐
b) 考试 ☐
c) 休息 ☐

五 小王想去四川菜馆的原因是什么？
a) 因为小王喜欢吃辣的 ☐
b) 因为价钱便宜 ☐
c) 因为汤姆想去 ☐

六 汤姆喜欢吃什么菜？
a) 甜的 ☐
b) 辣的 ☐
c) 清淡的 ☐

就餐广播

练习C 🔊　请听下面的就餐广播，然后根据广播内容，选出正确的答案。

生词	
guǎng bō 广播 *announcement*	chē xiāng 车厢 *carriage*
bō yīn 播音 *broadcast*	tè kuài liè chē 特快列车 *express train*
zhēn duì 针对 *be aimed at*	mǎ shàng 马上 *immediately; soon*
chéng kè 乘客 *passenger*	gōng yìng 供应 *to provide*
liáng cài 凉菜 *cold dish*	qīng zhēn shí pǐn 清真食品 *Islamic food*
dòu fu 豆腐 *tofu; bean curd*	xī cān 西餐 *western food*
huáng guā 黄瓜 *cucumber*	lǚ tú yú kuài 旅途愉快 *pleasant journey*

一 这条播音是针对什么人的？

　　a) 飞机上的乘客　☐

　　b) 餐馆里的顾客　☐

　　c) 火车上的乘客　☐

二 这些人要到哪里去？

　　a) 北京　☐

　　b) 西安　☐

　　c) 上海　☐

三 这条播音大概是在什么时间播出的？

　　a) 早上六点　☐

　　b) 中午十二点　☐

　　c) 晚上八点　☐

四 以下什么不在主食里？

　　a) 米饭　☐

　　b) 馒头　☐

　　c) 饺子　☐

五 热菜有什么？

　　a) 炒青菜　☐

　　b) 糖醋鱼　☐

　　c) 烤鸭　☐

六 凉菜有什么？

　　a) 豆腐　☐

　　b) 黄瓜　☐

　　c) 青菜　☐

七 餐厅在哪儿？

　　a) 三楼　☐

　　b) 三号车厢　☐

　　c) 一号车厢　☐

中华美食节

练习A 🖊

将于 2009 年 10 月
在北京大酒店举行，

欢迎喜爱中国食品
的朋友前来参加，

品尝各种中国美食！

第三届 中华美食节

如果您想订票或了解更多关于这次美食节活动的消息
请拨打：0086 10 8355 9988 或发电子邮件到：info@beijinghotel.cn

你刚刚参加完以上这个活动。请用中文给主持这次活动的人写一封 180-200 字的电子邮件，内容包括：

- 谢谢他们筹办这次活动
- 谈谈你对这次活动的哪些方面感兴趣，为什么？
- 谈谈你喜欢的中国食品
- 谈谈你对这次活动的意见和建议

健康饮食

练习B 🖊

健康饮食

越来越多人开始重视饮食健康，不单麦当劳等美式快餐店推出各种健康餐，现在连英国的中餐馆外卖店也说要吃得健康，菜要少油、少糖和少味精。

请你用中文写一篇 180-200 字的短文，来谈谈：

- 你常常吃中餐馆的外卖吗？你通常吃些什么菜？
- 你觉得这些菜的味道怎么样？
- 你觉得这些菜健康吗？为什么？
- 你的家人和朋友对中餐有什么看法？
- 你觉得中餐馆的外卖怎样做才能更健康？

生词

mài dāng láo
麦当劳
McDonald's

茶

茶 是中国的传统饮料，也是世界三大饮料之一（其他两种为咖啡和可乐）。中国茶主要分为绿茶、红茶、青茶和花茶。

一年四季气候不同，喝的茶也有不同。春季适合喝花茶；夏季适合喝绿茶；秋季适合喝青茶；冬季适合喝红茶。红茶含有很多的蛋白质，对健康很有好处，传统的英国茶就属于红茶。

生词

yǐn liào **饮料** *drink; beverage*	dàn bái zhì **蛋白质** *protein*
shì hé **适合** *suitable; appropriate for*	shǔ yú **属于** *to belong to*

请你用中文写一篇180–200字的短文，来谈谈：

- 你平常多喝什么饮料？

- 你和家人常常喝茶吗？你们喝什么茶？

- 你对中国茶有什么了解？

- 你觉得什么饮料最健康？

第二章 中国游

中国地理常识小测验

练习A 你到过中国旅游吗？你对中国的认识有多少？请阅读下面十个问题，选出你认为最佳的答案，然后进行双人或小组讨论。

一 长城在什么时候开始修建？

a) 六千年前

b) 两千五百多年前

c) 两百多年前

二 以下哪条河是中国最长的河？

a) 黑龙江

b) 黄河

c) 长江

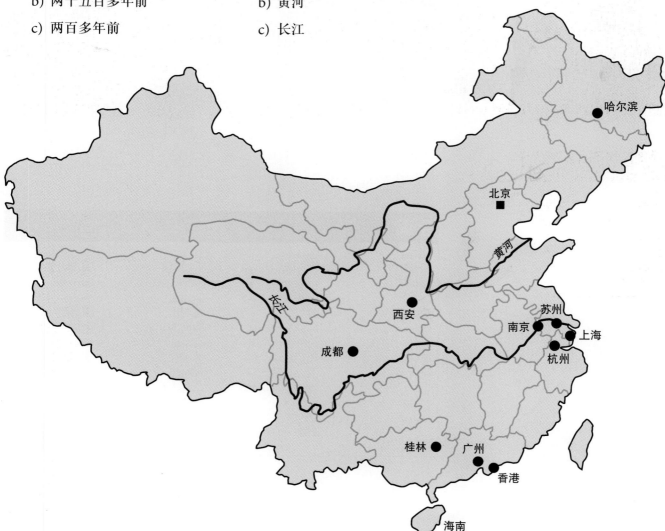

三 中国有多少个民族？

a) 十五

b) 三十一

c) 五十六

四 哪条河被称为中国的"母亲河"？

a) 长江

b) 黄河

c) 黑龙江

五 以下哪个是中国最年轻的城市？

a) 上海

b) 香港

c) 深圳

六 以下哪个不是沿海城市？

a) 上海

b) 广州

c) 西安

七 以下哪个名胜不在北京？

a) 长城

b) 故宫

c) 兵马俑

八 以下的中国城市，从北到南，哪个排列正确？

a) 西安——北京——上海——广州

b) 哈尔滨——北京——上海——香港

c) 北京——杭州——西安——苏州

九 以下哪个旅游城市的山水最有名？

a) 广州

b) 桂林

c) 西安

十 以下哪个关于中国旅游的说法不正确？

a) 在中国大部分地方，自来水不可以直接喝

b) 在中国，麦当劳等西式快餐比一般中餐便宜

c) 在中国，买往返机票跟买两张单程机票价钱差不多

生词

xiū jiàn **修建** to build	míng shèng **名胜** scenic spot	hā ěr bīn **哈尔滨** Harbin	zì lái shuǐ **自来水** tap water
mín zú **民族** nationality	gù gōng **故宫** Imperial Palace; Forbidden City	háng zhōu **杭州** Hangzhou	zhí jiē **直接** directly
mǔ qīn **母亲** mother	bīng mǎ yǒng **兵马俑** Terracotta Army	sū zhōu **苏州** Suzhou	wǎng fǎn jī piào **往返机票** return ticket
yán hǎi **沿海** coastal	xī ān **西安** Xian	guì lín **桂林** Guilin	

Shopping in Beijing

生词

gǔ wán 古玩 *antique*	jià gé 价格 *price*
fù zhì pǐn 复制品 *reproduction*	tǎo jià huán jià 讨价还价 *bargaining*
shǒu gōng yì pǐn 手工艺品 *handicraft*	jì qiǎo 技巧 *skill*
zhū bǎo shǒu shì 珠宝首饰 *jewellery*	bù kě 不可 shāng liáng de 商量的 *non-negotiable*
sī 丝 *silk*	

词组 / 表达法

hěn lìng rén xīng fèn
很令人兴奋
It's exciting.

hěn lìng rén gān gà
很令人尴尬
It's embarrassing.

wǒ duì   gǎn dào bù hǎo yì si
我对…感到不好意思
I'm a bit shy about …

bù sōng kǒu   bù ràng bù
不松口、不让步
don't give in

zǒu kāi
走开
to walk away

Shopping in Beijing is tremendously rewarding. Visitors can find many interesting and high-quality products there.

Among Beijing's best buys are art, antiques and reproductions, carpets, clothes, handicrafts, jewellery, silk and tea.

Prices in Beijing are generally very competitive, but that can depend on your bargaining skills. In places like department stores, prices are clearly marked and generally non-negotiable. However, in markets, bazaars and shops where prices are not indicated, bargaining is expected.

Please respond in Chinese to the bullet points below. You are *not* expected to refer to the full content of the above.

- State what the above article is referring to (a full summary is *not* required).

- Explain why the brochure says it is tremendously rewarding to shop in Beijing.

- What souvenirs do you usually buy?

- Have you ever bargained before? How do you feel about bargaining?

- Talk about one of your most memorable shopping experiences.

古都新城，天堂水乡七日游

请阅读下面一份旅行社的宣传单，然后用英文回答问题。

古都新城，天堂水乡七日游

中国国家旅行社：

古都新城，天堂水乡七日游

电话：80 8100 9508

西安、上海、苏州、杭州七日

1999 元

行程特色
西安：参观世界第八奇迹兵马俑
上海：游外滩，南京路购物
苏州：游览苏州园林
杭州：游览西湖美景

行程安排
第一天：北京——西安
从北京站乘火车硬卧到西安，宿
火车上。

第二天：西安
参观兵马俑、古城墙、大雁塔；
观看古典歌舞表演。宿西安宾馆。

第三天：西安——上海
参观回民街、钟楼，下午饺子宴，
晚上乘火车硬卧到上海。

第四天：上海
参观上海博物馆、玉佛寺及外滩，
宿友谊宾馆。

第五天：上海——苏州
南京路购物，下午乘火车到苏州。

第六天：苏州——杭州
游览苏州园林。晚上乘空调大
巴到杭州。宿西湖宾馆。

第七天：杭州——北京
游览西湖、宋城。晚上乘火车硬
卧回北京。结束愉快旅程！

行程基本信息
出发日期：每周二、五、六
出发地点：北京火车站
成人收费：1999 元／人（包括火
车票、景点门票、住宿及一日三
餐）
儿童：2 岁以下不占床位免费，
2–12 岁半价，12 岁以上按成人
收费

生词

gǔ dū 古都 ancient capital	wài tān 外滩 The Bund (an area of Huangpu district in Shanghai)	yìng wò 硬卧 hard sleeper (on a train)	huí mín jiē 回民街 Muslim Street (a street in Xi'an where there are many Muslim restaurants)	sòng chéng 宋城 Song City (a theme park reflecting the culture of the Song dynasty)	chéng rén 成人 adult
tiān táng 天堂 paradise; heaven	yóu lǎn 游览 to go sightseeing	sù 宿 to sleep	zhōng lóu 钟楼 bell tower; clock tower	jié shù 结束 to finish; to end	bāo kuò 包括 to include
shuǐ xiāng 水乡 region of rivers and lakes	yuán lín 园林 gardens	chéng qiáng 城墙 city wall		yú kuài 愉快 happy; pleasant	jǐng diǎn 景点 scenic spot
xíng chéng 行程 itinerary	ān pái 安排 arrangement; to arrange	dà yàn tǎ 大雁塔 Big Wild Goose Pagoda	yàn 宴 banquet; feast	jī běn 基本 basic	ér tóng 儿童 children
cān guān 参观 to visit	chéng 乘 to take (means of transport)	gǔ diǎn 古典 classic	yù fó sì 玉佛寺 Jade Buddha Temple	chū fā 出发 to set off	miǎn fèi 免费 free of charge
qí jì 奇迹 wonder; miracle			dà bā 大巴 coach		àn 按 in accordance with

练习A 📖 **Answer the following questions.**

一 The item you have just read is a …

a) travel itinerary

b) travel brochure

c) train timetable

二 Which of the following modes of transport will NOT be used in the trip?

a) plane

b) coach

c) train

三 How many nights do the tour party have to sleep on a train?

a) two

b) three

c) four

四 On which day will the tour party watch a performance?

a) Day 2

b) Day 3

c) Day 5

五 In which city will the tour party be given plenty of time to go shopping?

a) Xian

b) Shanghai

c) Hangzhou

六 Which of the following is NOT included in the tour package?

a) entrance fees to scenic spots

b) breakfast

c) insurance

七 What is the fee for a ten year old child?

a) free of charge

b) about 1000 yuan

c) about 500 yuan

八 Put the following activities into the right order according to the text. Write 1–6.

☐ eating dumplings

☐ visiting the West Lake

☐ going shopping

☐ visiting the Terracotta Army

☐ visiting a museum

☐ visiting famous gardens

中国旅游交通常识

请阅读下面一篇关于中国旅游交通常识的网上文章，然后用英文回答问题。

中国旅游交通常识

→ 飞机

到中国的各大城市旅游，一般都可乘飞机到达。和许多国家一样，每逢节假日时机票最贵，每天白天的机票比较贵，早上八点前或晚上八点后会便宜很多，常常可以买到七折甚至五折的机票。和西方国家不一样的是，在中国的国内航班，买一张往返机票并不比买两张单程机票更省钱，提前两、三天买的票也不一定比提前一个月买的票贵很多（节假日除外）。

→ 火车

火车是中国最主要的长途交通工具。乘火车的好处是方便、便宜。长途火车设有卧铺，卧铺分为硬卧和软卧。软卧的条件最好，但价格也最贵，不过比飞机票的价格还是便宜些。

→ 地铁

中国的北京、上海、广州等几个大城市都有地铁。地铁都很现代化，也很国际化，地铁里的指示牌，一般都是汉英对照。

→ 公共汽车

中国的公共汽车很方便，也很便宜，一般花一元或两元就可以从城市的一头坐到另一头。不过通常比较拥挤，而且冬天很冷，夏天很热；有些车条件较好，车上装有空调，也不太拥挤，这类车比普通的公共汽车稍贵一点儿。

→ 出租车

中国的出租车很方便，在街上招一招手就能叫到，而且价钱也很合理，一般起价费由五元到十二元不等，按公里计价，一般一公里两元左右。

→ 自行车

自行车是中国最普遍的日常交通工具。很多中国人每天骑自行车上班或上学。中国的马路有专门的自行车道，而且一般用花草树木或栅栏与汽车道隔开，所以比较安全。买一辆自行车并不费事，一般在各大商场都可以买到，而且价钱也很合理，便宜的只要一百多块钱（约值十英镑）。另外，很多旅游城市也都有出租自行车的服务。

→ 中国旅游交通最拥挤的时间

在中国旅游，最好避开几个主要节假日，尤其是春节（每年不同，一般是在一月底或二月初）、国庆节（十月一号）和劳动节（五月一号）。春节是中国人最重要的节日，春节前几天会有成千上万在外地工作的人赶回家过年，飞机票、火车票等不但很贵，也非常难买。在国庆节和劳动节这两个长假期，很多中国人都出去旅游，这期间各个旅游景点人山人海，非常拥挤。另外，每年的七月初和八月底正好是各大学学生放假和返校的时间，火车站也格外拥挤，最好避免这个时候坐火车。

jiāo tōng	wò pù	zhuāng yǒu	zuǒ yòu	ān quán	láo dòng jié
交通	卧铺	装有	左右	安全	劳动节
transport	*berth*	*to install*	*about; roughly*	*safe*	*Labour Day*

cháng shí	tiáo jiàn	pǔ tōng	pǔ biàn	fèi shì	chéng qiān shàng wàn
常识	条件	普通	普遍	费事	成千上万
common knowledge	*condition*	*normal*	*popular; widely used*	*troublesome; time or energy consuming*	*thousands of*

shěng qián	bù guò	shāo	rì cháng		wài dì
省钱	不过	稍	日常	chū zū	外地
to save money	*but; however*	*a little bit*	*daily*	出租	*part of the country other than where one's family is from*

tí qián	xiàn dài huà	chū zū chē	shàng bān	*rental*	rén shān rén hǎi
提前	现代化	出租车	上班	fú wù	人山人海
in advance	*modernised*	*taxi*	*to go to work*	服务	*huge crowds of people*

bù yī dìng	guó jì huà	zhāo shǒu	mǎ lù	*service*	zhèng hǎo
不一定	国际化	招手	马路	bì kāi	正好
not necessarily	*international*	*to wave*	*street; road*	避开	*as it happens*

chú wài	zhǐ shì pái	qǐ jià fèi	zhuān mén	*to avoid*	gé wài
除外	指示牌	起价费	专门	dǐ	格外
except	*signpost*	*starting price*	*special*	底	*exceptionally*

cháng tú	yī tóu	gōng lǐ	zhà lán	*at the end of*	bì miǎn
长途	一头	公里	栅栏	chū	避免
long-distance	*one end*	*kilometre*	*fence*	初	*to avoid*

shè yǒu	lìng	jì jià	gé kāi	*at the beginning of*	
设有	另	计价	隔开	guó qìng jié	
to equip with	*the other*	*to calculate the fare*	*to separate*	国庆节	

	yōng jǐ			*National Day*	
	拥挤				
	crowded				

练习B 📖 **Choose the best answers.**

一 How could you save money when buying a ticket for an internal flight?

   a) buy a ticket for a flight that departs late in the evening

   b) buy a ticket well in advance

   c) buy a return ticket rather than two singles

二 What is the main difference between buying plane tickets in China and buying them in the West?

   a) Buying a return ticket in China costs the same as buying two singles.

   b) Buying a return ticket in China is more expensive than buying two singles.

   c) Buying a return ticket in China is more difficult than buying two singles.

三 What is the main long-distance means of transport in China?

a) plane

b) train

c) coach

四 Which statement about the underground in China is NOT true?

a) It is very modern.

b) It has English signposting.

c) It can be found in most Chinese cities.

五 Which statement about Chinese buses is false?

a) They can be really hot in summer.

b) They are cheap but often crowded.

c) Air conditioned buses are comfortable but much more expensive than normal buses.

六 If you were in China, what would you quickly realise about the taxis?

a) It is very expensive to take a taxi.

b) You can hail a taxi anywhere in the street.

c) You pay a fixed price to take a taxi.

七 Which of the following is most widely used on a daily basis in China?

a) bus

b) underground

c) bike

八 Why is it relatively safe to ride a bike in China?

a) Because drivers always give way to cyclists.

b) Because drivers are very careful.

c) Because there are separate cycle lanes.

九 According to the article, during which of the following holidays would you be advised to avoid travelling in China?

a) Spring Festival

b) China's National Day

c) Mid-Autumn Festival

十 Why is it better not to travel by train in early July?

a) It is too crowded due to people going back to work.

b) It is too crowded due to university students going home.

c) It is too hot to travel by train.

故宫

请阅读下面一篇关于故宫的杂志文章，然后用英文回答问题。

北京故宫是明、清两代的皇宫，是过去皇帝工作和居住的地方，现在已成为博物院，开放供游客参观。

北京故宫是世界现存规模最大、最完整的古代皇宫。1987 年被联合国教科文组织列为"世界文化遗产"。

故宫建筑的许多细节都有着象征意义，处处体现中国的传统文化。比如数字"九"，传说故宫有九千九百九十九间房屋，每个门上的门钉也是横竖九个。这是因为"九"是数字中最大的一个，而古代中国人认为皇帝是人间最大的，所以必须用"九"。另外，"九"的谐音是"久"，寓意为皇帝活得长久、国家长久。

除了数字，故宫各个建筑的名称、颜色等也有不同的寓意，体现中国的传统文化思想。因此，了解故宫，也就是了解中国的传统文化。

生词

míng 明 *Ming dynasty (directly before the Qing dynasty)*	yí chǎn 遗产 *heritage*
qīng 清 *Qing dynasty*	xǔ duō 许多 *many*
dài 代 *generation; dynasty*	xì jié 细节 *details*
	chù chù 处处 *everywhere*
huáng gōng 皇宫 *palace*	tǐ xiàn 体现 *to embody*
huáng dì 皇帝 *emperor*	shù zì 数字 *number*
chéng wéi 成为 *to become*	dīng 钉 *nail*
kāi fàng 开放 *to open*	héng 横 *horizontal*
yóu kè 游客 *tourist*	gǔ dài 古代 *ancient*
xiàn cún 现存 *existing*	rèn wéi 认为 *to think; to regard*
guī mó 规模 *scale*	bì xū 必须 *must; have to*
wán zhěng 完整 *complete*	xié yīn 谐音 *homophone*
lián hé guó jiào kē wén zǔ zhī 联合国教科文组织 *the United Nations Educational, Scientific and Cultural Organization (UNESCO)*	jiǔ 久 *long-lasting*
	yù yì 寓意 *implied meaning*
	sī xiǎng 思想 *thinking; ideology*

练习C 📖 Answer the following questions in English.

一 What was the Imperial Palace used for in the past?

二 What is its use today?

三 What happened in 1987?

四 How many rooms are there in the Imperial Palace?

五 What is special about the doors in the Imperial Palace?

六 In the past, who did the Chinese consider to be the most important person in the world?

七 According to the article, what does the number nine symbolize in Chinese culture?

八 Why does the number nine have such a symbolic meaning?

九 Apart from numbers, in what other ways does the Imperial Palace reflect traditional Chinese culture?

十 Decide whether these statements are true or false. Correct the false statements.

a) The Imperial Palace is the biggest palace in China.

b) Number nine is a lucky number because it symbolizes good fortune.

c) To study the Imperial Palace is a good way to learn about Chinese culture.

场景对话

练习A 根据五段说话的内容，选出正确的答案。

生词

guān xi
关 系
relationship

fáng kǎ
房 卡
key card

zhàng dān
账 单
bill

diàn tī
电 梯
elevator; lift

一 这路公车的最后一站是哪儿？

a) 故宫

b) 前门

c) 北京火车站

二 对话中的男女是什么关系？

a) 汽车售票员和乘客

b) 出租车司机和游客

c) 游客和商店售货员

三 这段对话发生在什么地方？

a) 宾馆

b) 旅行社

c) 火车站

四 对话中的女士给了男士什么？

a) 房卡

b) 行李

c) 账单

五 学生爬长城要花多少钱？

a) 60元

b) 30元

c) 20元

订机票

练习B 根据电话对话的内容，选出正确的答案。

生词

shì fǒu
是 否
whether or not

háng bān
航 班
flight

liú xià
留 下
to leave (details)

fù qián
付 钱
to pay for

tōng zhī
通 知
to notify; to inform

一 大卫想去哪儿？

a) 北京

b) 上海

c) 西安

二 大卫最重视飞机的什么？

a) 时间

b) 票价

c) 是否送票

三 几点的飞机最便宜？

a) 早上八点

b) 下午三点

c) 晚上八点

四 大卫订票时，要告诉订票员些什么？

a) 他的信用卡号

b) 他的护照号

c) 他的姓名

五 大卫最后一共要付多少钱？

a) 600元

b) 620元

c) 800元

六 送票人最好在以下什么时候去送票？

a) 十一号中午十二点后

b) 十二号早上十点前

c) 二十号早上十点前

暑期计划

练习C 🔊 根据博文和马丽的谈话内容，选出正确的答案。

生词

zì yóu 自由 *freedom*	chú fēi 除非 *only if; unless*
tóng shì 同事 *colleague*	jǐn còu 紧凑 *well-organised;* *compact*
zhǔ yi 主意 *idea*	jiàn yì 建议 *recommendation;* *proposal*
kě xī 可惜 *pity*	

一 博文暑假想做些什么?

a) 打工赚钱

b) 出去旅游

c) 回家看父母

二 马丽想去中国哪几个城市?

a) 北京，杭州，广州，西安

b) 杭州，西安，桂林，苏州

c) 杭州，桂林，广州，西安

三 马丽为什么只能玩一周?

a) 因为她要准备考试

b) 因为她要写毕业论文

c) 因为她钱不够了

四 博文认为坐飞机有什么不好的地方?

a) 太贵

b) 不舒服

c) 不自由

五 马丽认为坐火车有什么不好的地方?

a) 人太多，太拥挤

b) 不够快

c) 太贵了

六 博文认为参加旅行团有什么好处?

a) 省钱

b) 舒服

c) 自由

七 根据对话，马丽第二天会去哪儿?

a) 火车站售票处

b) 飞机票售票处

c) 旅行社

八 根据对话，博文和马丽是什么关系?

a) 老师和学生

b) 朋友关系

c) 同事关系

你的旅游体会

练习A

亲爱的美美，

你好！我来英国一星期了，

一切还很新鲜！

英国和中国很不一样。英国

城市的街道都不大，也没有

中国城市那么多的高建筑，

但空气很新鲜，也很安静。

除了市中心，路上很少有行

人，有时问路都成问题！

请你用中文写一篇180–200字的短文，拿你住的地方和你最了解的一个亚洲的国家/地方来做比较，看看在以下几方面，有什么相同和不同的地方：

- 自然环境
- 人们的生活习惯、饮食等
- 交通
- 文化

中国游寻伴

练习B

请你用中文写一篇180–200字的电子邮件，内容包括：

- 你想去中国什么地方？为什么想去这些地方？
- 你打算什么时候去？你的行程计划是怎样的？
- 你打算怎样去？
- 你的个人爱好和性格是怎样的？

中国游寻伴

本人今年暑假想去中国旅游，想找一位中国朋友或懂中文的朋友与我同行。如果你感兴趣，请和我联系，我们可以一起计划这次中国之行。

大卫
电子邮件：davidchina@hotmail.com

你的旅游经验谈

练习C 你刚从一个地方旅游回来。你听说一位朋友下个月也要去那个地方，你想写信给他，谈一谈你的经验，告诉他要注意些什么。

请你用中文写一封180–200字的信给那位朋友，谈谈：

- 去那个地方要准备些什么？
- 那个地方有些什么名胜？你觉得哪些最有意思？
- 哪些事是一定要做的，为什么？
- 哪些事是要避免的，为什么？

第三章 教育

中国教育体系

练习A 你了解中国的教育体系吗？中、英学生的教育经历有什么相同和不同的地方？
请阅读下面十个问题，选出你认为最佳的答案，然后进行双人或小组讨论。

一 中国实施的是几年制义务教育？

a) 六年

b) 九年

c) 十二年

二 中国学校的学生要面对几次正式的考试？

a) 一次——高考入大学

b) 两次——中考和高考

c) 三次——小升初，初升高，高考入大学

三 英国的中等教育普通证书相当于中国的

a) 小学程度

b) 初中程度

c) 高中程度

四 英国的高等水平考试相当于中国的

a) 小学程度

b) 初中程度

c) 高中程度

五 为什么有人说"经过十二年寒窗苦读，才有希望进入高等学府"？

a) 中国的学制是十二年——小（6）+初（3）+高（3）

b) 中国学生勤奋辛苦，十二年紧绷弦

c) 以上全部正确

六 中国高中学生一般读多少科目？

a) 三科

b) 四科

c) 至少六科

生词

jiào yù tǐ xì 教育体系 education system	hán chuāng kǔ dú 寒窗苦读 hard life of a poor scholar
shí shī 实施 to carry out; to implement	qín fèn xīn kǔ 勤奋辛苦 diligent; hard-working
yì wù jiào yù 义务教育 compulsory education	jǐn bēng xián 紧绷弦 stressed; tense; uptight
miàn duì 面对 to face	shàng shù 上述 above-mentioned
xiāng dāng yú 相当于 correspond to	zhèng què 正确 correct
chéng dù 程度 level	fǎ bǎo 法宝 an effective tool; a secret weapon
chū zhōng 初中 junior high school	mìng gēn 命根 lifeblood; one's very life
gāo zhōng 高中 high school	
zhōng děng jiào yù 中等教育 pǔ tōng zhèng shū 普通证书 GCSE examination	yìng shì jiào yù 应试教育 exam oriented education
gāo děng shuǐ píng 高等水平 kǎo shì 考试 A-Level examination	sù zhì jiào yù 素质教育 education for all-round development

生词

continued from
page 29

孔子 kǒng zǐ
Confucius
(551–479 BC)

因材施教 yīn cái shī jiào
to teach according
to a student's
ability

内容 nèi róng
content

能力 néng lì
ability; capability

资源 zī yuán
resource

顺序 shùn xù
sequence; order

博士 bó shì
PhD

硕士 shuò shì
Master's degree

七 中国高中学生上一天的学，一般是从几点到几点？

a) 早上八点三十到下午三，四点钟

b) 早上七点到下午五点钟

c) 早上七点到晚上八，九点钟

八 "考，考，考 教师的法宝，分，分，分 学生的命根"的说法，反映了下面的哪一个特征？

a) 应试教育

b) 素质教育

c) 义务教育

九 中国古代教育家孔子提倡的"因材施教"，是什么意思？

a) 因应考试内容教学

b) 因应学生能力教学

c) 因应国家资源教学

十 中国大学学位的顺序是怎样的？

a) 学士，博士，硕士

b) 学士，硕士，博士

c) 硕士，学士，博士

Exam stress

练习B 请阅读婷婷发给她英国笔友的电子邮件，内容是关于学生如何应对学习压力的问题。

收件人：Susan

寄件人：Tingting

主题：Stressed

Hi Susan,

How are you? I'm stressed!

I'm finding high school life really difficult. The education system here is so exam-oriented. The top priority for every student is getting high marks in exams. There is a saying which goes:

'Exams, exams, exams,
The teachers' secret weapon.
Marks, marks, marks,
The students' life.'

That's how I feel at the moment. There are continuous exams and assessments and I feel under constant pressure.

A typical day for me starts at about seven o'clock and I have to study right up until eight or nine o'clock. Most mornings, I have to study. I have extra tuition in the evenings. I hardly have time to have lunch, and normally only take a short break for dinner. I take more than six courses a day, and I have to stay up late to finish all my homework. I have to spend all my weekends on school work so as to keep up with the other students and not get low marks in the exams.

生词

压力 / yā lì
紧张 jǐn zhāng
stress; pressure

有压力的 / yǒu yā lì de
紧张的 jǐn zhāng de
stressed

学校生活 xué xiào shēng huó
school life

轻重缓急 qīng zhòng huǎn jí
priority

持续不间断的 chí xù bú jiàn duàn de
continuous

评估 píng gū
assessment

不断的 bú duàn de
constant

温习 wēn xí
to study

补课 bǔ kè
extra tuition

熬夜 áo yè
stay up late

As you can see, I'm really stressed! I have such long days, large amounts of homework and never-ending exams. I have poor concentration and I get bad headaches. I am unable to attend to everything at once and find it hard to prioritise my work.

Can you give me some advice? How can I reduce my stress and become more efficient? What is school life in Britain like? Is it as stressful as in China? Do you have to work as hard as we do?

Write soon.

Your stressed friend,

Tingting ☺

生词

continued from page 30

wú xiū zhǐ de
无休止的,

méi wán de
没完的
never-ending

bù néng jí zhōng
不能集中

zhù yì lì
注意力
poor concentration

gù cǐ shī bǐ
顾此失彼
unable to attend to everything at once

fēn bié qīng zhòng
分别轻重

huǎn jí
缓急
prioritise

jiǎn yā
减压
reduce one's stress

yǒu xiào lǜ de
有效率的
efficient

Please respond in Chinese to the bullet points below.
You are *not* expected to refer to the full content of the above.

- State what the email is referring to (a full summary is *not* required).

- How do you feel about the writer's school life?

- Have you ever suffered from exam stress? If so, how did you cope with it?

- What are the differences between the British education system and the Chinese system?

- Imagine you are Tingting's penfriend. What advice would you give to help her reduce her stress?

词组 / 表达法

bù néng   wú fǎ zuò dào
不能 / 无法做到…
unable to …

cóng tóu zhì wěi   zì shǐ zhì zhōng
从头至尾,自始至终
right from the beginning

dà liàng de
大量的
a large amount of

nǐ shì guò   zhēng qǔ guò   ma
你试过 / 争取过…吗?
Have you tried …?

zěn me yàng   rú hé
…怎么样 / 如何?
What/How about …?

zǔ zhī
组织
organise/organisation

nǔ lì   fèn dòu
努力,奋斗
to struggle

wǒ tóng qíng
我同情…
I sympathise with …

校际交流，感受中国

请阅读下面一篇关于英国中学生访华感受的报道，然后用英文回答问题。

》校际交流，感受中国

在英国，越来越多的学校除了有中文课以外，还开展了英中学校的互访活动。每位访华老师和学生都有很多难忘的经历和感受：

》领队老师

每年带学生到中国，访问我们的友好学校，是一项非常有意义的活动。这项活动有助于学生多了解一些中国的情况，同时感受一下中国的文化和"活"的汉语。通过在中国的学习，以及和中国老师、学生的沟通与交流，学生们认识到两国教育体系的不同，也看到了许多新事物。

》访华学生

这里的人热情、友好，我们感到很受欢迎。我们参加了很多活动，譬如游览了当地的山水和有名的地方；参加了中国学生的夏令营；在中国家庭里学做中餐，如包饺子；观看国画和书法展览，还有太极和武术表演；制作陶器；参观学校和去教室听课。

我们印象最深刻的是中国的教学方式：
- 由于学生多，所以课堂大；
- 学生非常爱学习，特别勤奋；
- 基础知识良好；
- 上课时很安静，不经常插话，很少提问或与老师交流；
- 学生作业多，压力较大；
- 自由发展的空间不很大；
- 家长期望很高，老师对学生很严；
- 学生考试成绩很不错。

生词

gǎn shòu 感受 *to feel*	zhǎn lǎn 展览 *exhibition*
kāi zhǎn 开展 *to start; begin to develop*	tài jí 太极 *t'ai chi*
hù fǎng huó dòng 互访活动 *exchange visits*	wǔ shù 武术 *wushu; martial arts*
fǎng huá 访华 *to visit China*	táo qì 陶器 *pottery*
lǐng duì lǎo shī 领队老师 *visiting teacher*	yìn xiàng 印象 *impression*
yǒu yì yì de 有意义的 *meaningful*	jī chǔ zhī shi 基础知识
yǒu zhù yú 有助于 *to contribute to*	liáng hǎo 良好 *good basic knowledge*
gōu tōng yǔ jiāo liú 沟通与交流 *to communicate and exchange ideas*	chā huà 插话 *to chip in*
xià lìng yíng 夏令营 *summer camp*	qī wàng 期望 *expectation*

练习A 📖 Answer the following questions in English.

一 According to the visiting teacher in the article, what are the benefits of taking students on trips to China?

二 What does the teacher say her students gain from studying alongside Chinese students?

三 How did the exchange students describe Chinese people?

四 What activities did the exchange students participate in? List eight of them.

五 What impressed the exchange students most during their visit to China?

六 What do the exchange students think of the class size in the Chinese school they visited? Why?

七 What do the exchange students think of their Chinese counterparts' attitude towards studying?

八 What do the exchange students think of the interaction between teachers and students in Chinese classrooms?

九 What do the exchange students think of the attitudes of parents and teachers?

十 What do the exchange students think of their Chinese counterparts' exam results?

由"阴盛阳衰"想到"因材施教"

请阅读下面一篇关于男女学习差异的文章，然后用英文回答问题。

近年来，中英教育界的报道都在说"阴盛阳衰"、"女优于男"的事，例如"英国男女学童成绩的不同"、"女生成绩继续优于男生"等。2006年10月的报道说，英国中学的男生，平均水平比女生落后七年。从1999年到2006年，中国高考状元有560人，女生的人数占一半以上。到2007年，在中国30个省内共有66名高考状元，其中女生为46人，男生20人，女生人数接近70%。为此，许多人开始讨论，是什么让男生赶不上女生。有人说，现在的教育体系可能对女生有优势；越来越多的人发现，女生可能比男生更会学习；还有人觉得，男生的兴趣太多了。许多教育工作者都认为这是一个问题，需要研究。

目前中英两国所倡议的一些办法，都反映了中国古代最伟大的思想家、教育家孔子2 500多年前的教育思想——"有教无类"、"因材施教"、"因势利导"。例如受教育机会应该一样，每一位学生都应该得到帮助；进行男女分班教学，不让男生落后；给予个人学习指导等等。大家都知道，男女生的性格特点不同，例如女生比较安静、细心、专心；男生比较好动、不细心、兴趣分散。许多人认为，教师在教学中应该了解学生，先找出男生为什么赶不上女生的原因，然后提供帮助，让男生能像女生一样得到好成绩。

生词

yīn shèng yáng shuāi **阴盛阳衰** *women outshine men*	zhuàng yuán **状元** *Number One Scholar (title conferred on the one who comes first in the highest Imperial examination; the very best)*	yōu shì **优势** *advantage*	jǐ yǔ **给予** *to give; to provide*	zhuān xīn **专心** *undivided attention; concentration*
nǚ yōu yú nán **女优于男** *girls outshine boys*		yōu jiào wú lèi **有教无类** *to provide education for all people without discrimination*	gè rén zhǐ dǎo **个人指导** *individual guidance*	nài xìng **耐性** *patient*
píng jūn **平均** *average*	shěng **省** *province; to save*	yīn shì lì dǎo **因势利导** *give judicious guidance according to circumstances*	xì xīn **细心** *careful; attentive*	fēn sàn **分散** *scattered*
luò hòu **落后** *to fall behind*				

练习B 📖 **Answer the following questions in English.**

一 What is the main theme of this article?

二 Making use of the statistics in the article, explain the phenomenon of girls outshining boys.

三 What views are expressed in the article regarding the above-mentioned phenomenon?

四 According to the article, measures which reflect Confucius' thoughts on education are being carried out. Can you state what they are?

五 What are the different features of male and female students stated in the article?

六 What do people think teachers should do to sort this phenomenon out? Why?

"汉语热"持续升温

请阅读下面一篇关于学习汉语的新闻报道，然后用英文回答问题。

近年来，由于中国进一步扩大对外开放、经济迅速发展和国际地位日益提高，在全球各地兴起了学习汉语的热潮，称为"汉语热"。作为了解中国和与中国交往的重要工具，汉语受到各国越来越多人的重视。据报道，从2004年11月到2007年底，"孔子学院"的数量已增至210所，分布在64个国家和地区。到2006年，全世界已有2 500多所大学和上万所中小学开设了汉语课程，有3 000多万外籍人士在学习汉语，而且这个数字还在惊人地增长。中国国家汉语国际推广领导小组办公室（简称"汉办"）估计，到2010年，学习汉语的外国人将达到1亿。

在英国，"汉语热"持续升温，汉语学习风气越来越强劲。英、中之间的经贸联系，带动了两国的文化教育交流。越来越多教育专家认为学生应该学习汉语，以利中、英双方的交流。尽管英国到2006年已有大约100家中学开设了汉语课程，也出现了把中文列为必修课、一度成为热门新闻的中学，英国政府要求英国所有中学和大学在未来的5年内，都要在中国找到一家"姊妹学校"。有人估计，汉语将成为倍受英国学生欢迎的第二大外语，因为近年来，英国学生选修传统外语课的人次已有所减少。

许多人相信，如果学生能够熟练地运用中文，会为他们将来就业和发展事业增添优势。

生词

扩大 kuò dà *to widen*	**汉办** hàn bàn *The Office of Chinese Languages Council International (Hanban)*
经济 jīng jì *economy*	**估计** gū jì *to estimate*
迅速发展 xùn sù fā zhǎn *to develop rapidly*	**强劲** qiáng jìng *powerful*
地位 dì wèi *position; place; status*	**持续升温** chí xù shēng wēn *become more and more popular*
日益 rì yì *increasingly*	**经贸** jīng mào *economy and trade*
热潮 rè cháo *upsurge*	**专家** zhuān jiā *specialist*
称作 chēng zuò *to be called*	**双方** shuāng fāng *both sides*
交往 jiāo wǎng *contact*	**大约** dà yuē *about; approximately*
工具 gōng jù *tool; device*	**必修课** bì xiū kè *required course*
孔子学院 kǒng zǐ xué yuàn *Confucius Institute*	**一度** yí dù *once*
数量 shù liàng *number; amount*	**热门** rè mén *hot; popular*
开设 kāi shè *to open; to offer*	**政府** zhèng fǔ *government*
课程 kè chéng *course*	**姊妹学校** zǐ mèi xué xiào *partner school*
外籍人士 wài jí rén shì *foreigners*	

练习C **Answer the following questions in English.**

一 What is the article about?

二 Why has learning Chinese become so popular worldwide?

三 By 2010, how many people does Hanban estimate will be learning Chinese?

四 Why do some education specialists think that students should learn Chinese?

五 According to the article, what was the hot news in 2006?

六 What does the British government want every school, college and university to do within the next five years?

七 Why do some people think that Chinese will become British students' second language in the future?

八 What benefits do many people believe learning Chinese will bring them in the future?

为什么学中文？

练习 A 🔊 根据谈话的内容，选出正确的答案。

生词

yán jiū
研究
to study; to research

zhuān yè
专业
profession

hǎi wài
海外
overseas

diào chá biǎo
调查表
questionnaire

xué wèn
学问
learning

hài xiū
害羞
shy

xīn xiǎng shì chéng
心想事成
to get one's wish

一 这是在

a) 教室里的谈话 ☐

b) 校园里的谈话 ☐

c) 老师家里的谈话 ☐

二 谈话内容是关于学习汉语的

a) 感受 ☐

b) 方法 ☐

c) 目的 ☐

三 谁表示对汉字最感兴趣？

a) 汉纳 ☐

b) 约翰 ☐

c) 马丽 ☐

四 大卫想研究中国

a) 经济 ☐

b) 文学 ☐

c) 哲学 ☐

五 马丽的理想是将来当

a) 老师 ☐

b) 翻译 ☐

c) 商人 ☐

六 马修比较喜欢中国

a) 哲学 ☐

b) 经济 ☐

c) 历史 ☐

七 汉纳现在

a) 已经选好了专业 ☐

b) 还没选好专业 ☐

c) 已经决定将来要做什么 ☐

学好汉语的方法

练习B 📖 根据谈话的内容，在下面选出四个正确的句子，并在旁边的空格内打 **✗**。

生词

yòu liú lì yòu 又 流利 又 qīng chǔ 清楚 *fluently and clearly*	yǔ diào 语调 *intonation*
nào chū xiào huà 闹出笑话 *to make a funny mistake*	jìng 净 *only; merely*
sú yǔ 俗语 *common saying*	yáng qiāng yáng diào 洋腔洋调 *to speak with a foreign accent*
chéng gōng 成功 *to succeed*	gào sù 告诉 *to tell*
xí guàn 习惯 *be accustomed to*	shú néng shēng qiǎo 熟能生巧 *'Practice makes perfect'*
shōu huò 收获 *results*	yǒu zhì zhě 有志者 shì jìng chéng 事竟成 *'Where there's a will, there's a way'*
shēng diào 声调 *tone*	

一　现在是马丽、汉纳在中国的第十天。　□

二　汉纳现在说汉语说得又流利又清楚。　□

三　马丽觉得汉语的语法和汉字很难，发音不难。　□

四　马丽的发音不太好，闹出了"作业／昨夜；吃包子／吃报纸；杯子／被子"的笑话。　□

五　汉纳以前发音不太好，闹出了"作业／昨夜；吃包子／吃报纸；杯子／被子"的笑话。　□

六　汉纳的书包里有一本汉英词典。　□

七　马丽决心象汉纳那样多学、多练，用功学好汉语。　□

八　李亮用中国的一句俗语告诉马丽和汉纳，只要有决心就能成功。　□

到英国当交换生

练习 C 根据电话对话的内容，从括弧里的两个词语中，圈出正确的答案。

生词

zàn chéng 赞成 *to agree*	hù dòng 互动 *interaction*
zhì zào 制造 *to make; to produce*	diǎn bō 点拨 *to give a hint*
yī qiè 一切 *everything; all*	tīng huà 听话 *obedient*
jīng cǎi 精彩 *wonderful*	kàn zhòng 看重 *to regard something as important; to value*
bù xū cǐ xíng 不虚此行 *worthwhile trip*	yǐn sī 隐私 *private matters one wants to hide*
zhǐ shàng tán bīng 纸上谈兵 *to engage in idle theorising*	zhēn tàn 侦探 *detective*
bǎi wén bù rú 百闻不如 yī jiàn 一见 'It is better to see once than hear a hundred times'	fàng zòng 放纵 *to let somebody have his/her own way*
bīn bīn yǒu lǐ 彬彬有礼 *courteous*	suí chù kě jiàn 随处可见 *can be seen everywhere*
qì fēn 气氛 *atmosphere*	zì háo 自豪 *to be proud of*
qīng sōng 轻松 *relaxed*	

一 这是小明（第一次 / 第二次）到英国。

二 小明给妈妈打电话的时候，想告诉妈妈（这几天的 / 一天内的）事。

三 小明有很多话要说，妈妈让小明讲在英国见到的（主要 / 一切）事情。

四 小明这几天参观游览了许多地方，还去一所高中（听了一天的课 / 教了一天的汉语课）。

五 小明觉得英国学校的上课（内容 / 方式）很有趣。

六 小明觉得英国家长和孩子的关系是（平等的 / 孩子很听父母的话）。

七 小明（非常赞成 / 不太赞成）英国父母对子女的态度。

八 小明在英国看到（非常多 / 不太多）的中国留学生。

九 小明在商店里看到了许多商品上都有"中国制造"的（汉字 / 英文字）。

十 小明去开会之前还有大约（一个半小时 / 两个半小时）。

外面的世界很精彩

练习A

你在网上看到一篇题为"外面的世界很精彩"的报道。报道中，一些交换学生谈到在交换国家中所获得的经验和体会。你的学校也在准备安排学生到中国作交换生，为期21天，让学生亲自体会中国的文化和"活"的语言，从而增长见识、拓宽视野，毕业后能更好地计划未来。你希望能参予活动，看看外面的世界。

在报名以前，请你用中文写一封180–200字的信，告诉在中国的笔友：

- 你此时此刻的心情
- 你最想去哪一个城市？为什么？
- 你最希望能学到什么？为什么？
- 你课余时间最想做什么？为什么？
- 你现在要做好哪些准备？

"女优于男"的现象

练习B ✏

尽管中、英在学制、教学方法及教学侧重点上均有差异，但是近年来的教学成果，却显示出一个相似之处，就是"女优于男"。中等教育及高等水平考试成绩结果显示，女生表现优于男生。针对此种现象，许多教育工作者都认为这是一个值得关注的问题，他们认为，男女生在心理特点、思维方式等许多方面均有不同，因此在具体的学校教育中，应采用不同的教育方式，如因材施教。

请你用中文写一篇180–200字的短文，来谈谈上述问题：

- 据你所知，男女生在学习方面有哪些差异？对学习效果有什么影响？

- 你身边的人对此种现象有什么看法？

- 你认为这是什么原因造成的？

- 你对教学方法有什么建议？

网上学汉语

练习C ✏

汉办2006年的统计数据显示，全球有3000多万外籍人士学习汉语，2500所大学和上万所中小学开设了汉语课程。随着全球"汉语热"持续升温，汉语教师、汉语教材的需求量激增，汉语教学网站也相继问世。现在有越来越多的人上网学汉语。

请你用中文写一篇180–200字的短文，来谈谈：

- 你上网学汉语吗？从网上可以学些什么东西？

- 你觉得在网上学汉语和在教室里跟老师学汉语有什么不同？

- 在网上学汉语有什么利弊？

- 你的家人和朋友对网上学汉语有什么看法？

- 你对朋友在网上学汉语有什么建议？

第四章 中国的传统节日

中国传统节日知识小测验

练习A 🔊 中国是一个历史悠久的文明古国，文化源远流长，其丰富的民族传统节日，是不可或缺的重要内容。你对中国传统节日了解多少？请阅读下面十个问题，选出你认为最佳的答案，然后进行双人或小组讨论。

一 在端午节，中国人习惯吃

  a) 粽子

  b) 元宵

  c) 年糕

二 中秋节的时候，中国人除了吃月饼以外，还会

  a) 舞狮

  b) 赏月

  c) 吃饺子

三 春节的庆祝活动通常持续到

  a) 除夕

  b) 年初三

  c) 正月十五

四 如今的庙会

  a) 只是一种隆重的祭祀活动

  b) 只是一种娱乐活动

  c) 既弘扬民族文化，又发展民族经济

五 傣族过泼水节是因为

  a) 民族传说

  b) 天气热

  c) 宗教习惯

六 人们把重阳节登高的风俗看作是

  a) 老人的活动

  b) 免灾避祸的活动

  c) 健康长寿的活动

七 龙舟竞渡用的船，采用了龙的设计，因为

  a) 中国人喜欢龙

  b) 龙很美观

  c) 龙是中华民族的象征

八 在清明节，除了扫墓及祭祖外，还有很多风俗体育活动，例如

  a) 荡秋千

  b) 赛跑

  c) 打太极拳

九 七夕节有一个美丽的民间爱情传说，是关于

  a) 牛郎与织女

  b) 许仙与白娘子

  c) 梁山泊与祝英台

十 以下哪一个不是中国传统节日？

  a) 元宵节

  b) 复活节

  c) 清明节

生词

lì shǐ yōu jiǔ
历史悠久
have a long history

wén míng
文明
civilization

wén huà
文化
culture

yuán yuǎn liú cháng
源远流长
long standing

bù kě huò quē
不可或缺
essential

yuán xiāo
元宵
dumplings made of glutinous rice flour stuffed with different fillings

shǎng yuè
赏月
to observe the moon

chūn jié
春节
Spring Festival; Chinese New Year

chí xù
持续
to continue

zhēng yuè
正月
the first month of the lunar calendar

lóng zhòng
隆重
grand; solemn

jì sì
祭祀
to offer sacrifices to gods or ancestors

hóng yáng
弘扬
to spread; to introduce something to other parts of the world

fā zhǎn
发展
to develop

dǎi zú
傣族
Dai nationality

pō shuǐ
泼水
to splash water

chuán shuō
传说
legend

miǎn zāi bì huò
免灾避祸
to avoid disasters and misfortunes

cháng shòu
长寿
longevity

lóng zhōu jìng dù
龙舟竞渡
dragon boat race

cǎi yòng
采用
to use; to adopt

shè jì
设计
design

xiàng zhēng
象征
symbol; icon

chóng yáng jié
重阳节
Chong Yang Festival (9th day of the 9th lunar month)

qīng míng jié
清明节
Qing Ming Festival (5th day of the 4th lunar month)

sǎo mù
扫墓
to sweep the grave; to pay respect to the dead

jì zǔ
祭祖
to offer sacrifices to ancestors

dàng qiū qiān
荡秋千
to play on a swing

qī xī jié
七夕节
Qi Xi Festival (7th evening of the 7th lunar month)

fù huó jié
复活节
Easter

Lantern Festival

练习B 😊 请阅读下面一篇关于元宵节的文章。

生词

yuán xiāo jié	tuán jù
元 宵 节	团 聚
Lantern Festival;	*reunion*
Yuan Xiao Festival	
	qíng rén jié
fēng fù duō cǎi	情 人 节
丰 富 多 彩	*Valentine's Day*
rich and colourful	
	yóu rén péi bàn
cāi dēng mí	由 人 陪 伴
猜 灯 谜	*to chaperone*
to guess lantern	
riddles	wèi hūn
	未 婚
biǎo yǎn mín jiān wǔ	*unmarried*
表 演 民 间 舞	
to perform folk	
dances	

Falling on the fifteenth day of the first lunar month, the Lantern Festival is the first significant festival after Spring Festival. It is a rich and colourful festival. People go out at night carrying brightly lit lanterns, watch lantern parades in the streets, guess the meaning of riddles and perform folk dances. It is also an opportunity for family reunions. During the Lantern Festival, people gather together and eat 'yuanxiao', dumplings made of glutinous rice flour stuffed with different fillings. This is why the festival is also known as the Yuan Xiao Festival.

The Lantern Festival is regarded as China's Valentine's Day. In the past, unmarried young women were permitted to appear in public on that day. They would normally be chaperoned in the streets in the hope of finding love.

词组 / 表达法

mín jiān	
民 间	
among the people; folk	
nóng lì	
农 历	
the lunar calendar	
bèi kàn zuò	
被 看 作	
be regarded as	
xī yǐn	
吸 引	
to attract; to appeal	
shèng dàn jié	
圣 诞 节	
Christmas	
zhū shèng rì qián xī	wàn shèng jié
诸 圣 日 前 夕 ;	万 圣 节
Halloween	

Please respond in Chinese to the bullet points below. You are *not* expected to refer to the full content of the above.

- State what the above article is referring to (a full summary is *not* required).

- Have you experienced any Chinese festivals? If so, when and where?

- What is the significance of traditional food during Chinese festivals?

- What festivals do you celebrate locally? How?

- Talk in detail about a festival you have enjoyed.

清明节习俗

请阅读下面一篇关于清明节习俗的杂志文章，然后用英文回答问题。

中国传统的清明节大约有2500多年的历史。由于清明节与寒食的日子接近，而寒食是民间禁火扫墓的日子，渐渐两者便合二为一，因此清明节又称为"寒食节"。

除了"寒食节"，清明节还有"扫坟节"、"鬼节"、"冥节"等别称。清明节的主要习俗是扫墓。人们以为，逝者住在地下，坟墓就是他们的家。在扫墓时，人们会烧纸钱，并把鸡、鱼、肉、糕点、酒、水果等供品放在坟前，供先人享用。

清明节的习俗丰富有趣，除了禁火、扫墓，还有踏青、荡秋千、蹴鞠、打马球、插柳等活动。这个节日既有祭扫新坟的悲酸泪，又有踏青游玩的欢笑声，非常独特。

放风筝是清明节的另一风俗活动。人们不仅在白天放，夜里也会放。在风筝下或在拉线上挂一些五颜六色的小灯笼，在夜空中看起来，就像一闪一闪的小星星。有些人把风筝放上天空后，便剪断拉线，任其漂往天涯海角，据说这样能给自己带来好运。

生词

hán shí 寒食 *lit. cold food; here, name of a festival*	**chā liǔ** 插柳 *to plant willows*
jiē jìn 接近 *close to; near*	**jì yǒu…** 既有… **yòu yǒu…** 又有… *both … and …*
jìn 禁 *to forbid; to prohibit; to ban*	**bēi suān lèi** 悲酸泪 *tears of sorrow*
jiàn jiàn 渐渐 *gradually*	**huān xiào shēng** 欢笑声 *laughter*
chēng wéi 称为 *be called*	**dú tè** 独特 *special; unique*
guǐ 鬼 *ghost*	**fàng fēng zhēng** 放风筝 *to fly kites*
míng 冥 *the underworld*	**bù jǐn** 不仅 *not only*
shì zhě 逝者 *the dead; deceased*	**lā xiàn** 拉线 *string*
fén mù 坟墓 *grave (n.)*	**guà** 挂 *to hang; to put up*
gòng pǐn 供品 *offering (for the dead)*	**dēng long** 灯笼 *lantern*
xiān rén 先人 *ancestor*	**shǎn** 闪 *to twinkle; to glimmer; to flash*
yǒu qù 有趣 *interesting*	**jiǎn duàn** 剪断 *to cut off*
tà qīng 踏青 *to go for a walk in the countryside in spring (when the grass has just turned green)*	**rèn qí piāo wǎng** 任其漂往 **tiān yá hǎi jiǎo** 天涯海角 *to let it go to the ends of the earth*
cù jū 蹴鞠 *to kick a ball*	**jù shuō** 据说 *It is said that …; It is believed that …*

练习A 📖 **Answer the following questions in English.**

一 When did Chinese people start to celebrate the Qing Ming Festival?

二 Why is the Qing Ming Festival also called the *Han Shi*/Cold Food Festival?

三 What other names are there for the Qing Ming Festival?

四 What is the most important custom during this festival?

五 What is the reason behind the custom mentioned in question four?

六 Name three things that Chinese people offer their ancestors at the graveside during the festival.

七 What are some of the unique features associated with the Qing Ming Festival?

八 Other than sweeping graves, what activities do people do at the Qing Ming Festival? List three mentioned in the article.

九 What is special about the way kites are flown at night during this festival?

十 Why do some people cut off the strings of their kites while they are being flown?

中国的年文化

请阅读下面一篇关于庆祝春节的互联网文章，然后用英文回答问题。

中国的年文化

中国有很多古老的传统节日，如冬至、春节、元宵、清明、端午、七夕、中秋、重阳等。其中以庆祝春节的活动最为盛大、最为热闹。

春节又叫"过年"，传统的庆祝活动一般从除夕开始，一直到正月十五元宵节。在除夕那天，家家户户会欢聚一堂吃年夜饭，一起守岁。守岁的习俗，既有辞别过去，又有期待将来的意思。守岁从吃年夜饭开始，一直持续到深夜。春节时有各种辞旧迎新的活动，热闹得不得了。

在守岁时所吃的食品，不少都有特别含义，比如吃枣代表"春来早"、吃杏仁代表"幸福人"、吃长生果代表"长生不老"、吃年糕代表"一年比一年高"等等。人们用生活中常见的东西来表达自己的愿望。

生活中有欣喜，也有苦恼；有福，也有祸。无论是过去、现在还是将来，人人都有同样的愿望，就是"祈盼福气、躲避灾祸"。因此许多地方将"福"字倒过来贴在门上，表示"福到了"。由此可见，中国人过年的心理就是"驱邪降福"。

生词

dōng zhì 冬至 *Winter Solstice*	**biǎo dá** 表达 *to express; to show;* *to indicate*
qìng zhù huó dòng 庆祝活动 *celebration*	**yuàn wàng** 愿望 *wish; aspiration;* *desire*
chú xī 除夕 *New Year's Eve*	**xīn xǐ** 欣喜 *joy; happiness*
huān jù yī táng 欢聚一堂 *to gather together* *happily*	**kǔ nǎo** 苦恼 *worry; distress;* *trouble*
shǒu suì 守岁 *to stay up all night* *on New Year's Eve*	**fú** 福 *happiness; good* *fortune*
cí bié 辞别 *to bid farewell; to* *say goodbye*	**wú lùn** 无论 *regardless of;* *no matter what*
qī dài 期待 *to look forward to;* *to expect*	**qí pàn** 祈盼 *to hope; to wish*
tè bié 特别 *special*	**dào** 倒 *upside down*
zǎo 枣 *jujube; Chinese* *date*	**tiē** 贴 *to stick; to glue*
xìng rén 杏仁 *almond*	**xīn lǐ** 心理 *psychology;* *mentality*
xìng fú 幸福 *happiness*	**qū xié jiàng fú** 驱邪降福 *to expel evil and* *have good fortune*

练习B 📖 Answer the following questions in English.

一 Name five Chinese traditional festivals mentioned in the article.

二 How important is Chinese New Year among these festivals?

三 How long do the celebrations of Chinese New Year usually last?

四 What is the significance of the custom of staying up all night on Chinese New Year's Eve?

五 Name three things stated in the article that people do during Chinese New Year.

六 Name three kinds of food eaten at Chinese New Year.

七 What is the symbolic meaning of the food identified in question six?

八 What aspirations do people have for each coming year?

九 Why is the Chinese character 'fu' displayed upside down?

十 To most Chinese people, what is the deep-rooted meaning of celebrating New Year?

少数民族民间节庆

请阅读下面一篇关于少数民族民间节庆的杂志报道，然后用英文回答问题。

泼水节（傣族）

"泼水节"是傣族一个古老的传统节日，也是傣历新年，一般在傣历六月中旬（即农历清明前后十天左右）。每逢"泼水节"，傣族男女老少均会穿上节日的盛装，提着木桶和脸盆，互相追逐、泼水。被人泼得越多，代表得到的祝福也越多，因此被泼的人也就越高兴。

火把节（彝族）

"火把节"约在每年的农历六月二十四日，是彝族的传统节日。不仅彝族过"火把节"，纳西族、白族等少数民族也会庆祝这个节日。

"火把节"时，家家门前会竖一个火把，村口则竖一个高四、五丈的大火把。晚饭后，人们汇集在广场，点燃火把，欢呼声此起彼落。除了摔跤、斗牛比赛等传统节目以外，新增加的活动还包括歌舞、乐器、智力问答等。

三月三（黎族）

"三月三"是黎族的传统节日，在每年农历三月初三那天庆祝。节日当天，黎族人民会举行预祝"山兰"（山地的旱谷）和打猎丰收的活动，还有优美的"跳竹竿"。晚间，男女青年在广场上围着篝火起舞。黎族青年一般都把"三月三"作为定情的日子，象征他们的爱情似春天一样美好。

四月八（苗族）

"四月八"是苗族人的传统节日，又称"亚努节"。每逢这天，苗族人会举行各种活动，纪念古代英雄亚努。每年参加节日的人数在 20 万以上。人们在一起吹笙、跳舞、唱山歌、荡秋千、上刀梯、玩龙灯、舞狮子等，人山人海，非常热闹。

那达慕（蒙古族）

"那达慕"是中国蒙古族人喜爱的一种传统体育活动，每年农历六月初四开始，为期五天。"那达慕"是蒙古语的译音，意为"娱乐"或"游戏"。

"那达慕"大会期间有大型的物资交流会，晚上还举行各种娱乐活动。"那达慕"大大促进了体育活动的发展，因此深受牧区人民喜爱。

生词

shǎo shù mín zú
少数民族
*minority
nationality*

zhōng xún
中旬
*the middle ten days
of a month*

jí
即
that is (i.e.)

shèng zhuāng
盛装
*splendid attire;
best clothes*

tí
提
*to carry in one's
hand*

mù tǒng
木桶
wooden bucket

liǎn pén
脸盆
basin

hù xiāng zhuī zhú
互相追逐
to chase each other

yí zú
彝族
Yi nationality

nà xī zú
纳西族
Naxi nationality

bái zú
白族
Bai nationality

huǒ bǎ
火把
fire torch

shù
竖
to erect

zhàng
丈
*unit of length,
approximately
3.33 metres*

huì jí
汇集
to gather together

huān hū shēng
欢呼声
cheer; shout of joy

cǐ qǐ bǐ luò
此起彼落
*to rise one after
another*

shuāi jiāo
摔跤
wrestling

dòu niú
斗牛
bullfight

zēng jiā
增加
to add; to increase

yuè qì
乐器
*musical
instrument*

zhì lì wèn dá
智力问答
quiz

lí zú
黎族
Li nationality

hàn gǔ
旱谷
dry valley

dǎ liè
打猎
hunting

fēng shōu
丰收
*harvest; to have a
lot of prey*

yōu měi
优美
graceful

zhú gān
竹竿
bamboo pole

wéi
围
*to surround;
around*

gōu huǒ
篝火
bonfire

dìng qíng
定情
*to agree to marry
somebody*

sì
似
like; similar to

miáo zú
苗族
Miao nationality

yà nǔ
亚努
*Ya Nu, an ancient
hero of Miao
nationality*

yīng xióng
英雄
hero

chuī shēng
吹笙
*to play a reed pipe
wind instrument*

dāo tī
刀梯
knife ladder

měng gǔ zú
蒙古族
*Mongolian
nationality*

nà dá mù
那达慕
*Nadam Fair,
a traditional
Mongolian fair*

wéi qī
为期
to last

yì yīn
译音
transliteration

wù zī jiāo liú huì
物资交流会
trade fair

mù qū
牧区
pastoral area

cù jìn
促进
to promote

练习C 📖 **Answer the following questions.**

一 The Water Festival is ...

a) celebrated during New Year by the Dai minority.

b) another name for the Qing Ming Festival.

c) a modern Chinese festival.

二 Which minority nationalities celebrate the Torch Festival?

a) Yi, Naxi and Mongolian

b) Yi, Bai and Miao

c) Yi, Naxi and Bai

三 Where is the Torch Festival celebrated?

a) at the entrance of the village

b) in the village square

c) in front of the villagers' homes

四 Which of the following is a traditional activity during the Torch Festival?

a) wrestling

b) singing

c) doing quizzes

五 The Miao people do various activities during the Si Yue Ba Festival, including ...

a) singing pop songs and dancing

b) playing with dragon lanterns and lion dancing

c) sitting around a bonfire

六 Nadam is ...

a) a traditional Mongolian sport

b) a traditional Mongolian drama

c) a Mongolian festival for tourists

七 Why do people like splashing water over others during the Water Festival?

八 List three activities that people do during the San Yue San Festival.

九 Why is the San Yue San Festival a special day for young people?

十 What is the Si Yue Ba Festival also called? What is the origin of the name?

十一 What event takes place during the Nadam Fair?

十二 Why is the Nadam Fair so popular among Mongolian people?

庙会

生词
guàng miào huì 逛 庙 会 *to go to a* *temple fair*
zhǐ yī …之一 *one of …*
zǎo qī 早期 *early stage;* *early period*
xū yào 需要 *need; requirement*
jí shì jiāo yì 集市交易 *country/village* *trade fair*
mín sú 民俗 *folk custom*
zuì zhōng 最终 *ultimate*

练习A 🔊　根据广播节目内容，圈出正确的答案。

一 逛庙会是过年的重要习俗之一。　　　　　　　　　　　　　　　　　T / F

二 庙会只是一种隆重的祭祀活动。　　　　　　　　　　　　　　　　　T / F

三 庙会渐渐发展成人们喜爱的娱乐场所。　　　　　　　　　　　　　　T / F

四 人们喜欢逛庙会的主要原因，是他们可以在庙会上做生意。　　　　　T / F

五 庙会上能买到穿的和用的，却买不到吃的。　　　　　　　　　　　　T / F

六 如今的庙会，能让人感受到中华民族文化和民族经济的吸引力。　　　T / F

龙舟竞渡

生词

guó jì lóng zhōu **国际龙舟** lián hé huì **联合会** *International Dragon Boat Federation*	jǐn mì **紧密** *closely*
nóng hòu **浓厚** *profound*	hé zuò **合作** *to cooperate; to collaborate; to work together*
qǐ yuán **起源** *origin*	ài guó shī rén **爱国诗人**
wán měi **完美** *perfect*	qū yuán **屈原** *Qu Yuan, patriotic poet*
jié hé **结合** *combination; integration*	chéng lì **成立** *to found; to establish; to set up*
jí ní sī shì jiè **吉尼斯世界** jì lù dà quán **记录大全** *Guinness Book of World Records*	huá shǒu **划手** *rower* huá **划** *to row (a boat)*
jì zǎi **记载** *record*	duò shǒu **舵手** *steersman*
dūn **吨** *ton, approximately 2 240 pounds*	qí shǒu **旗手** *flag bearer*
yíng **赢** *to win*	luó gǔ **锣鼓** *gong and drum*

练习 B

根据关于龙舟竞渡的介绍，圈出正确的答案。

一 龙舟竞渡在何时举行？

a) 清明节

b) 中秋节

c) 端午节

二 龙舟竞渡是为了纪念哪位著名诗人？

a) 李白

b) 屈原

c) 杜甫

三 赛龙船的活动

a) 只在中国举行

b) 只在中国附近的地区和国家举行

c) 在中国及其附近的地区和国家举行

四 国际龙舟联合会的会员来自哪儿？

a) 全世界

b) 全中国

c) 亚洲各地

五 龙舟比赛是一项

a) 传统的民族体育运动

b) 历史活动

c) 文化活动

六 龙舟比赛前要举行什么活动？

a) 祭祀

b) 划船

c) 欢呼

七 龙舟按龙的形状设计，因为这个设计具有

a) 浓厚的文化色彩

b) 很强的美感

c) 文化跟艺术的完美结合

八 据吉尼斯世界纪录大全记载，世界上最大的龙舟

a) 长23米、宽2.38米、重0.7吨

b) 长69米、宽2.38米、重23吨

c) 长69米、宽0.7米、重2.38吨

九 龙舟船员有几种不同的分工？

a) 三种

b) 四种

c) 五种

十 要想赢得龙舟比赛，船员在比赛中必须做到什么？

a) 一起划船

b) 高声欢呼

c) 紧密合作

生词

héng jǐng 恒景 *Heng Jing, name of a person*	**hěn jiǔ yǐ qián** 很久以前 *a long time ago*
xiáng yāo 降妖 *to subdue an evil spirit*	**wǔ yì gāo qiáng** 武艺高强 *to excel in martial arts*
gōng fu 功夫 *kung fu; martial arts*	**zhū yú yè** 茱萸叶 *leaf of a cornel*
xiān zhǎng 仙长 *immortal master*	**jú huā** 菊花 *chrysanthemum*
wēn mó 瘟魔 *devil that spreads pestilence*	**bǎo jiàn** 宝剑 *precious sword*
dēng gāo 登高 *to walk up a hill or a mountain*	**dài** 带 *to take; to bring*

重阳节的传说

练习 C 🔊 根据重阳节的传说故事，回答下列问题。

一 恒景为什么要学习降妖功夫？

二 恒景跟谁学习功夫？

三 仙长给了恒景哪三件东西？

四 恒景学成了功夫以后，何时回到家乡？

五 恒景在九月初九那天，带人们到什么地方？

六 恒景是怎样降伏瘟魔的？

七 重阳节登高的意义是什么？

八 为什么重阳节又叫"老人节"？

七夕情人节

你从学校的简报上看到以下关于七夕节的介绍，觉得非常有意思，也感到很好奇。你很想多知道点关于牛郎和织女的事。请你用中文给中国朋友写一封180–200字的信，内容包括：

- 你想知道关于牛郎和织女的什么? 你为什么想知道这些?

- 知道了这个美丽的传说之后，你准备用它来做什么?

- 向你的朋友简述一个你喜欢的爱情传说。

- 比较两个故事，说说你更喜欢哪一个? 为什么?

- 注意书信的上下款

每年的农历七月初七，是中国传统的七夕节，民间称这节日为"女儿节"。说到七夕节，人们就会联想到牛郎织女这个美丽的民间传说，这是中国许多民间爱情传说之一。

在这天晚上，如果天空晴朗，我们会看到满天的星星，一道银河横贯南北。在银河的两边，各有一颗闪亮的星星，那就是牵牛星（Altair）和织女星（Vega）。传说在每年的这个夜晚，牛郎与织女都会在鹊桥相会。在中国传统节日中，七夕节是最具浪漫色彩的一个节日，是中国传统的情人节。

中秋节（农历八月十五）

农历八月十五日是中国传统的中秋节，这个节日是仅次于春节的第二大传统节日。

中秋节是个古老的节日，祭月和赏月是中秋节的重要习俗。每当中秋月亮升起时，一家人在院子里围着桌子坐下，一边吃月饼及瓜果，一边聊天赏月。

中秋节的另一习俗是吃月饼。月饼象征"团圆"，祭月之后，由家中长者将月饼切开，每人一块，如果有人不在家也要为其留下一份，表示全家团圆。

中秋节除了赏月、祭月、吃月饼等活动，还有各种赏月游乐活动。

你刚在杂志上读了一篇关于中秋节的短文。下星期六就是中秋节了，你的中国朋友邀请你那天去他／她家参加中秋晚会。请你用中文给中国朋友写一封180–200字的电子邮件，内容包括：

- 你接到中秋晚会的邀请时，心情怎么样？

- 你对这个中秋晚会有什么期待？

- 你准备带什么礼物去？为什么？

- 简述一下最近参加过的／或你自己举办过的一次聚会。

- 与中国的传统节日比较，说说你的聚会有什么相同或不同的地方。你最喜欢的是什么？为什么？

春节的习俗

练习C

春节是中国一个古老的节日，也是全年最重要的一个节日。千百年来，这个节日形成了不少习俗，下面介绍其中几个。

每逢春节临近，家家户户都要打扫房子，这代表了人们破旧立新的愿望。无论在城市还是农村，家家户户都喜欢贴上春联、窗花和年画等，为节日增添喜庆气氛。人们还把福字倒过来贴，表示"幸福已到"、"福气已到"。春节拜年时，长辈会把红包分给晚辈，表示把幸福和好运带给他们。晚辈得到压岁钱，就可以平平安安地度过一岁。红包、春联和窗花等都用的是红颜色，因为红色象征活力、愉快与好运。

上星期一，你和家人参观了一个关于中国文化的展览，了解了不少中国人过春节的习俗。老师请你为全班做一次"中、英文化比较"的演讲。请你用中文写一篇180–200字的演讲稿，内容包括：

- 分别简介中国人和英国人过年的习俗

- 两国的年文化各有什么特点？

- 比较两国的年文化，你觉得有什么相同或不同的地方？

- 你对这两种年文化的看法如何？

- 你打算怎样庆祝明年的新年？

复习一

练习A

请阅读下面十个问题，然后圈出正确的答案。

一 以下哪种材料跟其它的不同类?

  a) 黄瓜   b) 蒜   c) 盐
  d) 葱   e) 辣椒

二 以下哪种不是味道?

  a) 酸   b) 咸   c) 甜
  d) 瓣   e) 辣

三 "九"在以下哪个名胜中有象征意义?

  a) 故宫   b) 外滩   c) 兵马俑
  d) 苏州园林   e) 玉佛寺

四 以下哪个词语跟旅游和交通没有关系?

  a) 硬卧   b) 酱油   c) 免费
  d) 机票   e) 大巴

五 以下哪个不是城市?

  a) 浙江   b) 长江   c) 广州
  d) 山东   e) 湖南

六 以下哪个词有好的意义?

  a) 奋斗   b) 压力   c) 耐性
  d) 西安   e) 紧绷弦

七 以下哪个词语表示教育应想一想学生的全面发展?

  a) 素质教育   b) 应试教育   c) 义务教育
  d) 教育体系   e) 因材施教

八 "闹笑话"是什么意思?

  a) 玩笑   b) 城市里   c) 笑笑
  d) 说错   e) 笑着说话

九 中国人在以下哪个节日扫墓?

  a) 七夕节   b) 清明节   c) 中秋节
  d) 元宵节   e) 春节

十 以下哪个不是清明节的习俗?

  a) 放风筝   b) 守岁   c) 插柳
  d) 踏青   e) 蹴鞠

练习B

请将以下的词语与意思配对起来，有些单字曾在第一至四章中出现。（由于考试可能出现你从没见过的词语，因此你必须看懂单字，以判断词语的意思。）

一　玩笑　　　　　a) raw material

二　习惯　　　　　b) memory

三　消费　　　　　c) goods; merchandise

四　打鼓　　　　　d) to consume

五　赏玩　　　　　e) to look after someone

六　原料　　　　　f) trade

七　裁定　　　　　g) to admire the beauty of
　　　　　　　　　　　something; to enjoy

八　吉利　　　　　h) joke

九　贸易　　　　　i) scared; afraid

十　记忆　　　　　j) lucky; auspicious

十一　器材　　　　k) equipment

十二　产品　　　　l) to play the drum

十三　获得　　　　m) habit

十四　照顾　　　　n) to gain; to achieve; to win

十五　害怕　　　　o) ruling

练习C

请圈出正确的单字，完成以下句子。

一　她努力地练习，才能有如此 ● 彩的表演。

　　a) 静　　b) 精　　c) 清　　d) 情

二　春节时，中国人喜欢把"福"字 ● 贴在门上。

　　a) 正　　b) 挂　　c) 倒　　d) 壶

三　旅行团通常会为团员安排晚 ●。

　　a) 宴　　b) 旱　　c) 早　　d) 冥

四　元宵节的一个活动是 ● 灯迷。

　　a) 请　　b) 情　　c) 青　　d) 猜

五　四川菜的 ● 色是材料多包括辣椒、蒜和生姜。

　　a) 待　　b) 特　　c) 持　　d) 诗

六　小红既 ● 心又勤奋，因此才能考进北京大学。

　　a) 细　　b) 电　　c) 田　　d) 里

七　这本书 ● 载了邓小平的生平。

　　a) 裁　　b) 栽　　c) 记　　d) 纪

八　白族人在篝火前 ● 笙庆祝。

　　a) 你　　b) 欢　　c) 吹　　d) 观

九　每个人的兴趣和喜好都有 ● 异。

　　a) 差　　b) 盖　　c) 不　　d) 无

十　老师给你个人指导，你应该要 ● 心。

　　a) 传　　b) 砖　　c) 专　　d) 转

请在括号内填上正确的连接词。

不仅…也… 不但…而且… 一边…一边… 因为…所以… 除了…也…

一 过中秋节时，中国人喜欢（ ）赏月，（ ）吃月饼。

二 四川菜（ ）本地人欣赏，连外地人（ ）喜欢吃呢！

三 学习汉语，（ ）要注意发音，（ ）要注意语调。

四 游客（ ）会参观名胜古迹，（ ）还会品尝地道美味。

五 （ ）考试的压力太大，（ ）她时常头晕。

请在括号内填上正确的单字或词语。

才 把 被 并不 比 却 同时 因此 由于 然后

一 （ ）中国地大物博，所以不同地方的菜有不同的特色。

二 我们会先到故宫，（ ）才吃午饭。

三 我觉得素质教育（ ）应试教育好得多。

四 中国的经济起飞，（ ）越来越多人学习汉语。

五 他胃口大开，一个人（ ）六十个饺子全吃掉。

六 到了现代，故宫（ ）开放让老百姓进去。

七 妈妈喜欢吃辣的，我（ ）喜欢吃酸的。

八 我（ ）紧张的学校生活压得透不过气来。

九 在中国乘坐计程车（ ）特别昂贵。

十 在香港，学生要（ ）学习中文和英文。

请用第一至四章中出现过的词语，完成以下句子。括号内的英文为提示。

一 中国历史上，由于战争及其他原因，常常出现没有食物的情况，（ ）肚子便成了生存的最大问题（ ）。（ ）人们见面时说的第一句话多是："你吃了吗？"由于食物不多，为表示对他人的关心，人们就试试（ ）可吃的东西，并把它们做成（ ）可口的（ ）。
(therefore, dish, mix and stir-fry, (be) full, one of, delicious)

二 在英国某所新学校，校长让教师寻找（ ）的课题来做。那时一位老师（ ）把教汉语（ ）这样的课题。她的想法是，中文很有可能在未来成为世界上商界通用的语言，如果她的学生有（ ）学好中文，这会给他们的（ ）前景打开很多机会之窗。
(ability, meaningful, work, be regarded as, decide)

三 上海是中国最大的城市之一，（ ）也是一座（ ）的名城和有名的旅游城市。作为全国最大的（ ）中心，上海（ ）了中西（ ）的品质。它不仅现代化，而且还保持了中国的（ ）特色。
(at the same time, culture, economy, merge, traditional, ancient)

四 年画是中国一种（ ）的民间艺术，用来表达民众对未来的（ ）。过年时，人们除了贴（ ）字外，还喜爱在客厅里、卧室中贴年画。一张张年画给各家各户增添了快乐的节日（ ）。对许多老年人来说，年画是过年时（ ）的东西。
(ancient, atmosphere, indispensable, good fortune, wish)

请把以下的句子翻译成汉语。

一 Last year when Matthew visited Hangzhou, he was pleased that certain scenic spots were free of charge for adults as well as for children.

二 Due to continuous assessments and the pressure to achieve good results, nowadays many high school students are stressed.

三 One of the differences between trains in China and Britain is that trains in China have both hard and soft beds. In addition, long-distance train tickets are much cheaper in China than in Britain.

四 Chinese cooking involves stir-frying dishes in a wok. The main ingredients that produce the characteristic taste of China are garlic, ginger, spring onions and soy sauce.

五 Chinese New Year is regarded as an important time for family reunions. As huge crowds of people travel home to celebrate the festival, the price of train and plane tickets goes up.

六 In the past, the Chinese Emperor and his family lived in the Imperial Palace, but now it has been opened up to the public and has become a huge tourist attraction. As soon as you enter the Palace, you realise that the buildings all embody wonderful Ming dynasty architectural designs.

七 In the past, British school students used to have to study French, German or Spanish. However, many people now regard languages as being more difficult than other subjects. Consequently, the number of students studying them is decreasing.

八 Besides being a time for sweeping the graves of ancestors, the Qing Ming Festival is also a time for laughter among family members.

九 Chinese cuisine varies depending on which province you visit, since each area has its own distinctive style. In northern China, noodles are the staple food, whereas in the south, rice is regarded as the main part of a meal. Sichuan is famous for its hot and spicy dishes, whereas people in Shandong eat a lot of seafood.

十 No matter how expensive the taxis were, he avoided taking buses in the big cities because he liked to go anywhere he wanted at a time that suited him.

第五章 健康与健身

健康小测验

练习 A 😃 你知道如何保持身体健康吗？请阅读下面十个问题，选出你认为最佳的答案，然后进行双人或小组讨论。

一 为什么绿色蔬菜对身体健康很重要？

a) 它们的颜色好看

b) 它们能使牙齿闪亮

c) 它们含有维生素和矿物质

d) 它们比主食更有利于减肥

二 为什么我们要锻炼身体？

a) 保持我们的心脏健康

b) 使我们的肌肉强壮

c) 改善我们的体形

d) 以上全部正确

三 为什么我们要吃不同种类的水果？

a) 它们在胃里会变成水果沙拉

b) 吃同一种水果很单调

c) 不同水果含有不同的营养成份

d) 使我们的牙齿更健康

四 猪肉不含什么营养成分？

a) 蛋白质

b) 脂肪

c) 纤维

d) 维生素

五 以下哪种不是中国传统运动？

a) 太极

b) 拳击

c) 武术

d) 乒乓球

六 过量饮酒不会导致

a) 肝病

b) 癌症

c) 生育问题

d) 牙病

七 运动后，你更想吃哪种食物？

a) 含淀粉的食物

b) 含糖份的食物

c) 含蛋白质的食物

d) 含脂肪的食物

八 运动可以有效减肥吗？

a) 绝对可以，它减肥又快又好

b) 可以，但必须经常运动

c) 不可以，只靠运动是不行的

d) 绝对不可以，运动不能帮助减肥

九 以下哪种维生素可以从阳光中得到？

a) 维生素 A

b) 维生素 B

c) 维生素 C

d) 维生素 D

十 多吃以下哪种食物，可以减低患心脏病的机会？

a) 面条

b) 瘦肉

c) 鱼

d) 鸡肉

生词

jiàn kāng 健康 *health*	duàn liàn 锻炼 *to exercise*	yíng yǎng chéng fèn 营养成份 *nutrient*	ái zhèng 癌症 *cancer*
hán yǒu 含有 *to contain*	jī ròu 肌肉 *muscle*	zhī fáng 脂肪 *fat*	shēng yù wèn tí 生育问题 *birth problem*
wéi shēng sù 维生素 *vitamin*	qiáng zhuàng 强壮 *strong*	xiān wéi 纤维 *fibre*	diàn fěn 淀粉 *starch*
kuàng wù zhì 矿物质 *mineral*	gǎi shàn 改善 *to improve*	quán jī 拳击 *boxing*	yǒu xiào 有效 *effective; (-ly)*
yǒu lì yú 有利于 *advantageous to; favourable to*	tǐ xíng 体形 *body form*	dǎo zhì 导致 *to cause*	bì xū 必须 *must*
jiǎn féi 减肥 *to lose weight*	dān diào 单调 *monotonous*	gān bìng 肝病 *liver disease*	

生词

tǐ cāo 体操 *gymnastics*	líng huó 灵活 *flexible*
chì shǒu kōng quán 赤手空拳 *bare-handed*	tī 踢 *kick*
wǔ qì 武器 *weapon*	quán dǎ 拳打 *punch*
jì lǜ 纪律 *discipline*	yì lì 毅力 *stamina*
xiàn shēn jīng shén 献身精神 *dedication*	

Martial arts

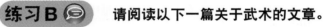 练习 B　请阅读以下一篇关于武术的文章。

Wushu, like kung fu, is a term which refers to Chinese martial arts. It has also become the name for a modern sport similar to gymnastics, which includes bare-handed forms and weapons in performance.

It tests practitioners' strength and stamina and is a good way to keep fit. To practice wushu, you need discipline and dedication. You also need a great deal of concentration when you are practising routines, and a sharp mind to remember all the forms. You need to be flexible and strong to do all the kicks, punches and high jumps, as well as having good stamina.

Please respond in Chinese to the bullet points below. You are *not* expected to refer to the full content of the article.

- State what the article is referring to (a full summary is *not* required).

- What does wushu test?

- What are the advantages of practising wushu?

- If you had the opportunity to take up martial arts, which one would you do? Why?

- Why do you think martial arts are becoming more and more popular outside Asia?

- Have you seen any of these films: *Star Wars*, *Crouching Tiger, Hidden Dragon*, *House of Flying Daggers* or *Hero*, which use wushu in many of the fighting scenes? Talk about a performance you have seen or experienced.

- Talk about a sports star that you like.

词组 / 表达法

jiàn shēn 健身 *to keep fit*	bǐ sài　jìng sài huó dòng 比赛；竞赛活动 *competition*	wò hǔ cáng lóng 《卧虎藏龙》 *Crouching Tiger, Hidden Dragon*
jiǎn qīng yā lì 减轻压力 *to relieve stress*	biǎo yǎn 表演 *performance*	shí miàn mái fú 《十面埋伏》 *House of Flying Daggers*
tǐ lì hé nǎo lì 体力和脑力 *physical and mental strength*	xīng qiú dà zhàn 《星球大战》 *Star Wars*	yīng xióng 《英雄》 *Hero*

血型与减肥

请阅读下面一篇关于血型与减肥的文章，然后用英文回答问题。

人的血型可以决定他们的身体适宜吃什么食物。美国的一位医生不但针对 O 型血、A 型血、B 型血和 AB 型血，提出了完整的饮食模式，而且还为不同血型的人，设计了完全不同的减肥食谱：

O 型血： 可以靠吃瘦肉、动物肝脏、海鲜和绿色蔬菜来控制体重。如果想靠吃玉米、谷物、卷心菜、土豆来减肥，那将没有效果。

A 型血： 要多吃蔬菜。某些植物蛋白质，如大豆蛋白质，是 A 型血人最佳的保健食品，常吃可预防心血管病和癌症。

B 型血： 这类人尤其适宜食用肉类和乳类食品。而鸡肉、玉米、西红柿、大部分坚果和种子类食物却不是他们的健康食品。

AB 型血： 既适宜吃动物蛋白，又适吃植物蛋白。这种血型的人消化系统比较敏感，他们适宜分多次吃高蛋白食物，每次吃少量。这类人士的健康食品是：鱼、豆腐、绿叶蔬菜和乳制品。

虽然这种说法很流行，但是也有人觉得它并不科学。

生词

xuè xíng 血型 *blood group*	kòng zhì 控制 *to control*	zuì jiā de 最佳的 *best*	jiān guǒ 坚果 *nut*
mó shì 模式 *model*	yù mǐ 玉米 *maize*	yù fáng 预防 *to prevent*	zhǒng zi 种子 *seed*
shí pǔ 食谱 *recipe*	gǔ wù 谷物 *cereal*	xīn xuè guǎn bìng 心血管病 *cardiovascular disease*	xiāo huà xì tǒng 消化系统 *digestive system*
kào 靠 *to depend on; to rely on*	juǎn xīn cài 卷心菜 *cabbage*	yóu qí 尤其 *especially*	mǐn gǎn 敏感 *sensitive*
gān zàng 肝脏 *liver*	xiào guǒ 效果 *effect*	rǔ lèi shí pǐn 乳类食品 *dairy product*	

练习A 📖 Answer the following questions in English.

一 According to the article, why is your blood group an important factor in determining a healthy diet?

二 What types of food are suitable for people with blood group O?

三 How can people with blood group A prevent cancer?

四 What food is not suitable for people with blood group B?

五 What should people with blood group AB be aware of when eating food high in protein?

中国针灸

请阅读下面一篇关于中国针灸的报刊文章，然后用英文回答问题。

中国针灸有几千年的历史，它不但在中国广泛使用，而且传到了世界各地。

针灸包括两种古老的治疗方法：针法和灸法。针法是用不同长度的针，按一定穴位，刺入病人体内以治疗疾病。灸法是把特殊植物的叶子燃烧，然后按一定的穴位，靠近皮肤或放在皮肤上，利用热的刺激来治疗疾病。哈佛大学科学家使用现代技术，证实了针灸可以缓解人的疼痛。他们发现，在针灸后几秒钟之内，患者大脑中的特定区域，血流会逐渐减少，让该区域镇静下来。

现代科学家所进行的实验，显示针灸对许多病症均有疗效。例如，德国的科学家近来证明了针灸对背疼的治疗，比现代医药更有效。另外，针灸可以帮助人更好地休息、增进饮食和调节情绪。你知道吗？据报道，很多名人曾使用过针灸。例如，Kate Moss 使用针灸戒毒，Gwyneth Paltrow 用它来减轻压力，Jim Carey 用针灸来延年益寿，其他名人则用针灸来减肥或抗衰老。

生词

zhēn jiǔ **针灸** *acupuncture and moxibustion*	pí fū **皮肤** *skin*	xiǎn shì **显示** *to show; to indicate*
zhì liáo **治疗** *treatment*	cì jī **刺激** *to stimulate*	zhèng míng **证明** *to prove*
zhēn **针** *needle*	hā fó dà xué **哈佛大学** *Harvard University*	zēng jìn **增进** *to increase*
cháng dù **长度** *length*	huǎn jiě **缓解** *to ease; to relieve*	tiáo jié qíng xù **调节情绪** *to regulate emotions*
xué wèi **穴位** *acupuncture point*	huàn zhě **患者** *patient*	jiè dú **戒毒** *drug rehabilitation*
cì rù **刺入** *to pierce*	dà nǎo **大脑** *brain*	yán nián yì shòu **延年益寿** *to prolong life*
rán shāo **燃烧** *to burn*	zhú jiàn **逐渐** *gradually*	kàng shuāi lǎo **抗衰老** *anti-aging*
tè shū **特殊** *special*	zhèn jìng **镇静** *to calm down; to cool down*	
kào jìn **靠近** *close to*	shí yàn **实验** *experiment*	

练习B 📖 **Answer the following questions in English.**

一 According to the article, what are acupunture and moxibustion? Identify the Chinese sentence which gives the definition.

二 What is the difference between acupuncture and moxibustion?

三 What is common between the two treatments?

四 How do acupuncture and moxibustion relieve a patient's pain?

五 According to the article, what has been proven by German scientists?

六 How can acupuncture and moxibustion help our well-being?

七 What have some celebrities used acupunture and moxibustion for?

校园集体舞

请阅读下面一篇关于青少年肥胖问题与集体舞的杂志文章，然后用英文回答问题。

近十年来，中国中小学生越来越胖。据有关部门公布，他们比 30 年前的同龄人平均高 2 英寸，重 6.5 磅。

许多人认为，导致青少年肥胖的原因，是中国有过多西方快餐店，尤其在北京和上海等大城市，你在每条街上，都会看到麦当劳、肯德鸡、比萨饼店。随着富有的中国人增多，70 多元人民币的意大利辣香肠比萨饼变得比较容易接受。

由于肥胖问题在中国越来越严重，政府因此提出了新的解决方法。从 2007 年秋季开学起，全国所有中小学生都要上舞蹈课，学习一套校园集体舞。教育部发布这个消息后在社会上引发了一连串热烈的讨论。

家长不太支持孩子参与这项活动。他们认为中小学生应该好好学习，跳双人舞会让男女学生有太多的身体接触，容易导致早恋。

大多数老师认为，集体舞的动作大方得体，在跳舞过程中会不断换舞伴，而不是固定一男一女搭配跳舞，不会造成一些人所担忧的身体接触导致早恋的问题。跳舞不但可以强身健体、预防疾病、避免肥胖，还可以放松心情，同时把美的一面展示给大家看。

教育部体育卫生与艺术教育司的官员说，如果学生不想跳舞，他们可以参加其他活动，比如：武术、游泳、踢足球、打篮球，而不是整日坐在教室里做功课。

生词

jí tǐ wǔ **集体舞** *group dancing*	yì dà lì **意大利** là xiāng cháng **辣香肠** *pepperoni*	tǎo lùn **讨论** *discussion*	dān yōu **担忧** *to worry about*
zhōng xiǎo xué shēng **中小学生** *(abbreviation for) middle school and primary school students*	jiē shòu **接受** *to accept; to receive*	zhī chí **支持** *to support*	qiáng shēn jiàn tǐ **强身健体** *to keep fit*
yīng cùn **英寸** *inch*	yán zhòng **严重** *serious*	shēn tǐ jiē chù **身体接触** *physical contact*	xīn qíng **心情** *feeling*
bàng **磅** *pound (in weight)*	jiě jué fāng fǎ **解决方法** *solution*	zǎo liàn **早恋** *romantic relationship at a young age*	zhǎn shì **展示** *to show*
kuài cān diàn **快餐店** *fast food shop*	tào **套** *set*	guò chéng **过程** *process; procedure*	guān yuán **官员** *an official*
suí zhe **随着** *with; to accompany*	fā bù **发布** *to announce*	bù duàn **不断** *constantly*	
fù yǒu **富有** *rich*	xiāo xī **消息** *news*	wǔ bàn **舞伴** *dancing partner*	
	xì liè **系列** *series*	gù dìng **固定** *fixed*	

练习 C 📖 **Answer the following questions in English.**

一 What facts show Chinese children are becoming fatter?

二 According to the article, what is the reason behind the obesity problem in China in this decade?

三 Which areas of China have serious obesity problems?

四 What is the Chinese government's new initiative to combat the obesity problem?

五 When and where will the new initiative be carried out?

六 What has been the response to the government's new initiative in society?

七 What do the parents think about the initiative?

八 What do teachers think about the parents' concerns?

九 What kind of benefits could students receive from this new initiative?

十 What are the alternatives if students do not wish to participate in the initiative?

你怎么了?

练习A 根据王明和丽丽的对话内容,
选出正确的答案。

生词

bú shū fu
不舒服
not feeling well

tóu yūn
头晕
dizzy

liáng tǐ wēn
量体温
to take somebody's temperature

yàn xuè
验血
blood test

dǎ zhēn
打针
injection

X- guāng
X 光
X-ray

zháo jí
着急
anxious

一 王明哪儿不舒服?

　　a) 头疼 ☐

　　b) 头晕 ☐

　　c) 背疼 ☐

二 王明没有做什么检查?

　　a) 量体温 ☐

　　b) 验血 ☐

　　c) 打针 ☐

三 王明的检查结果怎样?

　　a) 正常 ☐

　　b) 不正常 ☐

　　c) 严重 ☐

四 王明看的是什么医生?

　　a) 中医 ☐

　　b) 西医 ☐

　　c) 中西医 ☐

五 医生认为王明的病怎么样?

　　a) 严重 ☐

　　b) 没病 ☐

　　c) 没说 ☐

六 丽丽建议王明做什么?

　　a) 锻炼身体 ☐

　　b) 看中医 ☐

　　c) 多休息 ☐

看医生

练习B 王明听了丽丽的建议去看中医。
根据医生和王明的对话内容,
选出正确的答案。

生词

sǎng zi
嗓子
throat

mài bó
脉搏
pulse

pí juàn
疲倦
tired

yǎng chéng
养成
to develop

fā yán
发炎
inflammation

qì sè
气色
complexion

shàng huǒ
上火
to suffer from excessive internal heat

huī fù
恢复
to recover

xiū xián
休闲
relaxed; relaxation

一 王明病了多少天?

　　a) 一天 ☐

　　b) 两天 ☐

　　c) 三天 ☐

二 医生认为王明可能吃了什么?

　　a) 太热的东西 ☐

　　b) 不太热的东西 ☐

　　c) 太凉的东西 ☐

三 医生给王明检查了什么?

　　a) 嗓子 ☐

　　b) 牙齿 ☐

　　c) 脉搏 ☐

四 王明为什么会觉得疲倦?

　　a) 每天晚上学习 ☐

　　b) 每天晚上玩电脑 ☐

　　c) 每天晚上早睡 ☐

五 王明的病怎么样?

　　a) 严重 ☐

　　b) 不太严重 ☐

　　c) 没问题 ☐

六 医生怎样给王明治疗的?

　　a) 不用王明吃药,
　　　 叫他多休息 ☐

　　b) 叫他养成良好的
　　　 生活习惯 ☐

　　c) 开了中药给他吃 ☐

零食和健康

练习C 根据云云和方方关于零食的讨论，在下面选出正确的句子，并在旁边的空格内打 **✗**。

生词		
líng shí 零食 *snack*	**一** 方方正在吃五香豆腐干。	☐
rè liàng 热量 *energy*	**二** 云云不太爱吃巧克力。	☐
mì jué 秘诀 *key to success; secret*	**三** 方方认为炸土豆片的热量很高。	☐
lā jī shí wù 垃圾食物 *junk food*	**四** 方方认为鸭脖子是健康食品。	☐
jiù shēng quān 救生圈 *lifebuoy*	**五** 云云认为吃零食容易发胖。	☐
xīn kǔ 辛苦 *hard; laborious*	**六** 方方认为吃零食对身体好。	☐
miáo tiáo 苗条 *slim*	**七** 云云的减肥秘诀是少吃糖。	☐
	八 方方认为云云的减肥秘诀不好。	☐

看病日记

练习A

你刚去了医院看病。请你用中文写一篇180-200字的日记，来谈谈

- 你得病后的感觉

- 看医生的过程

- 医生给你什么建议，比如：多运动

- 今后你要如何保持身体健康

武术与健康

练习B

你在一场武术表演中得了第一名，获邀到一所学校去谈谈你的体会。请你用中文写一篇180-200字的讲话稿，来谈谈：

- 你喜欢吃什么营养食品？为什么？

- 你认为零食对你的健康有什么影响？

- 你平时做什么运动？

- 为什么你认为学习武术对青少年的健康有好处？

- 你会给新选手什么建议？

选菜单

练习C ✏ 两家公司为学校送来两份午餐菜单，请你比较并决定哪份较好。

A 公司的菜单

价钱：£2.10

主食：
油条 / 饺子 /
包子 / 面条 /
大米 / 鸡蛋炒饭

菜谱 / 菜：
炒肉片 / 鱼 / 青菜 /
古老鸡 / 宫保鸡丁

汤：
蛋花汤 /
菜汤 / 粥

B 公司的菜单

价钱：£1.70

主食：
比萨饼 / 三明治 /
面包 / 薯条 /
烤土豆 / 炸鸡腿 /
炸鱼 / 牛排 / 沙拉

甜食：
奶昔 / 冰淇淋 /
布丁 / 水果

汤：
西红柿汤

请你用中文写一篇180-200字的文章，来谈谈你选择的理由：

- 哪款饭菜的颜色好、味道香？哪个菜单更健康？为什么？

- 比较不同食物的做法，如炒、煮、炸、烤

- 比较不同食物的营养成份，如：蛋白质、脂肪、纤维、维生素、糖份

- 跟你同龄的人饮食习惯是什么样的？他们身体健康吗？为什么？

第六章 亚洲行

到亚洲旅游

练习A 💬 你愿意到亚洲旅游吗？外出旅游时，你会考虑些什么？请阅读下面十一个问题，然后进行双人或小组讨论。

一 外出旅游时，你希望住在

a) 豪华酒店

b) 露营地

c) 度假村 / 度假屋

d) 朋友家

二 你喜欢哪种类型的假期？

a) 以购物为主

b) 以品尝美食为主

c) 以休闲为主

d) 以看风景为主

三 外出旅游时，你喜欢到哪里用餐？

a) 在酒店里

b) 街边小店

c) 自己做

d) 到饭馆吃

四 度假时，你希望入住的酒店

a) 有运动设施，如高尔夫球场

b) 交通方便

c) 周围景色美丽

d) 娱乐设施好

五 你去过北京的四合院和胡同吗？去看北京的胡同，你认为哪种是最好的方式？

a) 走路

b) 骑自行车

c) 坐三轮车

d) 乘出租车

六 中国很多大城市均有堵车的问题，你认为什么引起了堵车？

a) 太多的私家车

b) 汽油太便宜

c) 自行车道不够

d) 马路太窄

七 你认为象胡同和四合院这些传统的东西应该保留吗？为什么？

八 香港的交通非常方便，你知道为什么吗？

九 台湾有很多著名景点，你能举出几个例子吗？

十 你知道东方明珠电视塔吗？请描述一下。

十一 亚洲很多国家和城市都有地铁，如北京、上海、广州、台北、香港和新加坡等。你乘坐过这些地方的地铁吗？它们的优点和缺点是什么？

生词

háo huá 豪华 *luxurious*	gòu wù 购物 *shopping*	gāo ěr fū qiú 高尔夫球 *golf*	yōu diǎn 优点 *advantage*
lù yíng 露营 *camping*	pǐn cháng 品尝 *to taste*	dǔ chē 堵车 *traffic congestion*	quē diǎn 缺点 *disadvantage*
yǐ wéi zhǔ 以…为主 *mainly*	shè shī 设施 *facility*	bǎo liú 保留 *to keep*	

Transcript

Transport

练习 B 💬 请阅读下面一篇关于中国交通的文章。

生词

zì xíng chē wáng guó 自 行 车 王 国 *bicycle kingdom*	bù wū rǎn 不 污 染 *non-polluting*
fù dān dé qǐ 负 担 得 起 *affordable*	jié néng 节 能 *energy efficient*
zuì huán bǎo de 最 环 保 的 jiāo tōng gōng jù 交 通 工 具 *greenest mode of transport*	

China's reign as the 'bicycle kingdom' is coming to an end as it now faces the rapid rise of the car. The improvement of the state economy has made cars affordable for many Chinese people. In 2008, Beijing will have three million cars competing for road space with some four million bicycles. Some of Beijing's bicycle lanes have been transformed into motor vehicle lanes as a result of the increasing demand from the large number of cars.

Like many big cities in the world, Beijing suffers from traffic congestion despite the effort made to have new roads constructed, old ones widened and new ring roads added. Some people suggest a move back to the old days with bicycles being the solution to the traffic problem. Cars cannot move once they get stuck on the road, but bicycles can. Bicycles are championed in the West as being the greenest mode of transport, since they are non-polluting, energy efficient, and also cheap to buy and look after.

词组 / 表达法

gōng gòng jiāo tōng 公 共 交 通 *public transport*
wǒ chéng zuò … shàng xúe 我 乘 坐 …上 学 *I take … to school*
wǒ huì xuǎn yòng 我 会 选 用 … *I would use …*
zhù zài dà chéng shì de rén 住 在 大 城 市 的 人 *people living in the big cities*
zhèng cè 政 策 *policy*
gǔ lì bié rén xuǎn yòng 鼓 励 别 人 选 用 … *to encourage people to use …*

Please respond in Chinese to the bullet points below. You are *not* expected to refer to the full content of the above.

- State what the above article is referring to (a full summary is *not* required).

- What modes of transport do you have locally?

- What mode of transport do you use to travel to school? What would you use if you could choose? Why?

- Why do you think many people in Beijing and some other big cities in China prefer cars to bicycles?

- What policy would you make to encourage the use of bicycles?

他们为什么喜欢香港?

请阅读下面一篇访问稿,然后用英文回答问题。

内地游客
李女士

香港是个购物天堂。在这里,商品琳琅满目,各色衣帽、箱包、电器、首饰、家具任你挑选。商店的营业时间很长,几乎所有商店一星期均七天营业。商场大都位于市中心,交通便捷。我每次来香港都满载而归。

在港工作的
美籍人士彼得

我最爱香港的美食。在这里,你能品尝到各色美味。海鲜是最有名的了,珍宝海鲜舫可以说是世界闻名。我还特别喜欢烤鹅,跟北京的烤鸭一样让人难忘。另外,街头小吃方便快捷花样多,又物美价廉,我经常和朋友一起去吃。

香港市民
吴先生

上酒楼是香港的地道饮食文化之一,也是我喜好的活动。和朋友、家人一起坐在酒楼里,一边聊天,一边品尝虾饺、烧卖等各种点心,真是人生一大享受。

留学生
吉姆

香港的公共交通非常方便,除了公车、电车,还有不堵车的地铁。要到不同岛屿,你可乘坐渡轮,不但速度快,还可以观赏香港的景色。新机场也很棒。

gòu wù tiān táng 购物天堂 *shopping paradise*	kuài jié 快捷 *quick*
shǒu shì 首饰 *jewellery*	wù měi jià lián 物美价廉 *cheap but good*
lín láng mǎn mù 琳琅满目 *a superb collection of beautiful things*	liáo tiān 聊天 *to chat*
yíng yè shí jiān 营业时间 *business hours*	rén shēng 人生 *one's life*
biàn jié 便捷 *convenient*	xiǎng shòu 享受 *enjoyment*
mǎn zài ér guī 满载而归 *return fully loaded; with fruitful results*	mì dù 密度 *density*
měi shí 美食 *good food*	gōng chē 公车 *bus*
zhēn bǎo hǎi xiān fǎng 珍宝海鲜舫 *Jumbo Seafood Restaurant*	dǎo yǔ 岛屿 *island*
shì jiè wén míng 世界闻名 *famous world wide*	sù dù 速度 *speed*
nán wàng 难忘 *unforgettable*	guān shǎng 观赏 *to enjoy the view*
	bàng 棒 *excellent*

练习A 📖 **Answer the following questions in English.**

一 Ms Li thinks Hong Kong is a great place for shopping. List two of her reasons from the article.

二 List three things in the article which you can buy in Hong Kong.

三 What does Peter say about the roast goose?

四 According to Peter, food sold in the streets is popular. Why?

五 What is Mr Wu's enjoyment in life?

六 Why does Jim think the ferries are good?

新加坡圣淘沙

请阅读下面一篇关于新加坡著名旅游胜地圣淘沙的简介，然后用英文回答问题。

圣淘沙是新加坡的度假胜地，它是一个长4.2公里，宽1公里的岛屿。它离新加坡本岛仅半公里，靠一座跨海大桥与本岛连接。圣淘沙在马来文中的意思是"和平安宁"。

圣淘沙有美丽的白沙和碧海，海滩娱乐和运动设施应有尽有。在这里，你可以骑车、划艇，还可以打高尔夫球。岛上鸟语花香，可以看到孔雀、猴子等野生动物。高37米的鱼尾狮塔是新加坡的旅游标志，在塔上你可鸟瞰圣淘沙及附近岛屿的美景。夜幕降临，备受欢迎的彩色音乐喷泉会带给你精彩的表演。当然这里还有大人和儿童都喜爱的海底海洋世界、蝴蝶公园及昆虫王国。

圣淘沙的住宿设备完善，既有服务一流的豪华大酒店，也有经济型的度假村和度假屋，你还可以选择露营营地。除此以外，岛上还有很多餐馆可供选择。

圣淘沙的道路四通八达，无论开车或使用公共交通工具均十分便利。

生词

shèng táo shā	kǒng què	pēn quán
圣淘沙	**孔雀**	**喷泉**
Sentosa (Singapore's island resort)	*peacock*	*fountain*

dù jià shèng dì	hóu zi	zhù sù
度假胜地	**猴子**	**住宿**
holiday resort	*monkey*	*accommodation*

lián jiē	yě shēng dòng wù	shè bèi wán shàn
连接	**野生动物**	**设备完善**
to join; to link	*wildlife*	*well equipped*

hé píng	yú wěi shī tǎ	jì yě
和平	**鱼尾狮塔**	**既…也**
peace	*Merlion (a statue with the head of a lion and the body of a fish)*	*not only … but also …*

ān níng		yī liú
安宁		**一流**
tranquility		*first class*

huá tǐng	biāo zhì	xuǎn zé
划艇	**标志**	**选择**
paddling	*sign; symbol*	*to choose*

rén gōng	niǎo kàn	biàn lì
人工	**鸟瞰**	**便利**
man-made; artificial	*to get a bird's-eye view*	*convenient*

练习 B Answer the following questions in English.

一 How big is Sentosa?

二 How is Sentosa connected to the mainland of Singapore?

三 According to the brochure, what sports facility can you find in Sentosa?

四 What is the icon of Singapore's tourism?

五 List the places both children and adults like visiting in Sentosa.

六 What types of accommodation can you find in Sentosa?

七 According to the brochure, is Sentosa easy to reach? Identify the sentence that provides the answer.

胡同和四合院

请阅读下面一篇关于北京胡同和四合院的报章介绍，然后用英文回答问题。

到了北京，除了一定要去看故宫、爬长城，也不能错过胡同和四合院，因为它们代表了老北京。在高楼大厦林立和满是宽阔街道的现代化北京城里，胡同和四合院是一道独特的风景。

四合院是北京传统住宅建筑的代表，它东西南北四面皆建有独立的房屋，四面的房屋合围，中间形成一个院落，故名"四合院"。坐北朝南的为正房，东西两边相对的是厢房，坐南朝北的为倒座，院门一般开在东南角。一般来说，家长居正房，晚辈住厢房，倒座一般用作书房和客厅。四合院一排排地相连，每排之间的间隔地带就是胡同，是住在四合院的人出入的通道。"胡同"这个词来自蒙古语，在忽必烈建元大都时出现。胡同的长短大小不一，最短的胡同大约为十来米长，叫"一尺大街"。最窄的胡同叫"钱市胡同"，它中间最窄处只44厘米。许多著名的胡同已被当作文物保留下来，它们为现代化的首都保存了一丝古老的色彩。著名作家老舍笔下曾无数次描写过四合院的生活，他曾居住过的小羊圈胡同，还保留着以前的样子。

去看胡同，你可以走路，也可以骑自行车。若要省时省力，还可以选择坐三轮车。逛累了，你可以进茶馆里歇歇脚，品一杯清香的绿茶，也许能听上一段京剧，那可是一种享受呢！

生词

cuò guò 错过 *to miss*	jiǎo 角 *corner*
hú tòng 胡同 *alley*	yòng zuò 用作 *be used for*
sì hé yuàn 四合院 *a compound with houses around a courtyard*	yī pái pái 一排排 *in rows*
dài biǎo 代表 *to represent*	jiàn gé 间隔 *in between*
gāo lóu dà shà 高楼大厦 *high buildings and large mansions*	dì dài 地带 *area*
	tōng dào 通道 *passageway*
zhù zhái 住宅 *residence*	hū bì liè 忽必烈 *Kublai Khan*
jiàn zhù 建筑 *building*	cháng duǎn 长短 *length*
jiē 皆 *all*	zhǎi 窄 *narrow*
dú lì 独立 *stand-alone; independent*	wén wù 文物 *historical relic*
yuàn luò 院落 *courtyard*	bǎo cún 保存 *to preserve; to keep*
cháo 朝 *facing*	wú shù 无数 *countless*
zhèng fáng 正房 *principal room (in a courtyard, usually facing south)*	shěng 省 *to save*
	guàng 逛 *to stroll*
xiāng fáng 厢房 *wing (usually of a one-storey house)*	xiē 歇 *to have a rest*

练习C 📖 Answer the following questions in English.

一 According to the writer, why is it important to visit hutongs when you are in Beijing?

二 Why are the unique buildings in Beijing called 'siheyuan'?

三 In a siheyuan, what is the house facing south called, and what is the one facing north called?

四 How are the houses in a siheyuan distributed among the family members?

五 Which house in a siheyuan is used as the living room and study?

六 How did hutongs come into being?

七 What is the shortest hutong called?

八 According to the article, why is it necessary to keep some old hutongs in modern Beijing?

九 Apart from walking, what other options do you have for touring the hutongs?

十 According to the writer, what could you do if you are tired during your hutong tour?

阿里山

生词

ā lǐ shān 阿里山 *Mount Ali or Alishan*	**pán xuán** 盘旋 *circle; to spiral*
qí guān 奇观 *(natural) wonder*	**dǐng** 顶 *top*
wēn hé 温和 *mild*	**rè dài** 热带 *torrid zone; the tropics*
jí shǐ 即使 *even though*	**wēn dài** 温带 *temperate zone*
shèng xià 盛夏 *midsummer*	**hán dài** 寒带 *frigid zone*
yī rán 依然 *still*	**hǎn jiàn** 罕见 *rare*
qīng shuǎng yí rén 清爽宜人 *fresh, cool and pleasant*	**chén liè** 陈列 *to display*
lǐ xiǎng 理想 *ideal*	**yīng huā** 樱花 *oriental cherry*
bì shǔ shèng dì 避暑胜地 *summer resort*	**wén míng** 闻名 *famous; well known*
zì … zhì … 自…至… *from … to …*	**luò yì bù jué** 络绎不绝 *in an endless stream*

练习A 🔊 根据电台的广播内容，选出正确的答案并回答问题。

一 阿里山在哪里？

   a) 上海 ☐

   b) 台湾 ☐

   c) 香港 ☐

二 阿里山的三大奇观包括：

   a) 松树、云海、森林 ☐

   b) 日出、云海、森林 ☐

   c) 云海、森林、博物馆 ☐

三 为什么在夏天，阿里山是一个好去处？

   a) 山里人不多 ☐

   b) 山里气候凉爽 ☐

   c) 交通方便 ☐

四 阿里山的火车可以带你看到哪几个气候带的植物？

五 在高山博物馆里，游人能看见些什么？

六 什么时候是看樱花的好季节？

新加坡和伦敦

练习B 🔊　根据文莉和朋友谈话的内容，从括弧里的两个词语中，圈出正确的答案，并回答问题。

生词	
jiàn qiáo 剑桥 *Cambridge*	jiè yú…zhì… 介于…至… zhì jiān 之间 *between … and …*
guǎn lǐ 管理 *management*	gōng yì 公益 *public welfare*
líng chén 凌晨 *before dawn*	

一　文莉从新加坡来剑桥（旅游／学习）。

二　文莉在剑桥（坐地铁／骑自行车）去上学。

三　文莉认为新加坡的地铁很方便，早班车（5.00/5.30）就开始了，末班车到（11.30/12.30）才结束。

四　伦敦地铁和新加坡地铁有哪些不同之处？

五　为什么文莉的朋友和家人都喜欢乘坐新加坡的地铁？

香港之行

练习C 🔊　根据说话的内容，在线上填上适当的词语。

生词	
dài lǐng 带领 *to take (people to different places); to lead*	yīng yǒu jìn yǒu 应有尽有 *to have everything that one expects to find*
dí sī ní lè yuán 迪斯尼乐园 *Disneyland*	tiāo xuǎn 挑选 *to choose; to select*
dǎo yóu 导游 *tour guide*	tǐ yàn 体验 *to experience*
jī huì 机会 *opportunity*	zhěng jié 整洁 *clean and tidy*
zuàn shí zhū bǎo 钻石珠宝 *diamonds and jewellery*	

一　陈美丽是这次香港之行的 ＿＿＿＿＿＿＿＿＿＿ 。

二　迪斯尼乐园是大人和 ＿＿＿＿＿＿＿＿＿＿ 都喜欢去的地方。

三　在香港你可以买到各种各样的东西，价钱 ＿＿＿＿＿＿＿＿＿＿ 。

四　香港人喜欢上酒楼 ＿＿＿＿＿＿＿＿＿＿ 和 ＿＿＿＿＿＿＿＿＿＿ 。

五　香港街边 ＿＿＿＿＿＿＿＿＿＿ 花样很多，价钱也不贵。

六　酒店离市区 ＿＿＿＿＿＿＿＿＿＿ ，交通很方便。

七　香港这几天的天气 ＿＿＿＿＿＿＿＿＿＿ 。

上海的南京路

练习A 🖊 你和朋友到上海观光，你们去逛了上海著名的南京路，买了很多东西，然后去一家餐馆吃晚餐，最后登上了东方明珠电视塔。

请你用中文写一篇180–200字的日记，记录：

* 你和朋友为什么选择到南京路去购物？你们都买了些什么？

* 在南京路的餐馆里，你们吃了哪几样东西？它们的味道怎么样？

* 南京路是怎样的？和你所居住城市的商业区有什么不同？

* 晚上在东方明珠电视塔上俯瞰上海，你看到了什么？

* 你愿意选择居住在上海吗？为什么？

到不同的地方旅游

练习B 🖊 你收到台湾笔友寄来的旅游册子，他还问了你一些问题。

日月潭是台湾最大和最有名的天然湖泊，一年四季风景如画。

阿里山的日出、云海、森林非常有名。

台北故宫博物院收藏了很多珍贵的文物。

请你用中文写一封180–200字的信，回答笔友的问题：

- 如果我来到你生活的城市／乡村，你会推荐哪些地方让我去游玩？

- 这些地方有什么特点？和台湾的景点相比，有什么相同和不同之处？

- 能够到不同的地方旅游，你觉得有什么好处？

解决堵车的问题

练习C 🖊

请你用中文写一篇180–200字的短文，来谈谈：

- 你家里有几辆车？一般由谁来开？

- 一般家庭都用车来做些什么？

- 拥有自己的车有什么利弊？

- 你对中国城市里出现越来越多的私家车，有什么看法？

- 你希望未来的车是什么样子的？

在广州，越来越多家庭拥有自己的车。这个城市最近一项民意调查显示，50.8%的市民赞成限制私家车的数量，以解决堵车的问题。

第七章 工作世界

工作世界

练习A 💬 人的一生，大约有五十年的时间用来工作。你想了解我们的工作世界是怎样一个纷繁复杂、多姿多彩的世界吗？请阅读下面十个问题，选出你认为最佳的答案，然后进行双人或小组讨论。

一 工作就是

　　a）完成一天的任务，快乐地活到太阳下山

　　b）该干什么，就干什么

　　c）一个人的谋生之道

二 面试时，经理只抬头看了你一眼，说声"请坐"，就埋头工作不再理你。你会

　　a）提醒经理你在等候

　　b）坐下静候

　　c）不辞而别

三 做什么样的家务最能使你放松？

　　a）做饭菜

　　b）看护婴儿

　　c）侍弄花草

四 你最崇拜的名人是

　　a）莫扎特

　　b）孔子

　　c）爱因斯坦

五 假如你是空档年学生，你想

　　a）去旅行

　　b）做带薪实习记者

　　c）去国外做义务英语教师

六 你的朋友对你的评价是

　　a）诚实勤奋、脚踏实地、有进取心

　　b）充满活力，有良好的人际沟通能力

　　c）有乐观自信、助人为乐的品质

七 什么人最适合做服装设计师？

　　a）敏感冲动、喜创新的人

　　b）能说会道、爱交友的人

　　c）细心负责、有理智的人

八 在你所做过的事情中，最有创造性的是什么？

　　a）演奏你自己谱写的曲子

　　b）设计你自己的房间

　　c）帮助你的同学竞选学生会主席

九 循循善诱是什么人的工作职责？

　　a）律师

　　b）教师

　　c）裁判

十 什么工作最好？

　　a）有优厚待遇、能赚大钱的工作

　　b）能周游世界的工作

　　c）自己喜欢的工作

fēn fán fù zá 纷繁复杂 complicated; complex	tí xǐng 提醒 to remind; reminder	kōng dàng nián 空档年 gap year	chōng mǎn huó lì 充满活力 energetic	néng shuō huì dào 能说会道 to have the gift of the gab	xué shēng huì 学生会 students' union

duō zī duō cǎi
多姿多彩
diverse and colourful

bù cí ér bié
不辞而别
to leave without saying goodbye

dài xīn
带薪
paid

rén jì gōu tōng
人际沟通
interpersonal communication

jiāo yǒu
交友
to make friends

zhǔ xí
主席
chairperson

rèn wu
任务
task

fàng sōng
放松
to relax

shí xí jì zhě
实习记者
trainee journalist

lè guān
乐观
optimistic

fù zé
负责
responsible

zhí zé
职责
(job) duties

móu shēng
谋生
to make a living

kān hù yīng ér
看护婴儿
to babysit

yì wù
义务
voluntary

zì xìn
自信
self-confident

lǐ zhì
理智
rational

lǜ shī
律师
lawyer

miàn shì
面试
interview

shì nòng huā cǎo
侍弄花草
to do the gardening

píng jià
评价
comment

zhù rén wéi lè
助人为乐
helpful

chuàng zào xìng
创造性
creativity

cái pàn
裁判
referee

jīng lǐ
经理
manager

chóng bài
崇拜
to adore; to idolise

chéng shí
诚实
honest

pǐn zhì
品质
quality

yǎn zòu
演奏
to play (a musical instrument)

yōu hòu dài yù
优厚待遇
excellent pay and benefits

mái tóu
埋头
to immerse oneself in something

míng rén
名人
celebrity

qín fèn
勤奋
hard-working; diligent

fú zhuāng
服装
shè jì shī
设计师
fashion designer

pǔ xiě
谱写
to compose

zhōu yóu
周游
to travel around

bú zài
不再
no longer

mò zhā tè
莫扎特
Wolfgang Amadeus Mozart

jiǎo tà shí dì
脚踏实地
earnest and practical

chōng dòng
冲动
impulsive

qǔ zi
曲子
song; tune; melody

lǐ
理
to pay attention to

ài yīn sī tǎn
爱因斯坦
Albert Einstein

yǒu jìn qǔ xīn
有进取心
with enterprising spirit

chuàng xīn
创新
innovative; creative

jìng xuǎn
竞选
to run for

Occupations

 练习B 请看下列图片：

Please respond in Chinese to the bullet points below.

- Identify and describe the occupations in the pictures.

- Talk about the income for each of the occupations.

- What duties does each of these jobs entail?

- What are the pros and cons of each job?

- Do you think people deserve the money they earn?

生词

zhí yè 职业 *occupation*	qǐ yè jiā 企业家 *entrepreneur*
zhōu jié lún 周杰伦 *Jay Chou,* *Taiwanese pop star*	shōu rù 收入 *income*
gē xīng 歌星 *pop star*	hǎo huài / yǒu lì 好坏 / 有利 hé bù lì 和不利 *pros and cons*
lǐ jiā chéng 李嘉诚 *Li Ka Shing,* *wealthy Hong* *Kong businessman*	

- What do you think people should be rewarded for: talent, ability or hard work?
- Why do you think there is a gap between the amount of money men and women earn?
- What kind of job do you want to do? Why?
- Talk about what you think is most important when choosing a career/job.

李嘉诚 香港企业家

教师

周杰伦 台湾歌星

词组 / 表达法

wǒ rèn wéi hǎo de fāng miàn shì
我认为好的方面是⋯
I think the pros of …

wǒ rèn wéi bù hǎo de fāng miàn shì
我认为不好的方面是⋯
I think the cons of …

wǒ xiǎng dāng zuò
我想当 / 做⋯
I would like to be …

zuì zhòng yào de shì
最重要的是⋯
The most important thing is …

wǒ rèn wéi zuò yī gè hǎo de jiàn zhù shī wài jiāo guān
我认为，做一个好的建筑师 / 外交官 /
biān jí yín háng jiā bì xū jù bèi
编辑 / 银行家，必须具备⋯
I think that to be a good architect/diplomat/editor/banker, you need …

做自己想做的工作

请阅读就业辅导员写给咨询人的一封信和一份随信附上的就业辅导资料，然后回答问题。

尊敬的杨先生：

您好！

谢谢您三月二十五日的来信。

关于如何选择合适的工作，我认为您应该首先认识自己的兴趣、需求及性格特点，因为不同类型的人适合不同类型的工作。

现附上一份就业辅导资料，敬请参考。

祝您成功！

此致

敬礼

林红

2007 年 3 月 26 日

一份合适的工作，可以使你的生活变得更加充实。对工作满意的秘诀就在于做你想做的工作。要知道自己想做什么，就要先了解自己。我们每个人，天生具有从事某种职业类型的特定性格。这好比我们分别使用自己的两只手写字一样，惯用的那只手写出来的字会比另一只好。

下面介绍几种常见的职业类型：

实际型

脚踏实地，喜欢从事需要使用工具的工作，如摄影师、木工、管道工、技术员等。

研究型

喜欢理性、独立和富有创造性的工作，如研究员、医生、工程师等。

艺术型

敏感冲动，追求完美和创新，适合当艺术家、设计师、建筑师等。

社会型

开朗活泼，喜欢有双向交流的工作，如教师、咨询员、公关员等。

企业型

乐观自信、能说会道、有敏锐的观察力，但独断。适合当经理、销售员、律师等。

常规型

细心负责，喜欢按计划办事，适合当秘书、会计、行政助理等。

生词

jiù yè fǔ dǎo 就业辅导 *career guidance*	lèi xíng 类型 *type; kind*	cóng shì 从事 *be engaged in*	mù gōng 木工 *carpenter*	kāi lǎng 开朗 *optimistic*	xiāo shòu yuán 销售员 *salesperson*
zī xún 咨询 *consultation*	zī liào 资料 *material*	mǒu zhǒng 某种 *some kind of; certain kind of*	guǎn dào gōng 管道工 *plumber*	huó pō 活泼 *lively; vivacious*	cháng guī 常规 *routine*
fù shàng 附上 *to attach; to enclose*	cān kǎo 参考 *for reference*	tè dìng 特定 *specific*	jì shù yuán 技术员 *technician*	shuāng xiàng jiāo liú 双向交流 *two-way communication; exchange*	jì huà 计划 *schedule; plan*
zūn jìng 尊敬 *respectable*	cǐ zhì jìng lǐ 此致敬礼 *with best wishes; respectfully*	fēn bié 分别 *respectively*	lǐ xìng 理性 *rational*	gōng guān yuán 公关员 *public relations officer*	mì shu 秘书 *secretary*
shǒu xiān 首先 *first of all*	chōng shí 充实 *fulfilled*	guàn yòng 惯用 *habitually practise; consistently use*	yán jiū yuán 研究员 *researcher*	mǐn ruì 敏锐 *sharp; keen*	kuài jì 会计 *accountant*
xū qiú 需求 *need; demand*	mǎn yì 满意 *satisfaction*	shí jì 实际 *realistic*	zhuī qiú wán měi 追求完美 *to pursue perfection*	guān chá lì 观察力 *observation*	xíng zhèng zhù lǐ 行政助理 *administration assistant*
xìng gé 性格 *personality; character*	tiān shēng 天生 *inborn; innate*	shè yǐng shī 摄影师 *photographer*	yì shù jiā 艺术家 *artist*	dú duàn 独断 *dictatorial*	

練習 A 📖 **Answer the following questions.**

一 What advice does Ms Lin give for pursuing the career that best suits you?

    a) get the proper training or education you need

    b) find out what type of person you are, and what your interests and needs are

    c) work out what experience you have

二 How can you tell if you are enjoying your job?

    a) You are doing what you dream of.

    b) You are doing what is available to you.

    c) You are doing what is decent and lucrative.

三 People with various personality traits are …

    a) more likely to achieve their goals.

    b) in a better position to become team leaders.

    c) better placed for certain jobs than others.

四 If you are creative and enjoy everything about food, a job …

    a) as an administration assistant at a cookery school could be for you.

    b) in the catering and hospitality industry could be for you.

    c) as a scientist in the food industry could be for you.

五 You could consider being a model or selling cosmetics if you are …

    a) attractive, impulsive and creative.

    b) observant, attractive and have the gift of the gab.

    c) practical, reasonable and have the gift of the gab.

六 Match the personality types to the careers indicated in the leaflet.

Personality type		Career
i) artistic	☐	a) teacher/consultant
ii) practical	☐	b) secretary/accounting clerk
iii) sociable	☐	c) designer/architect
iv) enterprising	☐	d) photographer/carpenter
v) routine	☐	e) doctor/engineer
vi) research	☐	f) lawyer/salesperson

一位青年钢琴家的故事

请阅读下面一篇关于中国天才青年钢琴家郎朗的杂志文章，然后回答问题。

> "择你所爱，爱你所做，你的一生不会有一天的工作。"

现在，让我们走近当今世界最年轻的著名职业钢琴家郎朗，看看他如何实践这句名言的。

郎朗，1982年出生于中国沈阳，3岁开始学习钢琴，13岁获得第二届柴科夫斯基国际青年音乐家比赛第一名，14岁进入美国一家著名的音乐学院深造。1999年，因紧急代替生病的美国钢琴家登台演出而一举成名。当时，一位著名的艺术大师向观众这样介绍道："你们将从这位中国男孩那里听到世界上最美妙、最有创造力的音乐。"

郎朗：弹着钢琴的时候，完全没有苦恼、没有劳累了。

对于从小便展露超凡音乐天分的郎朗来说，再也没有什么事情比弹琴更让他快乐的了。

郎朗：我喜爱观众，喜爱那种紧张气氛。这好比有很多人在观看一个伟大作品的创造，我同时充当翻译，架起一座通往观众心灵的桥。

天道酬勤，朗朗以杰出的才华和极好的口碑，赢得了全球每年约150场的演出。他还被美国杂志《青少年》选为20个将改变世界的青年人之一。

他的故事告诉我们，天才源自对职业的热爱。只要富于热情而脚踏实地，就能进入自己梦想中的职业而享乐无穷。

tiān cái 天才 *talented; genius*	shí jiàn 实践 *to practise*	yīn yuè xué yuàn 音乐学院 *conservatoire*	dà shī 大师 *master*	chāo fán 超凡 *supreme*	tiān dào chóu qín 天道酬勤 *hard-working people will be rewarded*
gāng qín jiā 钢琴家 *pianist*	shěn yáng 沈阳 *Shenyang (a city in the Liaoning province in Northeast China)*	shēn zào 深造 *further study*	guān zhòng 观众 *audience*	tiān fèn 天分 *talent; gift*	jié chū de cái huá 杰出的才华 *outstanding talent*
láng lǎng 郎朗 *Lang Lang (name of a virtuoso pianist)*		jǐn jí dài tì 紧急代替 *to replace somebody at the last minute*	měi miào 美妙 *wonderful*	wěi dà 伟大 *great*	kǒu bēi 口碑 *praise*
zé nǐ suǒ ài 择你所爱 *to choose what you love*	chái kē fū sī jī 柴科夫斯基 guó jì qīng nián 国际青年 yīn yuè jiā bǐ sài 音乐家比赛 *International Tchaikovsky Competition for Young Musicians*	dēng tái yǎn chū 登台演出 *to perform on stage*	tán 弹 *to play (a musical instrument)*	fān yì 翻译 *interpreter; translator*	fù yú rè qíng 富于热情 *full of passion*
ài nǐ suǒ zuò 爱你所做 *to love what you do*		yī jǔ chéng míng 一举成名 *to become famous overnight*	láo lèi 劳累 *tiredness*	jià qǐ 架起 *to build*	xiǎng lè wú qióng 享乐无穷 *endless enjoyment*
			zhǎn lù 展露 *to display; to show*	xīn líng 心灵 *heart; soul*	

练习 B 📖 **Answer the following questions.**

一 Correct the false statements.

a) If you find a job you enjoy, you'll never want to work a day in your life.

b) In 1999, Lang Lang followed his music dream to America.

二 How did Lang Lang's big break occur?

a) when he won the International Tchaikovsky Competition for Young Musicians

b) at an American conservatoire when he played the Tchaikovsky concerto

c) a last minute substitution for an American pianist playing the Tchaikovsky concerto

三 What does music mean to Lang Lang?

a) It's a bridge connecting the piano to the audience.

b) It's a language that connects an audience and the feeling from his soul.

c) It's an interpretation of great composition.

四 In what ways does Lang Lang win hearts and souls worldwide?

五 How does Lang Lang maintain a work-life balance?

快乐工作

请阅读以下一篇报刊文章，然后用英文回答问题。

有人说，工作的最高境界就是快乐工作。如果你把工作视作乐趣，人生就是天堂；如果你把工作视作负累，人生就是地狱。

在中国，现代上班族最流行的生存方式，就是把爱好与工作合二为一。他们认为，工作就是为了更快乐地生活。有迹象显示，越来越多年轻人开始懂得从工作中寻找生活的快乐。

在平衡中寻找快乐

王小丽，25岁，大学一毕业，就一脚踏进一周五天、朝九晚五的工作中。时间长了，她开始对这种重复的工作感到厌倦。于是她决定去旅游。"经过充沛的休息后再回到工作中，我感到一种从未有过的轻松和朝气。旅游——工作——旅游，这便是我最快乐的工作和生活方式。"

在充电中寻找快乐

李玉，24岁，年纪轻轻，已经是一家贸易公司小有名气的业务经理。然而半个月前，她却提出辞职，打算回到原先毕业的大学，进修商业管理硕士课程。"接受新的知识，不单能使我在今后的工作中如虎添翼，还能活跃我的思维。借此机会，我想对自己三年来的工作做一次全面总结，为下一个挑战做好准备。"

在转型中寻找快乐

杨刚，这个曾经当过高级经理的人，选择退出打工族，实践自己当老板的梦想。两年来，他有滋有味地经营着自己的网上旅游服务公司，成为一个完完全全的在家办公族青年。"在家工作不单可免却向公司报到的麻烦，还可以灵活地安排工作、生活以及与我家人相处的时间。"

人生是一个漫长的旅途，工作占据了当中三分之一的时间，是不可缺少的内容。只要你能做到乐在其中，快乐就是一个长长的过程！

生词

生词	拼音	英文
境界	jìng jiè	level
视作	shì zuò	to regard as
乐趣	lè qù	delight; pleasure
负累	fù lěi	burden
地狱	dì yù	hell
上班族	shàng bān zú	people who have a regular job
生存	shēng cún	to survive
合二为一	hé èr wéi yī	to combine two things as one
迹象	jì xiàng	sign
寻找	xún zhǎo	to look for; seek
平衡	píng héng	balance
一脚踏进	yī jiǎo tà jìn	to enter
朝九晚五	zhāo jiǔ wǎn wǔ	nine to five
重复	chóng fù	repetitive
厌倦	yàn juàn	tired of; exhausted
充沛	chōng pèi	abundant
从未有过	cóng wèi yǒu guò	never experienced before
轻松	qīng sōng	relaxation
朝气	zhāo qì	vitality
充电	chōng diàn	to recharge
小有名气	xiǎo yǒu míng qì	recognition amongst peers
业务	yè wù	business
辞职	cí zhí	resignation
原先	yuán xiān	original
进修	jìn xiū	to study further
商业管理	shāng yè guǎn lǐ	business management
今后	jīn hòu	in the future
如虎添翼	rú hǔ tiān yì	to strengthen (literary: like a tiger that has grown wings)
活跃	huó yuè	active
思维	sī wéi	thinking; thought
借此机会	jiè cǐ jī huì	to take the chance (to do something)
全面总结	quán miàn zǒng jié	comprehensive sum up
挑战	tiāo zhàn	challenge
转型	zhuǎn xíng	transformation
曾经	céng jīng	once
高级	gāo jí	senior
退出	tuì chū	to quit
打工族	dǎ gōng zú	group of employees
老板	lǎo bǎn	boss
有滋有味地	yǒu zī yǒu wèi de	enthusiastically
经营	jīng yíng	to manage; to run
完完全全	wán wán quán quán	complete; total
在家办公族	zài jiā bàn gōng zú	people who work at home
报到	bào dào	to report to somebody
与…相处	yǔ…xiāng chǔ	to get along with somebody
漫长	màn cháng	very long (time)
旅途	lǚ tú	journey; trip
占据	zhàn jù	to occupy
不可缺少	bù kě quē shǎo	indispensable
乐在其中	lè zài qí zhōng	to enjoy (doing something)

练习 C 📖   **Answer the following questions in English.**

一   Correct the false statements.

    a) The best work-life balance for Xiaoli Wang is to spend time doing leisure activities with her colleagues after a hectic work day.

    b) Yu Li quit her job to further her studies, so that in the future she would be able to find a better job.

    c) Gang Yang doesn't think the key to effective time management is to clarify your goals and purpose in life.

二   Match the statements to the three professionals mentioned in the article. Support your answers with the Chinese statements from the article.

    a) "I'm pursuing further study so that I can create more opportunities in my working life."

    b) "Doing what I really enjoy both at work and at home, I find my dreams and aspirations are taking shape."

    c) "I enjoy my job and maintain a good work-life balance by taking regular breaks to go on holiday."

三   According to the writer, what is the best achievement you can have at work? Support your answer with statements from the article.

四   Do you agree that we tend to get what we expect? Why? Support your answer with statements from the article.

五   According to Gang Yang, how does he find happiness in his career and life?

六   Why does the writer conclude that happiness will last a long time if you enjoy the job you do?

七   How do you obtain happiness at work? Answer this question in Chinese. You can answer this question based on the article or you can express your own opinion.

招聘广告

练习A 🔊 根据电台招聘广告的内容，选出正确的答案。

生词

zhāo pìn 招聘 recruitment	biǎo dá néng lì 表达能力 ability to express oneself
guǎng gào 广告 advertisement	tuán duì hé zuò 团队合作 jīng shén 精神 team spirit
cǎi fǎng 采访 to interview	
bào dào 报道 to report	cóng yè 从业 to engage in a business
yīng pìn rén 应聘人 applicant	bèi jǐng 背景 background
zhuān cháng 专长 expertise	yǒu yì zhě 有意者 people who are interested in a position/job
fú lì 福利 benefits	
guǎngzhōu yà yùn 广州亚运 zǔ wěi huì 组委会 Guangzhou Asian Games Organizing Committee (GAGOC)	qiú zhí xìn 求职信 application letter
	jiǎn lì 简历 curriculum vitae (CV)

一 招聘工作的职责是

a) 写新闻报道 ☐

b) 采访和翻译 ☐

c) 采访和报道 ☐

二 应聘人的性格必须是

a) 充满活力 ☐

b) 敏感冲动 ☐

c) 脚踏实地 ☐

三 要求应聘人

a) 能独立处事 ☐

b) 能与团队合作 ☐

c) 有体育专长 ☐

四 应聘人

a) 必须有丰富的经验 ☐

b) 不需任何经验 ☐

c) 最好有些经验 ☐

五 招聘人将提供

a) 采访所有体育明星的机会 ☐

b) 不错的收入和福利 ☐

c) 舒适的工作环境 ☐

六 招聘人的联系地址和电话是

a) 广州市临江大道3号发展中心，电话99638015 ☐

b) 中山市临江大道3号发展中心，电话99368015 ☐

c) 广州市临江大道30号发展中心，电话99630815 ☐

我想当记者

根据对话的内容，从括弧里的两个词语中，圈出正确的答案。

生词	
yǒu kǔ yǒu lè **有苦有乐** *pain and happiness*	háng yè **行业** *profession; trade*
yǒu qǐ yǒu luò **有起有落** *ups and downs*	xīn rén xīn shì **新人新事** *new faces and new happenings*
bào shè **报社** *general office of a newspaper*	tuī jiàn xìn **推荐信** *letter of recommendation*
duǎn qī gōng zuò **短期工作** shí xí **实习** *short-term internship*	xīn wén chù jué **新闻触觉** *ability to keep abreast of the news*
xié zhù **协助** *to assist*	cè huà **策划** *planning*
rén shǒu bú gòu **人手不够** *short-handed; short-staffed*	chū sè **出色** *outstanding* xiàng mù **项目** *project*

一 当体育（运动员／记者）是杨的（理想／谋生）职业。

二 如果得到（通知／聘用），这将是杨（第一次／第二次）做同样工作。

三 杨认为（一些／每个）行业都（有苦有乐／有起有落）。

四 杨在英国的实习工作（项目／职责）是（协助／独立）安排记者进行采访和拍摄工作。

五 杨在实习时就展露了新闻（写作／编辑）的（品质／才华）。

六 （招聘／应聘）时，除了要准备求职信外，还要准备（感谢信／推荐信）和（公司简介／个人简历）。

生词

gù zhǔ **雇主** *employer*	shèng rèn **胜任** *competent*
lù qǔ **录取** *to recruit*	líng huó gōng zuò zhì **灵活工作制** *flexible working hours*
zhí wèi **职位** *post; job*	xún qiú **寻求** *to seek*
diàn tái guǎng bō **电台广播** *radio broadcast*	shī zhǎn cái néng **施展才能** *to put one's abilities to good use*
quán chēng **全称** *full name*	
chóu bèi **筹备** *to prepare for*	wǔ tái **舞台** *stage*
zhǔ bàn **主办** *to host an event*	gòng xiàn **贡献** *contribution*
yè yú ài hào **业余爱好** *hobby*	jù tǐ **具体** *in detail*

工作面试

练习C 根据对话的内容，回答下面的问题。

一 杨从哪里知道招聘公司的？

二 杨为什么来中国？

三 杨在广州大学做什么？

四 杨的业余爱好是什么？

五 杨的性格有哪些优点？

六 杨为什么认为这份工作最适合他？

七 杨以前做过什么工作？

八 杨问了面试官什么问题？

九 杨何时可以收到雇主的答复？如获录取，何时可以开始上班？

生词

shū xiě gé shì **书写格式** *format of writing*	jī běn qíng kuàng **基本情况** *general information*
shǔ qī gōng **暑期工** *summer job*	tōng yòng **通用** *general application*
lǐ mào chēng hū **礼貌称呼** *polite address*	zhù míng **注明** *to note*

申请暑期工

练习A

根据下面正式信件的书写格式和内容提示，请你用中文写一封180-200字的求职信，申请一份暑期工。

书写格式

称呼：比一般书信的称呼要正规一些，如"尊敬的××"

正文：书信内容

结尾：可用"此致，敬礼"之类的通用词。

署名：可在署名前加上一些"你诚挚的××"、"你忠实的××"之类的形容词，也可以什么都不写，直接签上自己的名字。

日期：一般写在署名右下方，最好用阿拉伯数字写，并把年、月、日全写上。

内容提示

· 说明求职信息来源、应聘职位

· 介绍本人基本情况、工作经历等

· 写明希望对方给予答复，并盼望能有机会参加面试

小故事，大道理

练习B ✐

请阅读下面一则小故事，然后用中文写一篇180–200字的短文，来谈谈工作态度。

有人问三个木工："你们在做什么呢？"

第一个木工说："你没看见吗？我正在砌墙啊！"

第二个木工回答说："我正在做一项每小时12英镑的工作呢！"

第三个木工笑着说："老实告诉你吧，我正在建造这世界上最伟大的教堂！"

- 这个小故事讲述的大道理是什么？

- 你对工作态度的看法是什么？或者通过比较中国与你自己国家的年轻人的工作态度，说明自己的观点。

- 假如你得到一份工作，你具体应该怎么做？

寻找我的理想职业

练习C ✐

请用中文写一篇180–200字的短文，来谈谈：

- 我的兴趣有哪些？

- 我将来喜欢而且确定想从事的职业是什么？

- 我为什么选择上述职业？

- 我想从事的职业特性是什么？如工作环境、工作时间、待遇、所需具备的条件和能力，以及我应该要付出的努力。

- 我要做的决定是什么？

第八章 青少年文化

青少年文化小测验

练习A 你上Facebook（花名册）捅过别人吗？你到过中国的校内网www.xiaonei.com展示自己，结识新朋友吗？约会博弈是怎样玩的？你是个追星族吗？请做以下的青少年文化小测验找出答案。

一 以下哪种动物不属于中国的十二生肖？

a) 乌龟

b) 龙

c) 老鼠

二 你是个什么样的博客？

a) 开有自己的博客网站，天天写，网友留言必回

b) 有博客网站，但只是有空的时候才写几篇

c) 只用电子邮件，偶尔看看别人的博客

三 你熟悉社交网站吗？

a) 频繁上Facebook和YouTube视频播客网站捅别人，并聚合了一个社交圈

b) 偶尔上Facebook、YouTube视频播客网站或其它社交网站参加讨论

c) 听说过Facebook和YouTube视频播客网站，但从来没用过

四 用手机发短信已经成为时尚，你的手机

a) 天天收到熟人和陌生人的幽默群发短信，你再把这些短信群发给别人

b) 只阅读朋友的短信，一般不转发

c) 多只用来打电话，因为发信速度太慢

五 你如何跟心仪的男生／女生提出约会？

a) 提前两星期就邀约。穿很时髦的衣服，以吸引对方

b) 临时决定去溜冰，或者去看什么表演。穿整洁的牛仔裤和运动鞋，让人容易接受

c) 暗中喜欢，可又怕当着别人的面会尴尬，迟迟不敢提出约会

六 你听说过"辣妹"吗？"辣妹"是什么样的青春偶像？

a) 一队摇滚乐队

b) 一位现代艺术家

c) 一组英国流行歌手

七 你知道什么是"金马奖"吗？

a) 每年在台湾举行的中文电影奖

b) 每年在上海举行的世界华人音乐成就奖

c) 每年在香港举行的青少年计算机游戏比赛奖

八 一般青少年在考试前都会感到压力，考试前你如何给自己减压？

a) 丢开功课，猛睡一觉

b) 最后复习一遍，然后听音乐

c) 抓紧每分钟的时间复习，以防漏掉一点点什么

九 最近将有一位著名的歌星在你住的地区举行音乐会，但门票非常昂贵。对此你怎么看？

    a) 能亲自到现场观看自己喜爱的歌星表演，门票贵一点也值得

    b) 迟一点才在家里看电视重播，不花钱还舒服

    c) 不看也不要紧，反正以后可以买歌星的个人专辑

十 你的空闲时间主要花在

    a) 上社交网站，跟网上来来往往的人聊天

    b) 玩网上电脑游戏

    c) 在家里看电视

- 如果你的答案大部分是a，这说明你紧跟时尚，熟知当前青少年文化的热点。
- 如果你的答案大部分是b，这说明你了解一些青少年文化的特点，但不熟悉。
- 如果你的答案大部分是c，这说明你并不关心当前的青少年文化。不过，你何妨偶尔赶一次时髦，装一回酷的形象，让自己放松一下吧！

生词

tǒng 捅 to poke; to visit somebody's homepage, blog, etc.	ǒu ěr 偶尔 occasionally	yōu mò 幽默 humour; humorous
jié shí 结识 to get to know somebody	shú xi 熟悉 familiar	qún fā 群发 to send to people in a list
yuē huì bó yì 约会博弈 dating game	pín fán 频繁 frequently	zhuǎn fā 转发 to forward to
zhuī xīng zú 追星族 fan	shì pín bō kè 视频播客 video blogger	xīn yí 心仪 like; admire
shēng xiào 生肖 animal signs of the zodiac	jù hé 聚合 to get together; to foster; to have	yāo yuē 邀约 to invite
bó kè 博客 blogger	shè jiāo quān 社交圈 social circle	lín shí 临时 at the last moment
	mò shēng rén 陌生人 stranger	àn zhōng 暗中 secretly

gān gà 尴尬 embarrassing; embarrassed	chéng jiù 成就 achievement	zhí dé 值得 worthwhile
chí chí 迟迟 late	diū kāi 丢开 to put aside	chóng bō 重播 to replay
là mèi 辣妹 Spice Girls	měng shuì yī jiào 猛睡一觉 to have a good sleep	fǎn zhèng 反正 anyway
ǒu xiàng 偶像 idol	zhuā jǐn 抓紧 to grasp	zhuān jí 专辑 album
yáo gǔn 摇滚 rock and roll	yǐ fáng 以防 in case	lái lái wǎng wǎng 来来往往 to come and go
yuè duì 乐队 band	lòu diào 漏掉 to miss; to leave out	hé fáng 何妨 why not
jīn mǎ jiǎng 金马奖 Golden Horse Award	áng guì 昂贵 expensive	kù 酷 cool
		xíng xiàng 形象 image

Taipei Golden Horse Film Festival

The most prominent and most-watched film awards ceremony in the world is the Academy Awards, or as it is popularly known, the Oscars. But probably the most prestigious and spectacular ceremony in the Chinese-speaking world is the Taipei Golden Horse Film Festival. This ceremony has been held annually in Taiwan since 1962. Winners receive a golden horse statuette.

Modelled after the Academy Awards and other major film festivals worldwide, the Taipei Golden Horse Film Festival features mostly films from Taiwan and Hong Kong. It holds two major events: the film competition and film screenings, of which the latter includes showing nominated feature films and documentaries in the competition, alongside international productions. The equivalent award in mainland China is the Golden Rooster Award.

The Taiwanese director, Ang Lee, has won numerous Golden Horse Film awards for his films over the years, including Best Picture and Best Director for *Crouching Tiger, Hidden Dragon*, and Best Original Screenplay and Best Director for *The Wedding Banquet*. His most successful year was in 2007 when he took home seven awards for his controversial spy thriller *Lust, Caution*.

生词

tái běi jīn mǎ **台北金马** yǐng zhǎn **影展** *Taipei Golden Horse Film Festival and Awards*	jīn jī jiǎng **金鸡奖** *Golden Rooster Award*
ào sī kǎ jiǎng **奥斯卡奖** *Oscars*	lǐ ān **李安** *Ang Lee*
yǒu wēi wàng de **有威望的** *prestigious*	xǐ yàn **《喜宴》** *The Wedding Banquet*
yǐn rén zhù mù de **引人注目的** *spectacular*	yǒu zhēng yì de **有争议的** *controversial*
diǎn lǐ yí shì **典礼，仪式** *ceremony*	jiàn dié piàn **间谍片** *spy thriller*
mó fǎng **模仿** *modelled after*	sè jiè **《色，戒》** *Lust, Caution*

词组／表达法

yīng dé
应得
to deserve

cháng chu yōu diǎn
长处；优点
merit

diàn yǐng shè yǐng
电影摄影
cinematography

wǒ huì àn zhǔn zé lái fén yǔ jiǎng xiàng
我会按···准则来颁予奖项
I would judge the awards on …

Please respond in Chinese to the bullet points below. You are *not* expected to refer to the full content of the article.

- State what the article is referring to (a full summary is *not* required).

- What are the Academy Awards?

- Describe a recent awards ceremony you have watched or attended.

- Do you think holding awards ceremonies is worthwhile? Do you think that the winners deserve the awards? What do you think about the winners?

- Think of some Chinese films. What impression do those films give of China?

- What is your favourite Chinese film? Why?

- If you were awarding the Golden Horse Awards, what criteria would you judge the films on? Why are these criteria important?

- Have you watched any of Ang Lee's films? If so, which is your favourite? Do you think Ang Lee's films all have a common style? If you haven't watched any, who is your favourite Chinese director and why?

生肖属相性格运程大配对

请阅读下面一篇关于生肖性格的报纸文章，然后用英文回答问题。

属鼠的人（2008，1996，1984，1972，1960）聪明伶俐、反应快、环境适应能力强。天生乐观，但缺乏胆识且自私，不适合做领导。有晚睡习惯。

属牛的人（2009，1997，1985，1973，1961）诚实正直、富有忍耐力、责任心强。处事理性、脚踏实地，但比较固执。有婚姻上的麻烦。

属虎的人（2010，1998，1986，1974，1962）外表宽容、内心刚强。性格独立，爱冒险，意志力胜过常人。对自己充满信心，是天生的领袖型人物。容易树立敌人。

属兔的人（2011，1999，1987，1975，1963）为人温和有礼，有慈悲心。热爱团体生活，注重友情。记忆力强，工作成绩突出。常浪费金钱。

属龙的人（2012，2000，1988，1976，1964）具有伟大的理想，气质非凡。善思考，有奋斗精神，自信心强。追求完美，不容易与他人相处。

属蛇的人（2013，2001，1989，1977，1965）性格稳重，富有才智，能随机应变。敏感、细心、有计算头脑。爱嫉妒别人。女性好喝汤。

属马的人（2014，2002，1990，1978，1966）好动不好静，喜出风头。崇尚自由、无拘束的生活。容易得到朋友和同事的信赖。缺乏恒心，做事容易半途而废。

属羊的人（2015，2003，1991，1979，1967）有孝心、懂礼节。在温柔的外表下，藏着一颗坚毅的心，宗教信念较强。一生喜好居住在安静之处。不善于处理逆境和打击。

属猴的人（2016，2004，1992，1980，1968）活泼好动、聪明伶俐、拥有多方面的才能。爱帮助别人，愿意为他人的利益而放弃自己的事情。好说大话，太骄傲。

属鸡的人（2017，2005，1993，1981，1969）诚实有智慧，能与人交际。严守纪律，对自己和别人的要求同样严格。容易受异性引诱，恋爱的次数相当多。

属狗的人（2018，2006，1994，1982，1970）热情、有勇气、观察力敏锐。生性慷慨，不重视物质享受。虽不善于言谈，但能与朋友保持长久的友谊。

属猪的人（2019，2007，1995，1983，1971）性格正直、外表稳重、内心刚强、责任心强。待人热情，重视友谊并且极受别人欢迎。好享乐，好批评别人。

生词

shǔ xiàng 属相 *animal signs of the zodiac*	**gù zhí** 固执 *stubborn*	**jì yì lì** 记忆力 *memory*	**xǐ chū fēng tou** 喜出风头 *to enjoy being the centre of attention*	**wēn róu** 温柔 *gentle and soft*	**yì xìng** 异性 *opposite sex*
yùn chéng 运程 *fate; luck*	**má fan** 麻烦 *trouble*	**tū chū** 突出 *outstanding*	**chóng shàng** 崇尚 *to uphold; to advocate*	**yǐn cáng** 隐藏 *to hide; to conceal*	**yǐn yòu** 引诱 *to seduce*
shǔ 属 *to belong to one of the 12 zodiac animals*	**kuān róng** 宽容 *tolerant; lenient*	**làng fèi** 浪费 *to waste*	**wú jū shù** 无拘束 *unrestrained; free*	**nì jìng** 逆境 *adversity*	**yǒng qì** 勇气 *courage*
cōng míng líng lì 聪明伶俐 *clever; quick-witted*	**yì zhì lì** 意志力 *determination*	**shàn sī kǎo** 善思考 *good at thinking*	**xìn lài** 信赖 *trust*	**yuàn yì** 愿意 *willing to*	**kāng kǎi** 慷慨 *generous*
fǎn yìng 反应 *reaction*	**ài mào xiǎn** 爱冒险 *adventurous*	**fèn dòu jīng shén** 奋斗精神 *spirited*	**héng xīn** 恒心 *perseverance*	**lì yì** 利益 *benefit; interest*	**pī píng** 批评 *to criticise*
dǎn shí 胆识 *courage and determination*	**shèng guò** 胜过 *be superior to; better than*	**wěn zhòng** 稳重 *steady; sedate*	**bàn tú ér fèi** 半途而废 *to give up halfway; to leave something unfinished*	**fàng qì** 放弃 *to give up*	
zhèng zhí 正直 *upright*	**lǐng xiù** 领袖 *leader*	**cái zhì** 才智 *ability and wisdom*	**xiào xīn** 孝心 *filial affection; filial piety*	**jiāo ào** 骄傲 *proud; arrogant*	
rěn nài lì 忍耐力 *patience*	**shù lì dí rén** 树立敌人 *to make enemies*	**suí jī yìng biàn** 随机应变 *to act according to circumstances*	**dǒng lǐ jié** 懂礼节 *courteous*	**zhì huì** 智慧 *wisdom*	
	cí bēi xīn 慈悲心 *kindness*	**jí dù** 嫉妒 *jealous*		**yán shǒu jì lǜ** 严守纪律 *to observe discipline strictly*	

练习 A 📖 **Answer the following questions in English.**

一 According to the article, why are people born in the year of the rat not good leaders?

二 What kind of personality do people born in the year of the ox have?

三 People of which zodiac sign have natural leadership skills?

四 Do people born in the year of the rabbit get along well with others? Why?

五 What kind of eating habits do people born in the year of the snake have?

六 Are people born in the year of the ram always obedient? Why?

七 People of which zodiac sign fall in love easily?

八 Which zodiac sign do you belong to? Which part of the description in the passage fits your personality?

九 Which zodiac sign has the characters you would most like to have? Why?

十 Find out which zodiac signs your friends belong to. Compare the description in the passage with your friends' personalities. Describe similarities and differences.

火热的社交网站

请阅读下面一篇关于社交网站的报纸文章，然后用英文回答问题。

建明注册了成为 MySpace 的会员，这个中文在线社区以"友你友我"作口号，内容精彩繁多。建明每天做的一件事，就是登陆这个社交网站，将新内容全部浏览一遍，第一时间了解老友的最新动态。他也上载记录自己生活点滴的日志和相册，并阅读别人的留言。上社交网站已成为建明必不可少的活动，消磨了他大部分的娱乐时间。

社交网站的确有让人上瘾的魅力。它们就好像是小镇上最热闹的酒吧，成为最时髦的去处。网站聚集了一群 16–30 岁的消费者，他们是最追逐时尚，也是最善变的人。这些人通过个人主页、博客日志和留言板，扩大自己的朋友圈，形成了不断延伸的巨大社交网络。任何人也可以创建一个属于自己的部落，作为与朋友交流思想和保持联系的平台。社交网站具有了解他人和展示自己的双重功能。

作为一种新型的社交活动，社交网站日益火热。在这里，朋友随意交谈；单身人士邂逅同道；制片人与自己的"粉丝"交流；家人互相联系，勾画家族图谱；专业人士提升自己的人气；同学和学友则追忆当年。

社交网站成了联络乐迷的最有效途径。以前，乐队依赖音乐经纪人来为自己做宣传和推广。而现在，乐队可以自己在社交网站上发布演出日期和音乐样本，与他们的爱好者通过留言板进行直接交流。

目前中国最红火的一些青春偶像歌手，以及轰动全国的超级女声（简称"超女"，指一个少女业余歌手比赛的电视节目）获奖者，都在社交网站上有自己的一群铁杆粉丝。每场大型演出之前，社交网站上便会热闹非凡。

对很多社交网站的创办者来说，现在最重要的，是如何将旺盛的人气转化成现金。目前社交网站的收入来源主要靠商务广告。由于几家环球大型网络公司均进军社交网络市场，它们之间面临激烈的竞争和挑战。

生词

huǒ rè **火热** *feverish*	shēng huó diǎn dī **生活点滴** *daily occurrences*	shàn biàn **善变** *changeable*	fēn sī **粉丝** *fan*	yuè mí **乐迷** *fan of a singer,* *musician, etc.*	tiě gǎn **铁杆** *loyal; faithful*
shè jiāo wǎng zhàn **社交网站** *social networking* *site*	bì bù kě shǎo **必不可少** *essential*	yán shēn **延伸** *to extend*	jiāo liú **交流** *to exchange ideas,* *opinions, etc.*	tú jìng **途径** *way*	rè nào fēi fán **热闹非凡** *bustling with* *excitement*
zhù cè **注册** *register*	xiāo mó **消磨** *to pass (the time)*	shuāng chóng **双重** *double*	gōu huà **勾画** *to sketch*	jīng jì rén **经纪人** *agent*	wàng shèng de **旺盛的** *popularity*
zài xiàn **在线** *online*	shàng yǐn **上瘾** *addicted*	suí yì **随意** *at will; as one* *pleases*	jiā zú tú pǔ **家族图谱** *family tree*	xuān chuán **宣传** *to publicise*	rén qì **人气** *popularity*
dēng lù **登陆** *to log on*	mèi lì **魅力** *charm*	xiè hòu **邂逅** *to meet by chance*	zhuān yè rén shì **专业人士** *professional*	tuī guǎng **推广** *to promote*	zhuǎn huà **转化** *to transform*
liú lǎn yī biàn **浏览一遍** *to skim once*	jù jí **聚集** *to gather*	tóng dào **同道** *people sharing a* *common goal*	rén qì **人气** *popularity*	fā bù **发布** *to release*	lái yuán **来源** *source*
zuì xīn dòng tài **最新动态** *update*	xiāo fèi zhě **消费者** *consumer*	zhì piàn rén **制片人** *film producer*	zhuī yì **追忆** *to recollect*	hōng dòng **轰动** *to cause a stir*	jìn jūn **进军** *to advance*
shàng zǎi **上载** *to upload*	zhuī zhú shí shàng **追逐时尚** *to keep up with* *fashion*			chāo jí **超级** *super*	

练习B 📖 **Answer the following questions in English.**

一 What does the slogan for MySpace mean?

二 What does Jian Ming use this site for?

三 Who are the major users of social networking sites?

四 List two reasons mentioned in the article why social networking sites are attractive to people.

五 What methods do people use to make friends and show their own information on social networking sites?

六 List two social activities you can do on a social networking site.

七 Why did music bands need to rely on their agents in the past?

八 What opportunities do social networking sites offer bands?

九 What is 'Super Girl Voice'?

十 If you want to contact other fans of your favourite singer, what can you do?

十一 What are social networking site companies using their popularity for?

十二 What challenges are existing social networking site companies facing?

培养青少年足球运动员的尝试

请阅读下面一篇关于如何培养中国青少年足球运动员的报纸文章，然后用英文回答问题。

中国足球队连连失败，其落后的根源，在于缺乏优秀的青少年后备力量。

记者近日赴全国多个城市，针对我国青少年足球发展现状进行深入调查，所见所闻，令人忧虑。

中国有13亿人口，但当前注册的青少年足球运动员仅有5万多人。相比之下，邻国日本人口仅有中国的十分之一，但有60多万注册的青少年业余足球运动员。而在法国、英国、德国等足球强国，足球更是人人爱好的运动。

另外，中国目前的青少年足球培养方式大有问题。传统的做法是教练将有潜力的小球员从六、七岁开始一手带大。不少地方为了出成绩，习惯将球员早早就关起来，进行"同吃、同住、同训练"三集中式的强化训练。由于过分注重比赛，小球员心理负担很大，临场发挥反而不佳。专家对许多球员的成长进行跟踪研究，结果显示，青少年时期不宜过早进行封闭式训练，要让他们拥有正常人的生活，包括接受文化教育。这样才能使具备天赋的孩子从中脱颖而出，并解决大部分孩子被淘汰后的出路问题。

欧洲足球界的做法与我们恰恰相反。他们重视让小选手得到全面的培养。足球学校不仅有运动训练设施，还有学习和做作业的场所。球员每年参加比赛的数量也有限制。

其实，中国不乏杰出的球员。已经陆续有十多名中国球员加盟了英国足坛。2004年，刚18岁的小将董方卓以天价被曼联买入，成为其中最有发展潜力的一名前锋。目前22岁的他正期待着为曼联一队踢出喝彩。

中国足球协会正在筹组一个全新的青少年足球后备人才培养项目。这个项目在强化球员的足球基础技能的同时，将文化课程的学习放在同样重要的位置。教练李辉说，期望经过六年的培训后，这些小球员能在技术上达到进入职业俱乐部的资格。即使不去职业俱乐部，学生也能接受高等教育。

生词

péi yǎng **培养** *to train*	suǒ jiàn suǒ wén **所见所闻** *what has been seen and heard*	qiáng huà **强化** *to strengthen*	tiān fù **天赋** *talent; gift*	jiā méng **加盟** *to become a member of a union*	zhōng guó zú qiú **中国足球** xié huì **协会** *Chinese Football Association*
shī bài **失败** *failure*	yōu lǜ **忧虑** *worrying*	xùn liàn **训练** *training*	tuō yǐng ér chū **脱颖而出** *talent showing itself*	xiǎo jiàng **小将** *a young sports star*	jī chǔ jì néng **基础技能** *basic technique*
gēn yuán **根源** *root; source*	xiāng bǐ zhī xià **相比之下** *by comparison*	guò fèn **过分** *excessive; over*	táo tài **淘汰** *to eliminate through competition*	dǒng fāng zhuó **董方卓** *Dong Fangzhuo, Chinese footballer*	wèi zhi **位置** *place; position*
quē fá **缺乏** *lack; be short of*	yè yú **业余** *amateur*	fù dān **负担** *burden*	qià qià xiāng fǎn **恰恰相反** *on the contrary*	tiān jià **天价** *astronomical price*	lǐ huī **李辉** *Li Hui, Chinese football coach*
yōu xiù **优秀** *excellent*	qián lì **潜力** *potential*	lín chǎng fā huī **临场发挥** *performance during a contest*	xiàn zhì **限制** *limit*	màn lián **曼联** *Manchester United*	zī gé **资格** *qualification*
hòu bèi lì liang **后备力量** *reserve force*	guān **关** *to keep somebody away from other people*	gēn zōng yán jiū **跟踪研究** *follow-up study; trace study*	bù fá **不乏** *not short of*	qián fēng **前锋** *striker*	
fù **赴** *to go to*		bù yí **不宜** *unsuitable*		hè cǎi **喝彩** *cheer; applause*	

练习C 📖 **Answer the following questions in English.**

一 According to the article, what is the major reason behind Chinese football teams' failure?

二 How does the writer feel about China's young footballers' current performance?

三 What are the two main problems identified in the article that young Chinese footballers are facing?

四 How do Chinese coaches usually train young footballers?

五 What effect does the training method mentioned in question four have on young footballers in China?

六 What should Chinese coaches do to help young footballers?

七 What is the main difference between football training in Europe and in China?

八 What position does Dong Fangzhuo play in Manchester United?

九 What is the new project that China has initiated to train young footballers about?

十 What does the new project mentioned in question nine expect to achieve after six years of training?

十一 What could be the title for this article? Explain your answer.

生肖讨论

练习A 🔊 根据谈话的内容，圈出正确的答案。

生词

bàn xìn bàn yí 半信半疑 *half believing, half doubting*	shuì lǎn jiào 睡懒觉 *to sleep in; a long lie-in*
zhì lì 智力 *intelligence*	ná bù dìng zhǔ yì 拿不定主意 *cannot make up one's mind*
hú shuō bā dào 胡说八道 *nonsense*	dí què 的确 *indeed*
qī piàn 欺骗 *to cheat; to deceive*	qū bié 区别 *difference*
fú hé 符合 *to match; to conform to*	zhān biān 沾…边 *relevant; close to*
shí qíng 实情 *actual situation*	

一 刘建明对李兰所说的那篇文章，评价是

    a) 内容挺有意思

    b) 内容完全没有道理

    c) 内容让人半信半疑

二 李兰的生活习惯是

    a) 晚睡晚起

    b) 晚睡早起

    c) 早睡早起

三 李兰的性格是

    a) 诚实正直

    b) 自信心不够

    c) 独立性强

四 刘建明认为李兰考试成绩好是因为

    a) 她智力高

    b) 学习努力

    c) 能够集中精力

五 刘建明的性格是

    a) 崇尚自由

    b) 聪明活泼

    c) 稳重、可信赖

六 从对话推断，刘建明的生肖应该是

    a) 鼠

    b) 马

    c) 牛

全市青少年篮球比赛

练习 B 🔊 根据关于某城市青少年篮球比赛的新闻广播内容，圈出正确的答案。

生词	
tóu piào **投票** *to vote*	**sài shì** **赛事** *competition; event;* *tournament*
jiǎng jīn **奖金** *prize money*	**tuī chū** **推出** *to introduce*
lā lā duì **啦啦队** *cheerleading*	**xīn yì** **新意** *new*
chū xí **出席** *to attend*	**shè zhì** **设置** *to set up*
wén yú **文娱** *cultural and* *recreational*	**zhí bō** **直播** *live broadcast*
biāo tí **标题** *title*	**zhì dìng** **制定** *to draw up*
yī nián yī dù **一年一度** *annual*	**yǔn xǔ** **允许** *to allow; to let*

一 本届比赛的球员包括

    a) 来自中国和其他国家的职业运动员

    b) 来自中国各城市的青少年业余运动员

    c) 来自中国和其他国家的青少年业余运动员

二 观众可通过以下哪个途径投票？

    a) 网站

    b) 电视热线

    c) 电台热线

三 今年新的奖励方法允许

    a) 每位参赛运动员都得到奖金

    b) 每位获奖运动员得到 6 000 元奖金

    c) 最佳运动员得到 6 000 元奖金

四 百人啦啦队

    a) 专门支持表现好的球队

    b) 由小学生和中学生组成

    c) 将会表演舞蹈

五 在去年比赛，出席的名人包括

    a) 体育界名人

    b) 文娱界名人

    c) 不能确定

六 这篇报道比较合适的标题是

    a) 本届青少年篮球比赛新意多多！

    b) 本届青少年篮球比赛成功举行！

    c) 本届青少年篮球比赛大受欢迎！

刘美霞访谈

练习C 根据电台主持人与当代青春偶像刘美霞的访谈内容，用中文回答下列问题。

生词

miáo shù **描述** to describe	míng pái **名牌** famous brand
liú yán **流言** rumour	xū róng **虚荣** vanity
jiá nà diàn yǐng jié **戛纳电影节** Festival de Cannes; Cannes Film Festival	jiào dōu jiào bù xǐng **叫都叫不醒** cannot be woken up by others; deep sleep
chéng rèn **承认** to admit	bǎo zhèng **保证** to guarantee
rì sī yè xiǎng **日思夜想** to long for someone day and night	yùn yòng **运用** use
quán wú fǎn yìng **全无反应** without the slightest response	fù yǔ **赋予** to give
dān xiāng sī **单相思** unrequited love	bì jìng **毕竟** after all
	shì jué yì shù **视觉艺术** visual art

一 刘美霞为什么想读书？

二 刘美霞找男朋友的标准是什么？

三 刘美霞是怎样描述她对高中时代一个男孩子的感情的？

四 刘美霞怎样看待有关自己的流言？

五 有报道说刘美霞不喜欢戛纳电影节，她承认吗？为什么？

六 访谈中，刘美霞提到自己的生活习惯怎么样？这对她的工作有何帮助？

七 刘美霞喜欢弹奏什么乐器？为什么？

八 刘美霞在自己导演的影片中，追求什么风格？

感兴趣的青年活动

练习A 你在YouTube上看到Free Hugs campaign在中国兴起的视频，然后读到有关的一则博客：

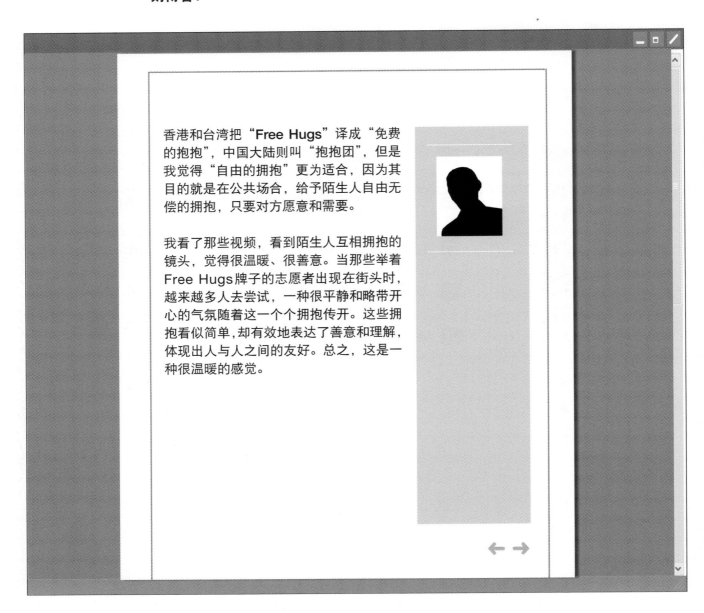

香港和台湾把"Free Hugs"译成"免费的抱抱"，中国大陆则叫"抱抱团"，但是我觉得"自由的拥抱"更为适合，因为其目的就是在公共场合，给予陌生人自由无偿的拥抱，只要对方愿意和需要。

我看了那些视频，看到陌生人互相拥抱的镜头，觉得很温暖、很善意。当那些举着Free Hugs牌子的志愿者出现在街头时，越来越多人去尝试，一种很平静和略带开心的气氛随着这一个个拥抱传开。这些拥抱看似简单，却有效地表达了善意和理解，体现出人与人之间的友好。总之，这是一种很温暖的感觉。

请你选一个自己感兴趣的青年活动，用中文写一篇180–200字的博客，来谈谈：

- 这个活动是什么？
- 你对这个活动持什么态度？
- 你觉得周围的人欢迎这个活动吗？为什么？
- 这个活动对社会有什么影响？

答复读者来信

练习B 你在学校报纸的"读者来信"栏中读到两封信：

我是一名高中二年级的学生，我数学不太好，但喜欢写作，用电脑记下自己的思想和某些不愿让大人知道的故事。可是，昨天我妈妈突击检查我的电脑，她不单把我的文稿全删掉，还骂了我一顿，说我不好好地复习功课，尽浪费时间写些没用的东西。那里有整整100多页，是我一年的心血啊！自以为秘密的内心家园，就这样被大人闯进和毁掉了！此刻，我的心情恶劣透顶。我真想完全放弃写作，但又不甘心。我该怎么办？

我读高三，是学校交响乐队的成员。一次中学汇演，我喜欢上了邻校的一个女孩，她的形象让我日思夜想，令我上课时无法集中精力。为了能看她一眼，跟她说上一句话，我精心计算她可能出现在校门前的时间，可是她对我好像全无反应，只打声招呼就走过去了。我知道我这是单相思，我的学习成绩也因此直线下降。如何才能赢得她的欢心，请朋友们给我出出点子。

请你选择其中一封信，用中文写一封180–200字的信答复对方，内容应包括：

- 介绍你自己。
- 建议对方应怎样做。
- 提醒对方要和家庭／学校妥协。
- 鼓励对方重新开始。

中学生开博客

练习C 🖊

最近，关于中学生开博客的问题引起了广泛的争议。中国的官方教育网站，专门为中学生开了一个博客频道，让青少年自由发表意见、倾诉烦恼、交流思想。有几所中学也建立了学生博客网，鼓励学生写作。虽然如此，很多家长却表示怀疑和忧虑。他们担心开博客网站会加剧很多已经存在的问题，如网络诈骗、网上聊天、色情、暴力等。

请你用中文写一篇180–200字的短文，对中学生开博客发表意见。内容应包括：

- 简要地介绍争论的焦点
- 表明你的观点，是支持还是反对？可用你的博客经验来说明你的观点
- 你对中学生开博客的建议
- 你觉得博客网站可以导致什么危险的情况？

复习二

选择有类似意思的词。

一 丰富多彩

    a) 活泼   b) 充沛   c) 彩声   d) 优秀

二 苦恼

    a) 忧虑   b) 乐趣   c) 敏感   d) 固执

三 出色

    a) 实际   b) 活跃   c) 张扬   d) 精彩

四 放松

    a) 休闲   b) 疲倦   c) 支持   d) 缓解

五 事先

    a) 过去   b) 顺序   c) 日常   d) 以前

六 紧张

    a) 压力   b) 减压   c) 奋斗   d) 耐性

七 赞成

    a) 持续   b) 自豪   c) 同意   d) 发展

八 流言

    a) 据说   b) 语调   c) 说明   d) 译音

九 消息

    a) 闻名   b) 休息   c) 新闻   d) 消化

十 患者

    a) 患难   b) 灾难   c) 病人   d) 大脑

练习B

下面的句子有拼音然后括弧里有两个词。根据拼音选择正确的词完成句子。

一 住在安徽省的企业家觉得酸味比（xián）（咸／鲜）味好吃得多。

二 因为丽丽是（shǔ）（竖／属）蛇的人她又细心又敏感。

三 杭州除了（sī）（似／丝）以外，还因为西湖著名。

四 如果你安排游览福建的话，那就一定计划品尝那儿的海鲜（yàn）（盐／宴）会。

五 钢琴家以他杰出的才华，弹奏出美妙的乐曲，（yíngdé）（赢得／应得）了观众的掌声。

六 清明节时，人们会把供品放在坟墓上，给住在 (míng)（明／冥）府的先人。

七 老师告诉我为了练习（wǔshù）（无数／武术）我（bìxū）（必须／必需）改善姿势与减肥。

八 春节是一个重要的中国传统节日，人们会回到故（xiāng）（乡／香）跟家人庆祝，并在家里放一些（jíxiáng）（吉祥／迹象）的东西。

九 过去，黄河的河岸领域（chēngwéi）（成为／称为）中国的"（wénmíng）（文明／闻名）摇篮"。

十 老板觉得（tuìchū）（退出／推出）工作进修有许多（lìyì）（利益／礼仪）。

练习 C

选择一个正确的答案。

一 哪一个不是吃的东西。

a) 种子　　　b) 坚果　　　c) 玉米
d) 喷泉　　　e) 谷物

二 针灸不会治疗下面的哪一个。

a) 延年益寿　b) 毅力　　　c) 戒毒
d) 调节情绪　e) 减轻压力

三 哪里不是亚洲的休闲游览地方之一。

a) 蒙古　　　b) 阿里山　　c) 圣淘沙
d) 剑桥　　　e) 迪斯尼乐园

四 哪一个不是交通工具。

a) 露营　　　b) 画舫　　　c) 巴士
d) 划艇　　　e) 大巴

五 哪个职业需要用比较多设备。

a) 律师　　　b) 秘书　　　c) 销售员
d) 公关员　　e) 摄影师

六 下面的一个词描述不积极的性格。哪一个。

a) 出色　　　b) 辛苦　　　c) 灵活
d) 朝气　　　e) 敏锐

七 下面的一个词描述积极的性格。哪一个。

a) 批评　　　b) 引诱　　　c) 骄傲
d) 嫉妒　　　e) 宽容

八 选择有"喜欢周围的人都看你，听你的话"一样意思的短语。

a) 喜出风头　b) 半途而废　c) 随机应变
d) 猛睡一觉　e) 脱颖而出

九 选择跟工作界没有关系的词。

a) 鬼魂　　　b) 招聘　　　c) 雇主
d) 退出　　　e) 同事

十 哪个不是个性特点。

a) 冲动　　　b) 崇拜　　　c) 细心
d) 活跃　　　e) 诚实

练习D

用英文翻译下面的句子。

一 为了改善体态，他正在减肥。

二 实验显示由于针灸的治疗，他的心理压力减轻了。

三 中国的少数民族不但有丰富多彩的服装，而且有历史悠久的喜庆节日。

四 无论一个国家的经济发展多么迅速，政府都必须提供基本的生活保障。

五 最近一位有名的歌星表演状态不佳，根据一些流言，她有吸毒的问题。

六 因为她的性格又活泼又伶俐，所以得到公司里高级领导的职位。

七 根据特快列车的广播，在五号车厢里你马上能买到饮料，凉菜，炒面，蛋炒饭和鱼香肉丝。

八 今日的名人一方面想获得媒体带来的利益，另一方面又想避免自己的私生活在杂志上被公开。

九 在大城市的商店里货物的价格不仅不可以商量，而且比乡村的市场贵得多。不过在大城市，手工艺品，珠宝首饰与古玩都很容易买。

十 随着互联网的不断壮大，你任何时候都可以浏览到感兴趣的最新消息。而且，对许多人来说，在家用电脑比出去买报纸方便得多。

练习E

用英文翻译下面的句子。

一 During his gap year Zhang Er decided to do some paid work experience with a law firm. After that, he plans to study law at university.

二 On the one hand the pianist loved what he did, on the other hand due to the number of performances he had to give each week, his tiredness led to unhappiness and eventually he didn't play in public at all.

三 As far as most young people are concerned, if you don't watch TV, or if you use books rather than the internet to do your research, and don't check your email daily or write blogs, then you're strange and definitely not cool!

四 Some parents worry about the rapid development and recent upsurge of social networking sites. If their children give out their details on one of these sites, there is huge potential for strangers to contact them and even lead them astray.

五 No matter how exhausted I am, whenever I visit Hong Kong, I spend hours strolling around the streets enjoying the variety of good food, superb collection of beautiful items in the shops and the vivacious atmosphere. When I've had enough of shopping, I jump on a boat to one of the islands and relax in the peace and tranquility of the hills.

六 According to the news, we should all be living a healthier lifestyle. Experts keep telling us we should make it a habit to exercise regularly, as well as eat a varied balanced diet which includes vitamins, carbohydrates, fibre, protein and fat. We should also insist on finding time to relax, so that our bodies can recover and recharge. As a result we should become more efficient in everything we do.

七 The world is a strange place nowadays! There are some people who enjoy and are full of passion for their jobs, because they have the opportunity to do something they love. However many people are stuck in a never-ending routine nine-to-five job they regard as hell. Is this fate?

八 He was so ill that the doctors first recommended he had blood tests, had his temperature taken and then go for an X-ray. They thought the problem might be liver disease, but later realised it was cancer. Luckily, he was treated quickly using a variety of medical techniques including acupuncture, and eventually he was cured.

九 If you visit China, you will see some unforgettable historical sites, taste wonderful and unusual flavours, experience traditional festivals and learn more about the different nationalities within China. You can stroll down the old alleys and imagine what living in one of the residences surrounding a courtyard during the Ming dynasty would have been like. After that you can walk between modernised skyscrapers chasing fashion in shopping paradise.

十 Celebrity spotters are always looking for optimistic, lively and quick-witted people with the determination and fighting spirit to succeed. If you can show that you have good interpersonal skills, are familiar with the latest trends, are willing to adapt to changing circumstances and are hardworking, you may meet a future employer by chance and become famous overnight.

语法

You are expected to study the grammatical system and structures of the Chinese language during your course. In the examination, you will be required to use actively and accurately grammar and structures appropriate to the task set, drawn from the following.

Comparisons

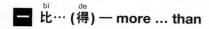

一 比… (得) — more … than

比 is a comparison marker. It indicates that two things are being compared. It can be used with both adjectives and adverbs with 得.

noun A	比	noun B	adjective
裤子	比	裙子	贵。
Trousers are more expensive than skirts.			
北京	比	桂林	冷。
Beijing is colder than Guilin.			

noun A	比	noun B	verb	得	adverb
哥哥	比	弟弟	跑	得	快。
My elder brother runs faster than my younger brother.					
妈妈	比	我	吃	得	健康。
Mum eats more healthily than me.					

二 有 / 没有… — (not) as …

有 sets out one item as a standard, and asks whether another item reaches that standard (or states, with 没, that it fails to reach that standard).

noun A	有 / 没有	noun B	adjective	
单板滑雪	有	滑雪	难	吗?
Is snowboarding as difficult as skiing?				
他	没有	我	聪明。	
He is not as intelligent as me.				

三 是…的

是…的 is used for emphasis with time, place, purpose and manner referring to past actions.

a) Emphasising adverb

To emphasise an adverb, 是 is placed directly before the adverb, with 的 at the end of the sentence.

subject	是	adverb	Rest of sentence	的
有名的乐队	是	很少	来布里斯托尔	的。
It is really infrequently that famous bands come to Bristol.				

b) Emphasising object

To emphasise an object, 是 comes before the object. If the verb refers to the past, 的 is placed between the verb and the object. Otherwise, it comes at the end of the sentence.

subject	verb	的	是	object
我昨天晚上	吃	的	是	宫保鸡丁。
I ate chicken and peanuts last night. (*lit.* It was chicken with peanuts that I ate last night.)				
老师	说	的	是	法语。
The teacher was speaking French. (*lit.* It was French that the teacher was speaking.)				

c) Emphasising subject

To emphasise the subject, 是 comes immediately before the subject, with 的 at the end of the sentence.

是	subject	verb	object	的
是	猫	打破了	花瓶	的。
It was the cat that broke the vase.				

Exclusion and inclusion

一 连…都（也）— even … can …

When talking about a group, 连…都（也）implies that the inclusion in the group of a particular subject is somehow surprising. 连…都（也）can be used with both positive and negative sentences. The structure 'brackets' the surprising group member, with the order of words in the rest of the sentence remaining flexible.

	连	surprising group member	都（也）	rest of sentence
说到新技术，	连	科学家	都	未必弄得懂。
When it comes to new technology, not even scientists can get their heads round it!				
	连	科学家	都	未必弄得懂新技术。
Not even scientists can get their heads round new technology!				
	连	我的小妹妹	也	会说汉语。
Even my little sister can speak Chinese.				

二 什么／谁／哪儿都（也）+ negative verb — anything; anybody; anywhere; nothing; nobody; nowhere

The question words 什么 (what), 谁 (who), and 哪 (where) can be negated by adding 都 or 也 and using a negative verb. The meaning is similar to 'nothing', 'nobody' and 'nowhere'.

Without the negative verb, they mean 'anything', 'anybody' or 'anywhere'.

subject	question word	都（也）	negation	verb
那个旅馆的卧室里	什么	都	没有。	
The rooms in that hotel have nothing in them.				
8 点以后，	谁	也	没	来过。
Nobody has come since eight o'clock.				
这几年，我	哪儿	也	没	去过。
I haven't been away anywhere these past few years.				
我的男朋友	什么	都		吃。
My boyfriend eats anything.				

三 一点…也 + negative verb — not even a little

一点也 emphasises the absoluteness of a negative verb.

subject	一点也	negative verb
佛教徒的饮食里，	一点肉也	没有。
There is no meat at all in Buddhist food.		
在这本就业辅导小册子里，	一点好的忠告也	没有。
There isn't one bit of good advice in this careers brochure.		
我住在加的夫，但是	一点威尔斯语也	不会说。
I live in Cardiff but I don't speak Welsh at all.		

四 除了…（以外），…也／还 — Apart from/Besides …, … also …

除了 includes a second idea with the first. It is neutral in tone, conveying no surprise at the second idea. Either a verb or a noun may follow 除了, but any noun following 除了 without its own verb must be governed by the final verb. The 以外 is optional, simply emphasising that the second idea is something different to the first. Both 也 and 还 mean 'also'. They are interchangeable.

除了	first idea	（以外），	subject	也／还	second idea with final verb
除了	武术	以外，	他	也	教太极拳。
Apart from wushu, he also teaches t'ai chi.					
除了	设计建筑物，		建筑师	还	负责监管建筑工程。
Besides designing buildings, architects also supervise their construction.					

五 不论…都 — Regardless of/No matter how …

不论……都 promises that there are no exceptions to the action described, although the circumstances might make the action difficult or surprising. The sentence starts with 不论, with the obstacle marked with 多.

不论	subject	degree of obstacle	subject	都		verb
不论		多累,	他	都	在每天早上五点	开始学习。
Regardless of how tired he is, he starts studying at 5a.m. every morning.						
不论	天气	多冷,	我们	都	天天	滑雪。
No matter how cold it is, we still go out skiing every day.						

六 不然 — otherwise

不然 is used to introduce a bad consequence.

excuse	otherwise	action
我感冒了,	不然	我会去远足。
I've caught a cold, otherwise I'd go hiking.		
功课太多了,	不然	我会给你帮忙。
I have so much homework to do, otherwise I'd help you around the house.		

七 否则 — or else; otherwise

否则 follows a warning and introduces the potential regrettable consequence.

warning	否则	regrettable consequence
注意少吃油腻菜,	否则	很容易会发胖。
You should be careful about eating greasy food, or else it'll be easy for you to become obese.		
你要更努力学习,	否则	成绩不会好。
You should study harder, otherwise your results won't be good.		

八 只有…才 — only (if)

只有…才 expresses that only if something is done, the result can then be achieved.

只有	action	subject	才	remainder of sentence
只有	每周练习,	我们	才	能唱好。
We will only be able to sing really well if we practise every week.				
只有	接受针灸治疗,	你	才	能好。
You will be cured only by undergoing acupuncture.				

Use of the adverb 就
see Conjunctions

Influencing people (Causative)

一 使 — to make somebody feel a certain way; to cause

使 is a verb used to indicate that someone's mood has been affected.

subject	使	person affected	adjective
考试的成绩	使	我	很高兴。
The exam results made me really happy.			
完成自己的博客	使	他	心满意足。
Finishing writing his own blog made him feel hugely satisfied.			

二 让 — to request; to let

让 is used when a person requests someone to do something. It is placed before the person of whom the request is being made.

subject	让	the person being requested	Action
大夫	让	我	每天多吃含蛋白质的食物。
The doctor asked me to eat more protein daily.			
傣族的朋友	让	我	跟她过泼水节。
My Dai friend asked me to celebrate the Water Festival with her.			

Time

一 才 — Only after ... (for some while)
_{cái}

才 expresses the idea that something needs to be done many times or for a long time until eventually the goal is achieved.

subject	time phrase	action	才	result
他	第五次	考试,	才	取得驾驶执照。
He took his driving test five times, then finally gained his licence.				
她	每周	跟不同的男人跳舞	才	找到合适的舞伴。
Every week she danced with a different man, then finally found a suitable dance partner.				

二 一边…一边… — ... while ...
_{yī biān yī biān}

一边…一边… expresses the idea that two actions are occurring simultaneously. Each 一边 is followed by one of the actions.

subject	一边	action 1	一边	action 2
她	一边	喝茶,	一边	看电视。
She watched TV while drinking tea.				
老师	一边	改作业,	一边	骂学生。
He scolded the student while marking his books.				

三 将 — will be; about to
_{jiāng}

将 is a future marker. It indicates that something is going to happen and is followed by the verb.

subject/time phrase	将	verb	noun
明天	将	有	雷雨。
There will be a storm tomorrow.			
政府的教育政策	将	会改变。	
The government's education policy is about to change.			

四 的时候 — when
_{de shí hòu}

Placed after a time phrase, 的时候 identifies a period of time when something happens/happened. Placed after a verb, it indicates when an action is/was taking place.

time phrase or verb	的时候	rest of sentence
年纪小	的时候,	他常常吃杏仁豆腐。
When he was young, he often ate almond tofu.		
唱歌	的时候,	弟弟总是口渴。
When he sings my brother is always thirsty.		

Presenting arguments

一 一方面…，另一方面… — on the one hand ..., on the other hand ...
_{yī fāngmiàn lìng yī fāngmiàn}

一方面…，另一方面… is used to describe something which has both a positive and negative slant. It is placed before the description.

subject	一方面	description 1	另一方面	description 2
人们	一方面	觉得毛泽东是天才,	另一方面	觉得他是暴君。
On one hand people consider Mao to be a genius, on the other hand he is considered a tyrant.				
游客	一方面	享受在香港购物,	另一方面	却不喜欢香港经常堵车。
On one hand tourists enjoy shopping in Hong Kong, on the other hand they think the traffic congestion there is horrific.				

if then ... sentences
see Useful phrases 如果… …就

Aspect markers

一 了
_{le}

了 indicates the completion of an action. It is used with the past tense or perfect tense.

a) Completion of an action (immediately after the verb)

subject	verb	了	rest of sentence
我	跑	了	一个小时。
I ran for an hour.			
他	吃	了	一个饺子。
He ate a dumpling.			

b) A brief happening (between a repeated verb or between a verb and 一会儿)

subject	verb	了	verb	rest of sentence
汤姆	想	了	想,	最后还是说不。
Tom thought for a while but he eventually said 'no'.				

c) Adjective used as verb

subject	adjective (used as verb)	了	rest of sentence
她的腰	宽	了	两寸。
Her waist has expanded by two inches.			
怀孕时她	重	了	十公斤。
She put on ten kilograms when she was pregnant.			

d) To express 'having had the experience'. In this case 了 is interchangable with the aspect marker 过.

subject	verb	了 / 过	rest of sentence
爸爸	去	了 / 过	马来西亚。
Dad has gone/been to Malaysia. (experienced going there)			
在四川我们	吃	了 / 过	辣面。
We ate spicy noodles in Sichuan. (experienced eating them)			

二 着 — '–ing' (steady state)

zhe

着 indicates an ongoing state or action. It is always used immediately after a verb.

a) An ongoing state resulting from an action

subject	verb	着	rest of sentence
他	穿	着	一双红皮鞋。
He is/was wearing red shoes. (He had put them on.)			
他结婚时	戴	着	爷爷的手表。
When he got married, he was wearing his grandfather's watch. (He had put it on.)			

b) A specific location (preceded by 在)

zài

subject	location marker	location	verb	着	rest of sentence
学生	在	图书馆里	忙	着	温习。
The students are/were busy revising in the library.					

c) A second action takes place during the course of the first action. The subject of both verbs must be the same.

subject	verb A	着	verb B	rest of sentence
孩子	哭	着	跑	了出去。
The child ran out crying.				

三 (正) 在 (…呢) — '–ing' (recurrent or unfinished)

zhèng zài

(正) 在 means something happening persistently, continuously or repeatedly. It often emphasises that the action is continuing at the particular time in question. Its meaning is similar to 'in the middle of' and 'in the process of'.

(正) 在 can be used for intermittent actions, e.g., My watch is ticking. (which is true even in between ticks.) It precedes the verb. 着 may also be added (again, immediately after the verb) without affecting the meaning.

subject	(正) 在	verb	(着)	rest of sentence
他	正在	戴		爷爷的手表。
He is putting on his grandfather's watch.				
坏了的水龙头	正在	滴	着	水呢！
The broken tap is dripping.				
学生	在	做		调查。
The students are/were conducting a survey.				

四 把 (Specific object marker)
bǎ

把 stresses that something was done to a particular object (the grammatical object of the verb). It is used mainly with action verbs. 把 denotes that we are dealing with a specific object. To give it added emphasis, 把 pulls the object forward from its normal position at the end of the sentence, so that it is in front of the verb. This leaves a void after the verb, which must be filled by a complement.

✓ The object of the sentence must be of specific reference. We must be able to work out exactly what/which one is being referred to.

✓ The verb must have a complement indicating result, location, direction, duration, manner or resultative state.

subject	把	object	verb + complement
小孩子	把	这个窗户	打破了。
The small child broke this window. (specific window, resultative state)			
姐姐	把	那个蛋糕	吃完了。
My older sister ate that entire cake. (specific cake, resultative state)			
我	把	牙齿	刷了一下。
I gave my teeth a (brief) brush. (duration. And although we've probably known whose teeth the writer is talking about, it's not actually specified in the sentence, so the next example is incorrect.)			
我	把	汉语	学了。(✗)
(My Chinese level may have changed, but the global state of Chinese itself hasn't been altered. No 'resultative state', duration, location, etc.)			
我	把	汉语	学了两年。(✗)
(Although this sentence gives a duration, we'd be hard pushed to be specific about what Chinese has been studied – it's too abstract an idea.)			

五 被 — by .../by means of ... (Agent marker)
bèi

被 is similar to the passive voice (something done by somebody) in English. The agent – whoever or whatever did the action – need not be specified.

It is often used to narrate an unpleasant, unfortunate or involuntary event; the speaker has effectively had no control over events (or at least may be disavowing having done it deliberately or maliciously – 'it's just one of those things').

✓ Verb should always be followed by a complement (see 把). bǎ

✓ To make the sentence negative, negate the 被 with a 没（有）in front of it. Do not negate the main verb.

subject	negative marker	被	agent	verb (+complement)
盐		被	我	用完了。
The salt was used up by me.				
盐		被		用完了。
The salt was used up (by someone).				
他	没（有）	被	西药	治愈。
He wasn't cured by Western medicine. (i.e. He may well have been cured, but it wasn't by western medicine.)				

六 的 — of ____ ownership/type (Possessive marker; attributive marker)
de

Possessive marker: added to nouns and pronouns (animate and inanimate) to indicate possession.

	owner	的	the possessed	rest of sentence
那是	妈妈	的	武术老师。	
That is Mum's martial arts teacher. (That is a martial arts teacher of 'mum' ownership/type.)				
这个	学校	的	屋顶	渗漏。
This school's roof is leaking (The roof of the 'this school' ownership/type is leaking.)				

Attributive marker: If we cheat and think of attributes as being possessions (e.g. the big blue house — the house 'owns' the bigness and the blueness), we can see how this 的 is what we need when linking an adjective with a noun. However, English and Chinese have a few philosophical differences. In Chinese, the bigness and the blueness own the house!

	owner, i.e. the adjective!	的	The possessed, i.e. the noun	rest of sentence
我住在	蓝色	的	大房子。	
I live in a big blue house. (I live in a house of the 'big blue' ownership/type.)				
我住在	大房子	的	蓝色。(✗)	
I live in a 'big blue' of the house's ownership/type. (✗)				
大夫用一支	长长	的	针	治好了病人。
The doctor used a long needle to cure the patient. (A needle of the 'long' ownership/type)				

七 地 (Adverb marker)

地 turns adjectives into adverbs. It is used after certain adjectives to denote the manner in which an action is carried out.

地 can only be used with:

a) disyllabic adjectives, e.g. 愤怒 (angry)

b) onomatopoeic words, e.g. 汩汩 (blub bubble gurgle bubble, or whatever noise your favourite stream makes)

c) reduplicated phrases or adjectives, e.g. 清清楚楚 (clear and distinct)

地 tends to be an objective description of the way something is done. (Compare 得 below, which tends to be more subjective.)

	adjective	地	verb	rest of sentence
她	愤怒	地	骂	丈夫。
She angrily scolded her husband. (No one can deny that she was angry.)				
河水	汩汩	地	流着。	
The river flowed along gurgling. (No one can argue that this wasn't the case.)				
我希望老师	清清楚楚	地	解释	语法。
I hope that the teacher explained the grammar clearly. (i.e. the clarity of the explanation had better not be in doubt)				

八 得 (Adverb marker)

得, like 地 (see above), introduces the manner in which an action is carried out, or a result. 得 tends to carry the nuance of a value judgement on the part of the speaker, whereas 地 is more objective. Word order is more flexible with 得 than with 地; 得 can be placed either after the verb or the adjective.

	adjective or verb	得	verb or 'adverbified' adjective	rest of sentence
我的女儿	漂亮	得		很。
My daughter is very beautiful. (That's not what the neighbours say.)				
他	吃	得	非常快。	
He ate extremely quickly. (But that's only going by my standards – it's all relative.)				

九 Adverbs of degree

Adverbs of degree do not have a marker in Chinese (see the last example above). English uses adverbs of degree to tell us the extent of an attribute: extremely quickly; absolutely fabulous; slightly mad. Chinese is economical and elegant here, needing nothing at all. For example,

degree	attribute
非常	快
extremely quick	
极	富有
fabulously rich	
相当	难
fairly difficult	

以 and some of its compounds

Chinese	English	examples			
		以	**noun**		
yǐ **以**	1) according to; in order of	**以**	年级	排队。	Line up according to your class.
	2) as	**以**	此	为证	use this as an evidence
		以	**verb**		
	3) so as to; in order to	**以**	应	学生的需要	to meet the needs of the students
yǐ biàn **以便**	so that; in order that	**means to achieve goal**	**以便**	**desired outcome**	
		舞台上的演员大声说话，	**以便**	后排的听众也能够听清楚。	The actor on stage spoke loudly so that even the audience in the back row could hear him.
yǐ miǎn **以免**	lest …; in order to prevent/ avoid … (can be used with requests and instructions)	**means to avoid problem**	**以免**	**problem**	
		营养家建议	要注意饮食健康，	**以免**	得癌症。 Nutritionists recommend eating healthy diets in order to avoid getting cancer.
yǐ lái **以来**	since	**time pointer**	**以来**		
		1949 年	**以来，**	老百姓也能进故宫了。	Ordinary people have been able to go in the Imperial Palace since 1949.
yǐ nèi **以内**	within (a period of time)	**time pointer**	**以内**		
		医生建议	两周	**以内**	接受针灸治疗。 The doctor suggested having acupuncture within two weeks.
yǐ zhì **以至**	consequently (unpleasant result)	**cause**	**以致**	**effect**	
		妹妹没有看清楚路面情况，	**以致**	撞了车。	My sister didn't check the road properly and consequently crashed her car.
yǐ jí **以及**	and also; as well as (appending another item	**list**	**以及**	**appended item**	
		饼干、巧克力、蛋糕、冰淇淋	**以及**	其它零食	biscuits, chocolate, cake, ice-cream, as well as other snacks

		thinker	以为	quoted thought	
以为 yǐ wéi	think that …	雇主	**以为**	毕业生的读写能力低，是严重的问题。	Employers think that the low literacy rate of graduating students is a serious problem.

		thinker	以	object of evaluation	为	how it is evaluated	
以…为 yǐ wéi	take … as …	北方人	**以**	面条	**为**	主食。	Northerners eat noodles as their staple food.

Useful phrases

Conjunctions 1

Chinese	English	Examples	
因为…所以 yīn wéi suǒ yǐ	because …, so …	**因为**奶奶生病了，**所以**他每天都去医院看望她。	Because his grandmother is ill, he goes to the hospital every day to see her.
因为… yīn wéi	since/as …, …	**因为**他不在，我便留下口信。	As he was out, I left a message.
不但…而且 bù dàn ér qiě	not only … but also …	老师**不但**懂武术，**而且**会做菜。	The teacher not only knows wushu, but also cooks well.
不仅…而且 bù jǐn ér qiě	not only … but also …	一些住在英国的中国人**不仅**庆祝春节，**而且**庆祝圣诞节。	Some Chinese people in Britain not only celebrate the Spring Festival, but also celebrate Christmas.
不仅…也 bù jǐn yě	not only … (but) also …	他**不仅**会唱流行歌，**也**会唱京剧。	Not only can he sing pop songs, he can also sing Beijing opera.
既然…便 / 就 jì rán biàn jiù	since/as …, …	**既然**你现在那么忙，我明天再来谈吧！	Since you are really busy right now, I'll come back tomorrow to talk.
虽然…但是 / 却 suī rán dàn shì què	although …, … … however, …	**虽然**我希望哪天能到中国学习，**但是**现在钱还不够。	Although I want to go to China to study some day, I don't have enough money at the moment.
尽管…还 jǐn guǎn hái	even though …, …	**尽管**下大雨，她**还**准备去远足。	Even though it's raining heavily, she still prepared to go hiking.
如果…就 rú guǒ jiù	if …, …	**如果**你有时间，明天**就**来帮我搬家吧！	If you have time, please come and help me move house tomorrow.
假如 / 要是…就 jiǎ rú yào shi jiù	if …, …	**假如 / 要是**天下雪，我**就**不来了。	If it snows, (then) I won't come.
要是 yào shì	if …, …	**要是**你学习得努力，你的成绩**就**会好了。	If you study hard, your results should be good.
先…然后 xiān rán hòu	first … then …	**先**完成作业，**然后**帮妈妈做家务。	Finish your homework first, and then help your Mum around the house.
一…就 yī jiù	as soon as …, … (right away)	妹妹**一**看见那个好看的男人，**就**脸红了。	As soon as my sister saw that good looking man, she blushed.
只要…就 zhǐ yào jiù	so long as …, …	**只要**你想学游泳，我**就**教你。	So long as you want to learn how to swim, I'll teach you.

bù guǎn hái shì 不管…还是	no matter / regardless of …	**不管**她多累，**还是**先照顾 孩子。	No matter how tired she is, she still looks after her children first.
wèi le 为了…	for; in order to; in order that	**为了**保持身体健康，必须 多加锻炼。	In order to keep fit, you must exercise more.

Conjunctions 2: and

Chinese	usage	examples	
hé 和	links two nouns, pronouns, adjectives and verbs	蒜**和**盐	garlic and salt
gēn 跟	links two nouns and pronouns	我**跟**他是好朋友。	He and I are good friends.
yǔ 与	links two nouns and pronouns more formal than 和	我**与**朋友在一起。	I am with my friends.
tóng 同	links two nouns and pronouns often used in southern and central China	你**同**他一起去。	You'll go with him.
ér 而	links two adjectives of similar meanings	乐观**而**自信	optimistic and self-confident
yòu yòu 又…又	links only adjectives	衣服**又**长**又**大	The clothes are big and long.

Other useful phrases

Chinese	English	Examples	
duì yú 对于	regarding; as far as … is concerned	**对于**我来说，应试教育是 考试压力大的原因。	As far as I'm concerned, exam-oriented education is the cause of exam stress.
suí zhe 随着	along with; in the wake of	**随着**社交网站的发展， 青少年不常到酒吧了。	In the wake of the development of social networking sites, young people don't often go out to bars.
yīn cǐ 因此	therefore; for this reason	春节是重要的家庭节日， **因此**家人都会聚在一起。	The Spring Festival is an important festival for families; for this reason the whole family will gather together.
yú shì 于是	as a result; consequently; thus	她吃了太多甜食和油腻的 快餐，**于是**最近出现过胖 的问题。	She ate too many sweet snacks and oily fast food; consequently, she has recently become obese.
gēn jù 根据	according to; based on	**根据**报纸报道，香港的商 店货品琳琅满目。	According to the newspaper, shops in Hong Kong have a superb collection of beautiful items.
rán hòu 然后	and then; after that	在新加坡的圣淘沙，游客 可以先划艇，**然后**打高尔 夫球。	At Sentosa in Singapore, tourists can row boats and then play golf.

dài tì 代替	instead of; in place of	一些政客认为，以素质教育**代替**应试教育，是教好学生的最有效方法。	Some politicians believe that adopting a system of education for all-round development in place of exam-oriented education is the most efficient way to teach students.
bù guò 不过	but; however; only	吃菜是很健康，**不过**，每天也应该吃点肉。	It is healthy to eat vegetables. However, there must be a little meat in your diet every day.
qí shí 其实	in fact; actually; as a matter of fact	**其实**，过分乐观并非好事。	As a matter of fact, being over-optimistic is not a good thing.
bìng 并	and; furthermore; moreover	他不单学习汉语，**并**教汉语的基础课程。	He's not merely studying Chinese, but also teaching it at a basic level.
bìng bù 并不	not	AB 血型的人**并不**适宜进食含蛋白质的食物。	Protein is not suitable for people with AB blood type.
bǐ jiào 比较	to compare	**比较**今天的青少年与五十年前的。	Compare today's young people with those of 50 years ago.
	quite	今天的午餐**比较**难吃。	The lunch today was quite awful.
què 却	yet; however; but	你明知道今天是他的生日，**却**忘了去拿生日蛋糕。	You knew it was his birthday today, yet you still forgot to bring a birthday cake.
dāng shí 当时	then; at that time	**当时**我很担忧，不知该怎么办。	At that time, I was really nervous. I didn't know what to do.
rú hé 如何	how	你打算**如何**跟她交朋友？	How are you going to make friends with her?
wèi le 为了	in order to; for the purpose of	**为了**去外国留学，他努力工作。	He worked hard so that he could go abroad to study.
tóng shí 同时	at the same time; simultaneously	除了要有纪律，练习武术**同时**要有灵活的身体。	Apart from having discipline, wushu also requires people to be flexible at the same time.
yóu yú 由于	due to; because of; owing to (See also Aspect markers)	**由于**他没看完就业辅导资料，所以他选择了一份不适合的工作。	Owing to the fact that he didn't finish reading the careers guidance booklet, he chose an unsuitable job.

生词表

汉 - 英

The page number indicates the first occurrence of the word in the book.

Character	Pinyin	English	Page
爱国诗人屈原	àiguóshīrénqūyuán	Qu Yuan	54
爱冒险	àimàoxiǎn	adventurous	105
爱你所做	àinǐsuǒzuò	to love what you do	93
爱因斯坦	àiyīnsītǎn	Albert Einstein	87
癌症	áizhèng	cancer	63
阿里山	ālǐshān	Mount Ali or Alishan	83
按	àn	in accordance with	18
昂贵	ángguì	expensive	101
安徽	ānhuī	Anhui Province	6
安宁	ānníng	tranquility	79
安排	ānpái	arrangement; to arrange	18
安全	ānquán	safe	20
暗中	ànzhōng	secretly	101
奥斯卡奖	àosīkǎjiǎng	Oscars	104
熬夜	áoyè	stay up late	31
白酒	báijiǔ	spirit distilled from sorghum or maize	10
百闻不如一见	bǎiwénbùrúyījiàn	'It is better to see once than hear a hundred times'	40
白族	báizú	Bai Nationality	50
瓣	bàn	clove of	4
磅	bàng	pound (in weight)	70
棒	bàng	excellent	77
拌上	bànshàng	to mix with	4
半途而废	bàntúérfèi	to give up halfway; to leave something unfinished	105
半信半疑	bànxìnbànyí	half believing, half doubting	111
保持	bǎochí	to maintain	6
保存	bǎocún	to preserve; to keep	81
报到	bàodào	to report to somebody	95
报道	bàodào	to report	97
宝剑	bǎojiàn	precious sword	55
包括	bāokuò	to include	18
保留	bǎoliú	to keep	75
报社	bàoshè	general office of a newspaper	98
保证	bǎozhèng	to guarantee	113
包子	bāozi	steamed bread with stuffing	8
八折	bāzhé	20 percent off	11
背景	bèijǐng	background	97
被看作	bèikànzuò	be regarded as	45
悲酸泪	bēisuānlèi	tears of sorrow	46
编辑	biānjí	editor	88
便捷	biànjié	convenient	77
便利	biànlì	convenient	79
表达	biǎodá	to express; to show; to indicate	48
表达能力	biǎodánénglì	ability to express oneself	97
表示	biǎoshì	to show; to express	1
标题	biāotí	title	112
表演	biǎoyǎn	performance	65
表演民间舞	biǎoyǎnmínjiānwǔ	to perform folk dances	45

Character	Pinyin	English	Page
标志	biāozhì	sign; symbol	79
必不可少	bìbùkěshǎo	essential	107
别放	biéfàng	do not put... in	10
毕竟	bìjìng	after all	113
避开	bìkāi	to avoid	20
避免	bìmiǎn	to avoid	20
彬彬有礼	bīnbīnyǒulǐ	courteous	40
兵马俑	bīngmǎyǒng	Terracotta Army	15
冰镇	bīngzhèn	refrigerated	10
比赛	bǐsài	competition	65
避暑胜地	bìshǔshèngdì	summer resort	83
必修课	bìxiūkè	required course	36
必需	bìxū	must	63
必须	bìxū	must; have to	23
博客	bókè	blogger	101
博士	bóshì	PhD/Doctorate	29
播音	bōyīn	broadcast	12
补	bǔ	to supplement	8
补充	bǔchōng	to replenish; to add	8
不辞而别	bùcíérbié	to leave without saying goodbye	87
不但…而且	bùdàn... érqiě	not only ... but also	6
不断	bùduàn	constantly	70
不断的	búduànde	constant	30
不乏	bùfá	not short of	109
不过	bùguò	but; however	20
不仅	bùjǐn	not only	46
补课	bǔkè	extra tuition	31
不可或缺	bùkěhuòquē	essential	44
不可缺少	bùkěquēshǎo	indispensable	95
不可商量的	bùkěshāngliángde	non-negotiable	17
不能	bùnéng	unable to ...	31
不能集中注意力	bùnéngjízhōngzhùyìlì	poor concentration	31
不舒服	bùshūfu	not feeling well	72
不松口, 不让步	bùsōngkǒu, bùràngbù	don't give in	17
不污染	bùwūrǎn	non-polluting	76
不相同	bùxiāngtóng	different	6
不虚此行	bùxūcǐxíng	worthwhile trip	40
不宜	bùyí	unsuitable	109
不一定	bùyídìng	not necessarily	20
不再	bùzài	no longer	87
步骤	bùzhòu	procedure; step	4
菜	cài	dish	4
猜灯谜	cāidēngmí	to guess lantern riddles	45
采访	cǎifǎng	to interview	97
材料	cáiliào	ingredient	4
裁判	cáipàn	referee	87

Character	Pinyin	English	Page
菜谱	càipǔ	recipe	4
菜系	càixì	cuisine	6
采用	cǎiyòng	to use; to adopt	44
才智	cáizhì	ability and wisdom	105
参观	cānguān	to visit	18
参考	cānkǎo	for reference	90
餐桌礼仪	cānzhuōlǐyí	table manners	1
策划	cèhuà	planning	98
曾经	céngjīng	once	95
插	chā	to stick into	1
茶壶	cháhú	teapot	1
插话	chāhuà	to chip in	32
柴可夫斯基国际青年音乐家比赛	cháikěfūsījīguójìqīngniányīnyuèjiābǐsài	International Tchaikovsky Competition for Young Musicians	93
插柳	chāliǔ	to plant a willow	46
长处	chángchù	merit	104
长度	chángdù	length	68
长短	chángduǎn	length	81
常规	chángguī	routine	91
常识	chángshí	common knowledge	20
长寿	chángshòu	longevity	44
长途	chángtú	long-distance	20
朝	cháo	facing	81
炒	chǎo	to stir-fry	4
超凡	chāofán	supreme	93
超级	chāojí	super	107
炒面	chǎomiàn	fried noodles	3
差异	chāyì	difference	1
乘	chéng	to take (means of transport)	18
盛出	chéngchū	to dish out food	4
程度	chéngdù	level	29
成功	chénggōng	to succeed	39
成就	chéngjiù	achievement	101
乘客	chéngkè	passenger	12
成立	chénglì	to found; to establish; to set up	54
城墙	chéngqiáng	city wall	18
成千上万	chéngqiānshàngwàn	thousands of	20
成人	chéngrén	adult	18
承认	chéngrèn	to admit	113
诚实	chéngshí	honest	87
成为	chéngwéi	to become	23
称为	chēngwéi	to be called; to be known as	6
橙汁	chéngzhī	orange juice	10
称作	chēngzuò	to be called	36
陈列	chénliè	to display	83
车厢	chēxiāng	carriage	12
吃饱	chībǎo	full	1
迟迟	chíchí	late	101
吃掉	chīdiào	to eat up; to devour	4
吃法	chīfǎ	way of eating	4
赤手空拳	chìshǒukōngquán	bare-handed	65
持续	chíxù	to continue	44
持续不间断的	chíxùbùjiànduànde	continuous	30
持续升温	chíxùshēngwēn	become more and more popular	36
崇拜	chóngbài	to adore; to idolise	87
重播	chóngbō	to replay	101
充电	chōngdiàn	to recharge	95
冲动	chōngdòng	impulsive	87
重复	chóngfù	repetitive	95
充满活力	chōngmǎnhuólì	energetic	87
充沛	chōngpèi	abundant	95
崇尚	chóngshàng	to uphold; to advocate	105
充实	chōngshí	fulfilled	91
重阳节	chóngyángjié	Chong Yang Festival	44

Character	Pinyin	English	Page
筹备	chóubèi	to prepare for	99
初	chū	at the beginning of	20
创新	chuàngxīn	innovative; creative	87
创造性	chuàngzàoxìng	creative	87
传说	chuánshuō	legend	44
传统	chuántǒng	tradition; traditional	8
处处	chùchù	everywhere	23
出发	chūfā	to set off	18
除非	chúfēi	only if; unless	26
吹笙	chuīshēng	to play a reed pipe wind instrument	50
春节	chūnjié	Spring Festival; Chinese New Year	44
春卷	chūnjuǎn	spring roll	3
出色	chūsè	outstanding	98
除外	chúwài	except	20
除夕	chúxī	New Year's Eve	48
出席	chūxí	to attend	112
初中	chūzhōng	junior high school	29
出租	chūzū	rental	20
出租车	chūzūchē	taxi	20
慈悲心	cíbēixīn	kindness	105
辞别	cíbié	to bid farewell; to say goodbye	48
刺激	cìjī	to stimulate	68
此起彼落	cǐqǐbǐluò	to rise one after another	50
刺入	cìrù	to pierce	68
辞职	cízhí	resignation	95
此致敬礼	cǐzhìjìnglǐ	with best wishes; respectfully	90
葱	cōng	spring onion	4
聪明伶俐	cōngmínglínglì	clever; quick-witted	105
从事	cóngshì	be engaged in	91
从头至尾	cóngtóuzhìwěi	right from the beginning	31
从未有过	cóngwèiyǒuguò	never experienced before	95
从业	cóngyè	to engage in a business	97
促进	cùjìn	to promote	50
蹴鞠	cùjū	to kick a ball	46
错过	cuòguò	to miss	81
大巴	dàbā	coach	18
大概	dàgài	probably; maybe	6
打工族	dǎgōngzú	group of employees	95
代	dài	generation; dynasty	23
带	dài	to take; to bring	55
代表	dàibiǎo	to represent	81
代表性	dàibiǎoxìng	representative	6
带领	dàilǐng	to take (people to different places); to lead	84
带薪	dàixīn	paid	87
傣族	dǎizú	Dai nationality	44
打开	dǎkāi	to open	1
大量的	dàliàngde	a large amount of	31
打猎	dǎliè	hunting	50
大脑	dànǎo	brain	68
蛋白质	dànbáizhì	protein	14
蛋炒饭	dànchǎofàn	egg fried rice	3
单调	dāndiào	monotonous	63
荡秋千	dàngqiūqiān	to play on a swing	44
胆识	dǎnshí	courage and determination	105
单相思	dānxiāngsī	unrequited love	113
担忧	dānyōu	to worry about	70
倒	dào	to pour	1
倒	dào	upside down	48
刀梯	dāotī	knife ladder	50
导游	dǎoyóu	tour guide	84
岛屿	dǎoyǔ	island	77
导致	dǎozhì	to cause	63
搭配	dāpèi	combination; to arrange in pairs or groups	4
大师	dàshī	master	93

Character	Pinyin	English	Page
打算	dǎsuàn	to plan	11
大雁塔	dàyàntǎ	Big Wild Goose Pagoda	18
大约	dàyuē	about; approximately	36
打针	dǎzhēn	injection	72
等	děng	such; and so on; etc.	6
登高	dēnggāo	to walk up a hill or a mountain	55
灯笼	dēnglong	lantern	46
登陆	dēnglù	to log on	107
登台演出	dēngtáiyǎnchū	to perform on stage	93
底	dǐ	at the end of	20
滴	dī	a drop of	4
点拨	diǎnbō	to give a hint	40
淀粉	diànfěn	starch	63
典礼	diǎnlǐ	ceremony	104
电台广播	diàntáiguǎngbō	radio broadcast	99
电梯	diàntī	elevator; lift	25
电影摄影	diànyǐngshèyǐng	cinematography	104
调查表	diàochábiǎo	questionnaire	38
地带	dìdài	area	81
顶	dǐng	top	83
钉	dīng	nail	23
定情	dìngqíng	to agree to marry somebody	50
的确	díquè	indeed	111
迪斯尼乐园	dísīnílèyuán	Disneyland	84
丢开	diūkāi	to put aside	101
地位	dìwèi	position; place; status	36
地狱	dìyù	hell	95
董方卓	Dǒngfāngzhuó	Dong Fangzhuo	109
懂礼节	dǒnglǐjié	courteous	105
冬至	dōngzhì	Winter Solstice	48
豆腐	dòufu	tofu; bean curd	12
豆浆	dòujiāng	soya milk	8
斗牛	dòuniú	bullfight	50
锻炼	duànliàn	to exercise	63
短期工作实习	duǎnqīgōngzuòshíxí	short-term internship	98
堵车	dǔchē	traffic congestion	75
独断	dúduàn	dictatorial	91
度假胜地	dùjiàshèngdì	holiday resort	79
独立	dúlì	stand-alone; independent	81
吨	dūn	ton, approximately 2,240 pounds	54
舵手	duòshǒu	steersman	54
多姿多彩	duōzīduōcǎi	diverse and colourful	87
独特	dútè	special; unique	46
儿童	értóng	children	18
法宝	fǎbǎo	an effective tool; a secret weapon	29
发布	fābù	to announce	70
发布	fābù	to release	107
翻炒	fānchǎo	to mix and stir-fry	4
放风筝	fàngfēngzhēng	to fly kites	46
访华	fǎnghuá	to visit China	32
房卡	fángkǎ	key card	25
放弃	fàngqì	to give up	105
放松	fàngsōng	to relax	87
放纵	fàngzòng	to let somebody have his/her own way	40
翻译	fānyì	interpreter; translator	93
反映	fǎnyìng	to reflect	8
反应	fǎnyìng	reaction	105
反正	fǎnzhèng	anyway	101
发胖	fāpàng	to put on weight	8
发现	fāxiàn	to discover	1
发炎	fāyán	inflammation	72
发展	fāzhǎn	to develop	44
费事	fèishì	troublesome, time or energy consuming	20

Character	Pinyin	English	Page
分别	fēnbié	respectively	91
分别轻重缓急	fēnbiéqīngzhònghuǎnjí	prioritise	31
奋斗	fèndòu	to struggle	31
奋斗精神	fèndòujīngshén	spirited	105
纷繁复杂	fēnfánfùzá	complicated; complex	87
丰富多彩	fēngfùduōcǎi	rich and colourful	45
丰盛	fēngshèng	rich; sumptuous	8
丰收	fēngshōu	harvest; to have a lot of prey	50
坟墓	fénmù	grave (n.)	46
分散	fēnsàn	scattered	34
粉丝	fěnsī	fan	107
福	fú	happiness; good fortune	48
赴	fù	to go to	109
负担	fùdān	burden	109
负担得起	fùdāndéqǐ	affordable	76
符合	fúhé	to match; to conform to	111
复活节	fùhuójié	Easter	44
福建	fújiàn	Fujian Province	6
负累	fùlěi	burden	95
福利	fúlì	benefits	97
付钱	fùqián	to pay for	25
附上	fùshàng	to attach; to enclose	90
服务	fúwù	service	20
服务员	fúwùyuán	waiter; waitress	1
富有	fùyǒu	rich; be full of	70
赋予	fùyǔ	to give	113
富于热情	fùyúrèqíng	full of passion	93
负责	fùzé	responsible	87
付帐	fùzhàng	to pay the bill	1
复制品	fùzhìpǐn	reproduction	17
服装设计师	fúzhuāngshèjìshī	fashion designer	87
钙	gài	calcium	8
概括	gàikuò	to summarise	8
改善	gǎishàn	to improve	63
盖子	gàizi	lid	1
赶	gǎn	to rush	11
肝病	gānbìng	liver disease	63
尴尬	gāngà	embarrassing; embarrassed	101
干干净净	gāngānjìngjìng	cleanly, without leaving anything behind	1
钢琴家	gāngqínjiā	pianist	93
感受	gǎnshòu	to feel	32
肝脏	gānzàng	liver	66
高等水平考试	gāoděngshuǐpíngkǎoshì	A Level examination	29
高尔夫球	gāoěrfūqiú	golf	75
高级	gāojí	senior	95
高楼大厦	gāolóudàshà	high buildings and large mansions	81
告诉	gàosù	to tell	39
高中	gāozhōng	high school	29
各	gè	every	6
隔开	gékāi	to separate	20
根	gēn	unit for long thin objects such as spring onions	4
根源	gēnyuán	root; source	109
跟踪研究	gēnzōngyánjiū	follow-up study; trace study	109
个人指导	gèrénzhǐdǎo	individual guidance	34
格外	géwài	exceptionally	20
歌星	gēxīng	pop star	89
宫保鸡丁	gōngbǎojīdīng	Kungpao chicken	10
公车	gōngchē	bus	77
功夫	gōngfu	kung fu; martial arts	55
公共交通	gōnggòngjiāotōng	public transport	76
公关员	gōngguānyuán	public relations officer	91
工具	gōngjù	tool; device	36
公里	gōnglǐ	kilometre	20

Character	Pinyin	English	Page
供品	gòngpǐn	offering (for the dead)	46
贡献	gòngxiàn	contribution	99
公益	gōngyì	public welfare	84
供应	gōngyìng	to provide	12
勾画	gōuhuà	to sketch	107
篝火	gōuhuǒ	bonfire	50
沟通与交流	gōutōngyǔjiāoliú	to communicate and exchange ideas	32
购物	gòuwù	shopping	75
购物天堂	gòuwùtiāntáng	shopping paradise	77
挂	guà	to hang; to put up	46
关	guān	to keep somebody away from other people	109
观察力	guānchálì	observation	91
管道工	guǎndàogōng	plumber	91
逛	guàng	to stroll	81
广播	guǎngbō	announcement	12
广泛	guǎngfàn	wide range of; widely	6
广告	guǎnggào	advertisement	97
逛庙会	guàngmiàohuì	to go to the temple fair	53
广州亚运组委会	guǎngzhōuyàyùn zǔwěihuì	Guangzhou Asian Games Organizing Committee (GAGOC)	97
管理	guǎnlǐ	management	84
观赏	guānshǎng	to enjoy the view of	77
关系	guānxì	relationship	25
惯用	guànyòng	habitually practise; consistently use	91
官员	guānyuán	official (n.)	70
观众	guānzhòng	audience	93
顾此失彼	gùcǐshībǐ	unable to attend to everything at once	31
古代	gǔdài	ancient	23
古典	gǔdiǎn	classic	18
固定	gùdìng	fixed	70
古都	gǔdū	ancient capital	18
故宫	gùgōng	Imperial Palace; Forbidden City	15
鬼	guǐ	ghost	46
归类	guīlèi	to classify	7
桂林	guìlín	Guilin	15
规模	guīmó	scale	23
估计	gūjì	to estimate	36
顾客	gùkè	customer	10
古老肉	gǔlǎoròu	sweet and sour pork	3
鼓励别人选用	gǔlìbiérénxuǎn yòng	to encourage people to use ...	76
锅	guō	pan; wok	4
过程	guòchéng	process; procedure	70
过分	guòfèn	excessive; over	109
国际化	guójìhuà	international	20
国际龙舟联合会	guójìlóngzhōu liánhéhuì	International Dragon Boat Federation	54
国庆节	guóqìngjié	National Day	20
过去	guòqù	in the past	8
古玩	gǔwán	antique	17
谷物	gǔwù	cereal	66
固执	gùzhí	stubborn	105
雇主	gùzhǔ	employer	99
哈尔滨	Hā'ěrbīn	Harbin	15
哈佛大学	hāfódàxué	Harvard University	68
海外	hǎiwài	overseas	38
害羞	hàixiū	shy	38
汉办	hànbàn	The Office of Chinese Language Council International (Hanban)	36
寒窗苦读	hánchuāngkǔdú	hard life of a poor scholar	29
寒带	hándài	frigid zone	83
航班	hángbān	flight	25
旱谷	hàngǔ	dry valley	50

Character	Pinyin	English	Page
行业	hángyè	profession; trade	98
杭州	hángzhōu	Hangzhou	15
罕见	hǎnjiàn	rare	83
寒食	hánshí	lit. cold food; here, name of festival	46
含有	hányǒu	to contain	63
豪华	háohuá	luxurious	75
好坏	hǎohuài	pros	89
好久	hǎojiǔ	long time	11
好运	hǎoyùn	good luck/fortune	3
喝彩	hècǎi	cheer; applause	109
合二为一	héèrwéiyī	to combine two things as one	95
何妨	héfáng	why not	101
合理	hélǐ	reasonable	11
横	héng	horizontal	23
恒景	héngjǐng	Heng Jing	55
恒心	héngxīn	perseverance	105
很久以前	hěnjiǔyǐqián	a long time ago	55
和平	hépíng	peace	79
合作	hézuò	to cooperate; to collaborate; to work together	54
轰动	hōngdòng	to cause a stir	107
弘扬	hóngyáng	to spread; to introduce something to other parts of the world	44
后备力量	hòubèilìliang	reserve force	109
猴子	hóuzi	monkey	79
划	huá	to row (a boat)	54
皇帝	huángdì	emperor	23
皇宫	huánggōng	palace	23
黄瓜	huángguā	cucumber	12
欢呼声	huānhūshēng	cheer; shout of joy	50
缓解	huǎnjiě	to ease; to relieve	68
欢聚一堂	huānjùyītáng	to gather together happily	48
欢笑声	huānxiàoshēng	laughter	46
患者	huànzhě	patient	68
划手	huáshǒu	rower	54
划艇	huátǐng	paddling	79
花样	huāyàng	variety	6
忽必烈	hūbìliè	Kublai Khan	81
互动	hùdòng	interaction	40
互访活动	hùfǎnghuódòng	exchange visits	32
恢复	huīfù	to recover	72
汇集	huìjí	to gather together	50
回民街	huímínjiē	Muslim Street (a street in Xi'an where there are many Muslim restaurants)	18
湖南	húnán	Hunan Province	6
活	huó	to live	8
火把	huǒbǎ	fire torch	50
活泼	huópō	lively; vivacious	91
火热	huǒrè	feverish	107
活跃	huóyuè	active	95
胡说八道	húshuōbādào	nonsense	111
胡同	hútòng	alley	81
互相追逐	hùxiāngzhuīzhú	to chase each other	50
即	jí	that is (i.e.)	50
既…也	jì … yě	not only ... but also	79
家常	jiācháng	homely	4
价格	jiàgé	price	17
加盟	jiāméng	to become a member of a union	109
戛纳电影节	jiánàdiànyǐngjié	Festival de Cannes; Cannes Film Festival	113
坚持	jiānchí	to insist	1
简单	jiǎndān	briefly	6
间谍片	jiàndiépiàn	spy thriller	104
剪断	jiǎnduàn	to cut off	46
减肥	jiǎnféi	to lose weight	63

Character	Pinyin	English	Page
间隔	jiàngé	in between	81
奖金	jiǎngjīn	prize money	112
江苏	jiāngsū	Jiangsu Province	6
坚果	jiānguǒ	nut	66
酱油	jiàngyóu	soy sauce	4
渐渐	jiànjiàn	gradually	46
健康	jiànkāng	health	63
简历	jiǎnlì	curriculum vitae (CV)	97
剑桥	jiànqiáo	Cambridge	84
减轻压力	jiǎnqīngyālì	to relieve stress	65
健身	jiànshēn	to keep fit	65
减压	jiǎnyā	reduce one's stress	31
建议	jiànyì	recommendation; proposal	26
建筑	jiànzhù	building	81
建筑师	jiànzhùshī	architect	88
角	jiǎo	corner	81
交	jiāo	to hand in	11
骄傲	jiāoào	proud; arrogant	105
叫都叫不醒	jiàodōujiàobùxǐng	cannot be woken up by others; deep sleep	113
交流	jiāoliú	to exchange ideas, opinions etc.	107
脚踏实地	jiǎotàshídì	earnest and practical	87
交通	jiāotōng	transport	20
交往	jiāowǎng	contact	36
交友	jiāoyǒu	to make friends	87
教育体系	jiàoyùtǐxì	education system	29
饺子	jiǎozi	dumpling	3
架起	jiàqǐ	to build	93
价钱	jiàqian	price	11
家务	jiāwù	housework	87
家族图谱	jiāzútúpǔ	family tree	107
基本	jīběn	basic	18
基本情况	jīběnqíngkuàng	general information	99
基础技能	jīchǔjìnéng	basic technique	109
基础知识良好	jīchǔzhīshiliánghǎo	good basic knowledge	32
记得	jìde	to remember	4
嫉妒	jídù	jealous	105
皆	jiē	all	81
节能	jiénéng	energy efficient	76
介于…至…之间	jiè...yú...zhì...zhījiān	between ... and ...	84
杰出的才华	jiéchūdecáihuá	outstanding talent	93
借此机会	jiècǐjīhuì	to take the chance (to do something)	95
戒毒	jièdú	drug rehabilitation	68
结合	jiéhé	combination; integration	54
接近	jiējìn	close to; near	46
解决方法	jiějuéfāngfǎ	solution	70
结识	jiéshí	to get to know somebody	101
接受	jiēshòu	to accept; to receive	70
结束	jiéshù	to finish; to end	18
计划	jìhuà	schedule; plan	91
机会	jīhuì	opportunity	84
计价	jìjià	to calculate the fare	20
纪律	jìlǜ	discipline	64
禁	jìn	to forbid; to prohibit; to ban	46
紧绷弦	jǐnbēngxián	stressed; tense; uptight	29
紧凑	jǐncòu	well-organised; compact	26
净	jìng	only; merely	39
精彩	jīngcǎi	wonderful	40
景点	jǐngdiǎn	scenic spot	18
经济	jīngjì	economy	36
境界	jìngjiè	level	95
经纪人	jīngjìrén	agent	107
经理	jīnglǐ	manager	87
经贸	jīngmào	economy and trade	36
竞赛活动	jìngsàihuódòng	competition	65
竞选	jìngxuǎn	to run for	87
经营	jīngyíng	to manage; to run	95
今后	jīnhòu	in the future	95
吉尼斯世界记录大全	jínísīshìjièjìlùdàquán	Guinness Book of World Records	54
紧急代替	jǐnjídàitì	to replace somebody at the last minute	93
金鸡奖	jīnjījiǎng	Golden Rooster Award	104
进军	jìnjūn	to advance	107
金马奖	jīnmǎjiǎng	Golden Horse Award; golden horse statuette	101
紧密	jǐnmì	closely	54
进行	jìnxíng	to take place; to carry out	11
进修	jìnxiū	to study further	95
紧张	jǐnzhāng	stress	31
紧张的	jǐnzhāngde	stressed	31
技巧	jìqiǎo	skill	17
既然	jìrán	since	1
肌肉	jīròu	muscle	63
即使	jíshǐ	even though	83
集市交易	jíshìjiāoyì	fair	53
技术员	jìshùyuán	technician	91
祭祀	jìsi	to offer sacrifices to gods or ancestors	44
集体舞	jítǐwǔ	group dance	70
久	jiǔ	long-lasting	23
就连	jiùlián	even	4
救生圈	jiùshēngquān	lifebuoy	73
就业辅导	jiùyèfǔdǎo	career guidance	90
吉祥	jíxiáng	auspicious	3
迹象	jìxiàng	sign	95
记忆力	jìyìlì	memory	105
既有… 又有…	jìyǒu... yòuyǒu...	both ... and ...	46
给予	jǐyǔ	to give; to provide	34
记载	jìzǎi	record	54
祭祖	jìzǔ	to offer sacrifices to ancestors	44
卷心菜	juǎnxīncài	cabbage	66
聚合	jùhé	to get together; to foster; to have	101
菊花	júhuā	chrysanthemum	55
聚集	jùjí	to gather	107
俱佳	jùjiā	(things mentioned) are all very good	6
据说	jùshuō	It is said that ...; It is believed that ...	46
具体	jùtǐ	in detail	99
开放	kāifàng	to open	23
开朗	kāilǎng	optimistic	91
开设	kāishè	to open; to offer	36
开展	kāizhǎn	to start; begin to develop	32
慷慨	kāngkǎi	generous	105
抗衰老	kàngshuāilǎo	anti-aging	68
看护婴儿	kānhùyīng'ér	to babysit	87
看似奇怪	kànsìqíguài	to appear strange	4
看重	kànzhòng	to regard something as important; to value	40
靠	kào	to depend on; to rely on	66
靠近	kàojìn	close to	68
烤肉	kǎoròu	roast meat	3
课程	kèchéng	course	36
可口	kěkǒu	tasty	6
可惜	kěxī	pity	26
空档年	kōngdàngnián	gap year	87
孔雀	kǒngquè	peacock	79
控制	kòngzhì	to control	66
孔子	kǒngzǐ	Confucius	29
孔子学院	kǒngzǐxuéyuàn	Confucius Institute	36
口碑	kǒubēi	praise	93

Character	Pinyin	English	Page
口味	kǒuwèi	a person's taste	6
酷	kù	cool	101
快餐店	kuàicāndiàn	fast food shop	70
会计	kuàijì	accountant	91
快捷	kuàijié	quick	77
筷子	kuàizi	chopsticks	1
矿物质	kuàngwùzhì	mineral	63
宽容	kuānróng	tolerant; lenient	105
苦恼	kǔnǎo	worry; distress; trouble	48
扩大	kuòdà	to widen	36
辣	là	hot; spicy	6
来来往往	láiláiwǎngwǎng	to come and go	101
来源	láiyuán	source	107
辣椒	làjiāo	chilli	6
垃圾食物	lājīshíwù	junk food	73
啦啦队	lālāduì	cheerleading	112
辣妹	làmèi	Spice Girls	101
浪费	làngfèi	to waste	105
郎朗	lánglǎng	Lang Lang	93
老板	lǎobǎn	boss	95
劳动节	láodòngjié	Labour Day	20
劳累	láolèi	tiredness	93
拉线	lāxiàn	string	46
乐观	lèguān	optimistic	87
类	lèi	kind; type	6
类型	lèixíng	type; kind	90
乐趣	lèqù	delight; pleasure	95
乐在其中	lèzàiqízhōng	to enjoy (doing) something	95
理	lǐ	to pay attention to	87
李安	Lǐ'ān	Ang Lee	104
凉菜	liángcài	cold dish	12
量体温	liángtǐwēn	to take somebody's temperature	72
联合国教科文组织	liánhéguójiàokēwénzǔzhī	the United Nations Educational, Scientific and Cultural Organization (UNESCO)	23
连接	liánjiē	to join; to link	79
脸盆	liǎnpén	basin	50
了解	liǎojiě	to understand; to know	1
聊天	liáotiān	to chat	77
李辉	Lǐhuī	Li Hui	109
礼貌	lǐmào	good manners	1
礼貌称呼	lǐmàochēnghu	polite address	99
临场发挥	línchǎngfāhuī	performance during a contest	109
另	lìng	the other	20
凌晨	língchén	before dawn	84
领队老师	lǐngduìlǎoshī	visiting teacher	32
灵活	línghuó	flexible	64
灵活工作制	línghuógōngzuòzhì	flexible working hours	99
零食	língshí	snack	73
领袖	lǐngxiù	leader	105
琳琅满目	línlángmǎnmù	a superb collection of beautiful things	77
临时	línshí	at the last moment	101
历史悠久	lìshǐyōujiǔ	have a long history	44
留	liú	to remain; to leave	1
浏览一遍	liúlǎnyībiàn	to skim once	107
留下	liúxià	to leave (details)	25
流言	liúyán	rumour	113
理想	lǐxiǎng	ideal	83
理性	lǐxìng	rational	91
利益	lìyì	benefit; interest	105
理智	lǐzhì	rational	87
黎族	lízú	Li nationality	50
隆重	lóngzhòng	grand; solemn	44
龙舟竞渡	lóngzhōujìngdù	dragon boat race	44
漏掉	lòudiào	to miss; to leave out	101

Character	Pinyin	English	Page
论文	lùnwén	dissertation	11
锣鼓	luógǔ	gong and drum	54
落后	luòhòu	to fall behind	34
络绎不绝	luòyìbùjué	in an endless stream	83
录取	lùqǔ	to recruit	99
律师	lǜshī	lawyer	87
旅途	lǚtú	journey; trip	95
旅途愉快	lǚtúyúkuài	pleasant journey	12
露营	lùyíng	camping	75
麻	má	to numb	6
麻烦	máfan	trouble	105
脉搏	màibó	pulse	72
麦当劳	màidāngláo	McDonald's	13
埋头	máitóu	to immerse oneself in something	87
马路	mǎlù	street; road	20
漫长	màncháng	very long (time)	95
忙得要死	mángdeyàosǐ	very busy	11
曼联	mànlián	Manchester United	109
馒头	mántou	steamed bread	8
满意	mǎnyì	satisfaction	91
满载而归	mǎnzàiérguī	return fully loaded; with fruitful results	77
马上	mǎshàng	immediately; soon	12
每当	měidāng	whenever	4
魅力	mèilì	charm	107
美妙	měimiào	wonderful	93
美食	měishí	good food	77
没完的	méiwánde	never-ending	31
美味	měiwèi	delicious food; delicacy	4
蒙古族	měnggǔzú	Mongolian nationality	50
猛睡一觉	měngshuìyījiào	to have a good sleep	101
面对	miànduì	to face	29
免费	miǎnfèi	free of charge	18
面试	miànshì	interview	87
免灾避祸	miǎnzāibìhuò	to avoid disasters and misfortune	44
描述	miáoshù	to describe	113
苗条	miáotiáo	slim	73
苗族	miáozú	Miao nationality	50
密度	mìdù	density	77
秘诀	mìjué	key to success; secret	73
明	míng	Ming dynasty	23
冥	míng	the underworld	46
敏感	mǐngǎn	sensitive	66
命根	mìnggēn	lifeblood; one's very life	29
名牌	míngpái	famous brand	113
名人	míngrén	celebrity	87
名胜	míngshèng	scenic spot	15
民间	mínjiān	among the people; folk	45
敏锐	mǐnruì	sharp; keen	91
民俗	mínsú	folk custom	53
民族	mínzú	nationality	15
秘书	mìshu	secretary	91
模仿	mófǎng	modelled after	104
陌生人	mòshēngrén	stranger	101
模式	móshì	model	66
谋生	móushēng	to make a living	87
某种	mǒuzhǒng	some kind of; certain kind of	91
莫扎特	mòzhātè	Wolfgang Amadeus Mozart	87
木工	mùgōng	carpenter	91
母亲	mǔqīn	mother	15
牧区	mùqū	pastoral area	50
木桶	mùtǒng	wooden bucket	50
拿不定主意	nábùdìngzhǔyì	cannot make up one's mind	111
那达慕	nàdámù	Nadam Fair	50
耐性	nàixìng	patient	34
难忘	nánwàng	unforgettable	77

Character	Pinyin	English	Page
闹出笑话	nàochūxiàohuà	to make a funny mistake	39
纳西族	nàxīzú	Naxi Nationality	50
内容	nèiróng	content	29
能力	nénglì	ability; capability	29
能量	néngliàng	energy	8
能说会道	néngshuōhuìdào	to have the gift of the gab	87
鸟瞰	niǎokàn	to get a bird's eye view	79
逆境	nìjìng	adversity	105
浓厚	nónghòu	profound	54
农历	nónglì	the lunar calendar	45
努力	nǔlì	to struggle	31
女优于男	nǚyōuyúnán	girls outshine boys	34
偶尔	ǒuěr	occasionally	101
偶像	ǒuxiàng	idol	101
盘旋	pánxuán	to circle; to spiral	83
盘子	pánzi	dish	1
配	pèi	to go with	8
培养	péiyǎng	to train	109
喷泉	pēnquán	fountain	79
皮肤	pífū	skin	68
疲倦	píjuàn	tired	72
品尝	pǐncháng	to taste	75
频繁	pínfán	frequently	101
评估	pínggū	assessment	30
平衡	pínghéng	balance	95
评价	píngjià	comment	87
平均	píngjūn	average	34
平时	píngshí	normally	4
品质	pǐnzhì	quality	87
批评	pīpíng	to criticise	105
泼水	pōshuǐ	to splash water	44
普遍	pǔbiàn	popular; widely used	20
普通	pǔtōng	normal	20
谱写	pǔxiě	to compose	87
前锋	qiánfēng	striker	109
强化	qiánghuà	to strengthen	109
强劲	qiángjìng	powerful	36
强身键体	qiángshēnjiàntǐ	to keep fit	70
强壮	qiángzhuàng	strong	63
潜力	qiánlì	potential	109
敲	qiāo	to tap; to knock	1
恰恰相反	qiàqiàxiāngfǎn	on the contrary	109
期待	qīdài	to look forward to; to expect	48
切成	qiēchéng	to cut into …	4
切碎	qiēsuì	to crush	4
气氛	qìfēn	atmosphere	40
奇观	qíguān	(natural) wonder	83
气候	qìhòu	climate	6
奇迹	qíjì	wonder; miracle	18
起价费	qǐjiàfèi	starting price	20
勤奋	qínfèn	hard-working; diligent	87
勤奋辛苦	qínfènxīnkǔ	diligent; hard-working	29
清	qīng	Qing dynasty	23
清淡	qīngdàn	not greasy or strongly flavoured; light	6
清明节	qīngmíngjié	Qing Ming Festival	44
轻轻	qīngqīng	lightly; gently	1
情人节	qíngrénjié	Valentine's Day	45
清爽	qīngshuǎng	light and refreshing	6
清爽宜人	qīngshuǎngyírén	fresh, cool and pleasant	83
轻松	qīngsōng	relaxed; relaxation	40
清真食品	qīngzhēnshípǐn	Islamic food	12
轻重缓急	qīngzhònghuǎnjí	priority	31
庆祝	qìngzhù	to celebrate	3
庆祝活动	qìngzhùhuódòng	celebration	48
祈盼	qípàn	to hope; to wish	48
欺骗	qīpiàn	to cheat; to deceive	111
气色	qìsè	complexion	72
旗手	qíshǒu	flag bearer	54
求职信	qiúzhíxìn	application letter	97
期望	qīwàng	expectation	32
七夕节	qīxījié	Qi Xi Festival	44
企业家	qǐyèjiā	entrepreneur	89
起源	qǐyuán	origin	54
其中	qízhōng	among which	6
全称	quánchēng	full name	99
拳打	quándǎ	punch	64
拳击	quánjī	boxing	63
全面总结	quánmiànzǒngjié	comprehensive sum up	95
全无反应	quánwúfǎnyìng	without the slightest response	113
区别	qūbié	difference	111
缺点	quēdiǎn	disadvantage	75
缺乏	quēfá	lack; be short of	109
群发	qúnfā	to send to people in a list	101
去皮	qùpí	to remove the skin	4
驱邪降福	qūxiéjiàngfú	to expel evil and have good fortune	48
曲子	qǔzi	song; tune; melody	87
燃烧	ránshāo	to burn	68
热潮	rècháo	upsurge	36
热带	rèdài	torrid zone; the tropics	83
热量	rèliàng	energy	73
热门	rèmén	hot; popular	36
热闹非凡	rènàofēifán	bustling with excitement	107
仍	réng	still	1
人工	réngōng	man-made; artificial	79
人际沟通	rénjìgōutōng	interpersonal communication	87
忍耐力	rěnnàilì	patience	105
人气	rénqì	popularity	107
任其漂往天涯海角	rènqípiāowǎngtiānyáhǎijiǎo	to let it go (to the ends of the earth)	46
人山人海	rénshānrénhǎi	huge crowds of people	20
人生	rénshēng	one's life	77
人手不够	rénshǒubúgòu	short-handed; short-staffed	98
认为	rènwéi	to think; to regard	23
任务	rènwu	task	87
日常	rìcháng	daily	20
日思夜想	rìsīyèxiǎng	to long for someone day and night	113
日益	rìyì	increasingly	36
融合	rónghé	to mix together, merge	6
软滑	ruǎnhuá	soft and smooth	6
如虎添翼	rúhǔtiānyì	to strengthen (literary: like a tiger that has grown wings)	95
乳类食品	rǔlèishípǐn	dairy product	66
赛事	sàishì	competition; event; tournament	112
嗓子	sǎngzi	throat	72
扫墓	sǎomù	to sweep the grave; to pay respect to the dead	44
《色，戒》	sèjiè	Lust, Caution	104
闪	shǎn	to twinkle; to glimmer; to flash	46
善变	shànbiàn	changeable	107
山东	shāndōng	Shandong Province	6
上班	shàngbān	to go to work	20
上班族	shàngbānzú	people who have a regular job	95
上火	shànghuǒ	to suffer from excessive internal heat	72
上述	shàngshù	above-mentioned	29
商业管理	shāngyèguǎnlǐ	business management	95
上瘾	shàngyǐn	addicted	107
赏月	shǎngyuè	to observe the moon	44
上载	shàngzǎi	to upload	107
善思考	shànsīkǎo	good at thinking deeply	105
山西	shānxī	Shanxi Province	6
稍	shāo	a little bit	20

Character	Pinyin	English	Page
烧饼	shāobǐng	baked dough; similar to pitta bread; sesame seed cake	8
少数民族	shǎoshùmínzú	minority nationality	50
设备完善	shèbèiwánshàn	well equipped	79
设计	shèjì	design	44
社交圈	shèjiāoquān	social circle	101
社交网站	shèjiāowǎngzhàn	social networking site	107
省	shěng	province;	34
		to save	81
生存	shēngcún	to survive	95
圣诞节	shèngdànjié	Christmas	45
声调	shēngdiào	tone	39
胜过	shèngguò	be superior to; better than	105
生活点滴	shēnghuódiǎndī	daily occurrences	107
生活习惯	shēnghuóxíguàn	habits and customs	6
生姜	shēngjiāng	ginger	10
省钱	shěngqián	to save money	20
胜任	shèngrèn	competent	99
圣淘沙	shèngtáoshā	Sentosa	79
盛夏	shèngxià	midsummer	83
生肖	shēngxiào	animal signs of the zodiac	101
生育问题	shēngyùwèntí	birth problem	63
盛装	shèngzhuāng	splendid attire; best clothes	50
深受…喜爱	shēnshòuxǐài	well received by ...	6
身体接触	shēntǐjiēchù	physical contact	70
沈阳	shěnyáng	Shenyang City	93
深造	shēnzào	further study	93
设施	shèshī	facility	75
摄影师	shèyǐngshī	photographer	91
设有	shèyǒu	to equip with	20
设置	shèzhì	to set up	112
失败	shībài	failure	109
是否	shìfǒu	whether or not	25
适合	shìhé	suitable; appropriate for	14
视作	shìzuò	to regard as	95
实际	shíjì	realistic	91
实践	shíjiàn	to practise	93
世界闻名	shìjièwénmíng	famous worldwide	77
视觉艺术	shìjuéyìshù	visual art	113
侍弄花草	shìnònghuācǎo	to do the gardening	87
《十面埋伏》	shímiànmáifú	House of Flying Daggers	65
视频播客	shìpínbōkè	video blogger	101
食谱	shípǔ	recipe	66
实情	shíqíng	actual situation	111
实施	shíshī	to carry out; to implement	29
事先	shìxiān	beforehand	1
实习记者	shíxíjìzhě	trainee journalist	87
实验	shíyàn	experiment	68
施展才能	shīzhǎncáinéng	to put one's abilities to good use	99
逝者	shìzhě	the dead; deceased	46
适中	shìzhōng	moderate, just right	6
首都	shǒudū	capital	6
手工艺品	shǒugōngyìpǐn	handicraft	17
收获	shōuhuò	results	39
收入	shōurù	income	89
首饰	shǒushì	jewellery	77
守岁	shǒusuì	to stay up all night on New Year's Eve	48
首先	shǒuxiān	first of all	90
竖	shù	vertical	1
竖	shù	to erect	50
属	shǔ	to belong to one of the 12 zodiac animals	105
摔跤	shuāijiāo	wrestling	50
双重	shuāngchóng	double	107
双方	shuāngfāng	both sides	36

Character	Pinyin	English	Page
双向交流	shuāngxiàng jiāoliú	two-way communication; exchange	91
睡懒觉	shuìlǎnjiào	to sleep in; a long lie-in	111
水乡	shuǐxiāng	region of rivers and lakes	18
数量	shùliàng	number; amount	36
树立敌人	shùlìdírén	to make enemies	105
熟能生巧	shúnéngshēng qiǎo	'Practice makes perfect'	39
顺序	shùnxù	sequence; order	29
硕士	shuòshì	Master's degree	29
暑期工	shǔqīgōng	summer job	99
熟悉	shúxi	familiar	101
属相	shǔxiàng	animal signs of the zodiac	105
书写格式	shūxiěgéshì	writing format	99
属于	shǔyú	to belong to	14
数字	shùzì	number	23
似	sì	like; similar to	50
丝	sī	silk	17
四川	sìchuān	Sichuan Province	6
四合院	sìhéyuàn	a compound with houses around a courtyard	81
思维	sīwéi	thinking; thought	95
思想	sīxiǎng	thinking; ideology	23
宋城	sòngchéng	Song City	18
宿	sù	to sleep	18
蒜	suàn	garlic	4
酸	suān	sour	6
酸奶	suānnǎi	yoghurt	8
速度	sùdù	speed	77
随处可见	suíchùkějiàn	can be seen everywhere	40
随机应变	suíjīyìngbiàn	to act according to circumstances	105
随意	suíyì	at will; as one pleases	107
随着	suízhe	with; to accompany	70
所见所闻	suǒjiànsuǒwén	what has been seen and heard	109
俗语	súyǔ	common saying	39
素质教育	sùzhìjiàoyù	education for all-round development	29
苏州	sūzhōu	Suzhou	15
台北金马影展	táiběijīnmǎyǐng zhǎn	Taipei Golden Horse Film Festival and Awards	104
太极	tàijí	t'ai chi	32
弹	tán	to play (a musical instrument)	93
糖醋鱼	tángcùyú	sweet and sour fish	10
套	tào	set	70
讨价还价	tǎojiàhuánjià	bargaining	17
讨论	tǎolùn	discussion	70
陶器	táoqì	pottery	32
淘汰	táotài	to eliminate through competition	109
踏青	tàqīng	to go for a walk in the countryside in spring (when the grass has just turned green)	46
特别	tèbié	special	48
特定	tèdìng	specific	91
特快列车	tèkuàilièchē	express train	12
特色	tèsè	characteristic	6
特殊	tèshū	special	68
提	tí	to carry in one's hand	50
甜	tián	sweet	6
添	tiān	to add	1
天才	tiāncái	talented; genius	93
天道酬勤	tiāndàochóuqín	hard-working people will be rewarded	93
天分	tiānfèn	talent; gift	93
天赋	tiānfù	talent; gift	109
天价	tiānjià	astronomical price	109
天生	tiānshēng	inborn; innate	91
天堂	tiāntáng	paradise; heaven	18

Character	Pinyin	English	Page
条件	tiáojiàn	condition	20
调节情绪	tiáojiéqíngxù	to regulate emotions	68
挑选	tiāoxuǎn	to choose; to select	84
挑战	tiǎozhàn	challenge	95
体操	tǐcāo	gymnastics	64
贴	tiē	to stick; to glue	48
铁杆	tiěgǎn	loyal; faithful	107
体力和脑力	tǐlìhénǎolì	physical and mental strength	65
听话	tīnghuà	obedient	40
提前	tíqián	in advance	20
体现	tǐxiàn	to embody	23
提醒	tíxǐng	to remind; reminder	87
体形	tǐxíng	body form	63
体验	tǐyàn	to experience	84
捅	tǒng	to poke; to visit somebody's homepage, blog, etc.	101
同道	tóngdào	people sharing a common goal	107
通道	tōngdào	passageway	81
同事	tóngshì	colleague	26
通用	tōngyòng	general application	99
通知	tōngzhī	to notify; to inform	25
投票	tóupiào	to vote	112
头晕	tóuyūn	dizzy	72
团队合作精神	tuánduìhézuò jīngshén	team spirit	97
团聚	tuánjù	reunion	45
突出	tūchū	outstanding	105
退出	tuìchū	to quit	95
推出	tuīchū	to introduce	112
推广	tuīguǎng	to promote	107
推荐信	tuījiànxìn	letter of recommendation	98
途径	tújìng	way	107
脱颖而出	tuōyǐngérchū	talent showing itself	109
外地	wàidì	part of the country other than where one's family is from	20
外交官	wàijiāoguān	diplomat	88
外籍人士	wàijírénshì	foreign people	36
外滩	wàitān	The Bund	18
往返机票	wǎngfǎnjīpiào	return ticket	15
旺盛的人气	wàngshèngde rénqì	popularity	107
完美	wánměi	perfect	54
万圣节	wànshèngjié	Halloween	45
完完全全	wánwánquánquán	complete; total	95
完整	wánzhěng	complete	23
围	wéi	to surround; around	50
味	wèi	taste	6
伟大	wěidà	great	93
未婚	wèihūn	unmarried	45
味精	wèijīng	monosodium glutamate (MSG)	10
胃口大开	wèikǒudàkāi	to have a good appetite	4
为期	wéiqī	to last	50
维生素	wéishēngsù	vitamin	63
位置	wèizhì	place; position	109
温带	wēndài	temperate zone	83
温和	wēnhé	mild	83
文化	wénhuà	culture	44
文明	wénmíng	civilization	44
闻名	wénmíng	famous; well known	83
瘟魔	wēnmó	devil that spreads pestilence	55
温柔	wēnróu	gentle and soft	105
文物	wénwù	historical relic	81
温习	wēnxí	to study	30
文娱	wényú	cultural and recreational	112
稳重	wěnzhòng	steady; sedate	105
《卧虎藏龙》	wòhǔcánglóng	*Crouching Tiger, Hidden Dragon*	65
卧铺	wòpù	berth	20
我同情	wǒtóngqíng	I sympathise with ...	31
舞伴	wǔbàn	dancing partner	70
物产	wùchǎn	product	6
无法做到…	wúfǎzuòdào	unable to ...	31
无拘束	wújūshù	unrestrained; free	105
无论	wúlùn	regardless of; no matter what	48
物美价廉	wùměijiàlián	cheap but good	77
武器	wǔqì	weapon	65
无数	wúshù	countless	81
武术	wǔshù	wushu; martial arts	32
舞台	wǔtái	stage	99
无休止的	wúxiūzhǐde	never-ending	31
武艺高强	wǔyìgāoqiáng	to excel in martial arts	55
物资交流会	wùzījiāoliúhuì	trade fair	50
X光	xguāng	X-ray	72
夏令营	xiàlìngyíng	summer camp	32
鲜	xiān	fresh	6
咸	xián	salty	6
西安	Xīān	Xian	15
现存	xiàncún	existing	23
现代化	xiàndàihuà	modernised	20
香	xiāng	aroma; pleasant smell	6
相比之下	xiāngbǐzhīxià	by comparison	109
相当于	xiāngdāngyú	correspond to	29
厢房	xiāngfáng	wing (usually of a one-storey house)	81
享乐无穷	xiǎnglèwúqióng	endless enjoyment	93
项目	xiàngmù	project	98
香喷喷	xiāngpēnpēn	savoury; appetising	4
享受	xiǎngshòu	enjoyment	77
降妖	xiángyāo	to subdue an evil spirit	55
象征	xiàngzhēng	symbol; icon	44
象征意义	xiàngzhēngyìyì	symbolic meaning	3
鲜嫩	xiānnèn	delicious and tender	6
先人	xiānrén	ancestor	46
献身精神	xiànshēnjīngshén	dedication	65
显示	xiǎnshì	to show; to indicate	68
纤维	xiānwéi	fibre	63
鲜榨	xiānzhà	freshly squeezed	10
仙长	xiānzhǎng	immortal master	55
限制	xiànzhì	limit	109
消费者	xiāofèizhě	consumer	107
效果	xiàoguǒ	effect	61
消化	xiāohuà	to digest	8
消化系统	xiāohuàxìtǒng	digestive system	66
小将	xiǎojiàng	a young sports star	109
消磨	xiāomó	to pass (the time)	107
销售员	xiāoshòuyuán	salesperson	91
消息	xiāoxī	news	70
孝心	xiàoxīn	filial devotion; filial piety	105
小有名气	xiǎoyǒumíngqì	recognition amongst peers	95
西餐	xīcān	western food	12
喜出风头	xǐchūfēngtou	to enjoy being the centre of attention	105
歇	xiē	to have a rest	81
邂逅	xièhòu	to meet by chance	107
谐音	xiéyīn	homophone	23
协助	xiézhù	to assist	98
习惯	xíguàn	be accustomed to	39
西红柿	xīhóngshì	tomato	4
细节	xìjié	details	23
系列	xìliè	series	70
形	xíng	appearance	6
形成	xíngchéng	to form	6
行程	xíngchéng	itinerary	18
幸福	xìngfú	happiness	48
性格	xìnggé	personality; character	90
《星球大战》	xīngqiúdàzhàn	*Star Wars*	65

Character	Pinyin	English	Page
杏仁	xìngrén	almond	48
形象	xíngxiàng	image	101
行政助理	xíngzhèngzhùlǐ	administrative assistant	91
辛苦	xīnkǔ	hard; laborious	73
信赖	xìnlài	trust	105
心理	xīnlǐ	psychology; mentality	48
心灵	xīnlíng	heart; soul	93
心情	xīnqíng	feeling	70
新人新事	xīnrénxīnshì	new faces and new happenings	98
新闻触觉	xīnwénchùjué	ability to keep abreast of the news	98
欣喜	xīnxǐ	joy; happiness	48
心想事成	xīnxiǎngshìchéng	to get one's wish	38
心血管病	xīnxuèguǎnbìng	cardiovascular disease	66
心仪	xīnyí	like; admire	101
新意	xīnyì	new	112
修建	xiūjiàn	to build	15
休闲	xiūxián	relaxed; relaxation	72
细心	xìxīn	careful; attentive	34
《喜宴》	xǐyàn	*The Wedding Banquet*	104
吸引	xīyǐn	to attract; to appeal	45
需要	xūyào	need to	8
宣传	xuānchuán	to publicise	107
选择	xuǎnzé	to choose	79
许多	xǔduō	many	23
学生会	xuéshēnghuì	students' union	87
穴位	xuéwèi	acupuncture point	68
学问	xuéwèn	learning	38
学校生活	xuéxiàoshēnghuó	school life	30
血型	xuèxíng	blood group	66
训练	xùnliàn	training	109
寻求	xúnqiú	to seek	99
迅速发展	xùnsùfāzhǎn	to develop rapidly	36
寻找	xúnzhǎo	to look for; seek	95
需求	xūqiú	need; demand	90
虚荣	xūróng	vanity	113
虚伪	xūwěi	hypocritical	1
须要	xūyào	must; have to	8
需要	xūyào	need; requirement	53
压力	yālì	stress; pressure	30
盐	yán	salt	4
宴	yàn	banquet; feast	18
养成	yǎngchéng	to develop	72
洋腔洋调	yángqiāngyáng diào	to speak with a foreign accent	39
沿海	yánhǎi	coastal	15
研究	yánjiū	to study; to research	38
研究员	yánjiūyuán	researcher	91
厌倦	yànjuàn	tired of; exhausted	95
延年益寿	yánniányìshòu	to prolong life	68
延伸	yánshēn	to extend	107
严守纪律	yánshǒujìlù	to observe discipline strictly	105
亚努	yànǔ	Ya Nu, an ancient hero of Miao Nationality	50
验血	yànxuè	blood test	72
严重	yánzhòng	serious	70
演奏	yǎnzòu	to play (a musical instrument)	87
摇滚	yáogǔn	rock and roll	101
要求	yāoqiú	to request	10
邀约	yāoyuē	to invite	101
野生动物	yěshēngdòngwù	wildlife	79
业务	yèwù	business	95
业余	yèyú	amateur	109
业余爱好	yèyúàihào	hobby	99
以…为主	yǐ…wéizhǔ	mainly	75
一般	yìbān	generally; usually	8
遗产	yíchǎn	heritage	23
意大利	yìdàlì	Italy	6

Character	Pinyin	English	Page
意大利辣香肠	yìdàlìlàxiāng cháng	pepperoni	70
一度	yīdù	once	36
以防	yǐfáng	in case	101
一脚踏进	yījiǎotàjìn	to enter	95
一举成名	yījǔchéngmíng	to become famous overnight	93
毅力	yìlì	stamina	65
一连	yìlián	in a row	4
一流	yīliú	first class	79
因材施教	yīncáishījiào	to teach according to a student's ability	29
隐藏	yǐncáng	to hide; to conceal	105
因此	yīncǐ	therefore; so	6
赢	yíng	to win; to gain	54
英寸	yīngcùn	inch	70
应得	yīngdé	to deserve	104
樱花	yīnghuā	oriental cherry	83
应聘人	yīngpìnrén	applicant	97
应试教育	yìngshìjiàoyù	exam oriented education	29
硬卧	yìngwò	hard sleeper (on a train)	18
英雄	yīngxióng	hero	50
营养	yíngyǎng	nutritious	4
营养成份	yíngyǎngchéngfèn	nutrient	63
营业时间	yíngyèshíjiān	business hours	77
应有尽有	yīngyǒujìnyǒu	to have everything that one expects to find	84
银行家	yínhángjiā	banker	88
一年一度	yīniányīdù	annual	112
饮料	yǐnliào	drink; beverage	14
引人注目的	yǐnrénzhùmùde	spectacular	104
阴盛阳衰	yīnshèngyáng shuāi	women outshine men	34
因势利导	yīnshìlìdǎo	give judicious guidance according to circumstances	34
隐私	yǐnsī	private matters one wants to hide	40
印象	yìnxiàng	impression	32
引诱	yǐnyòu	to seduce	105
音乐学院	yīnyuèxuéyuàn	conservatoire	93
一排排	yīpáipái	in rows	81
一切	yīqiè	everything; all	40
依然	yīrán	still	83
仪式	yíshì	ceremony	104
艺术家	yìshùjiā	artist	91
一头	yìtóu	one end	20
义务	yìwù	voluntary	87
义务教育	yìwùjiàoyù	compulsory education	29
异性	yìxìng	opposite sex	105
译音	yìyīn	transliteration	50
意志力	yìzhìlì	determination	105
彝族	yízú	Yi Nationality	50
拥挤	yōngjǐ	crowded	20
勇气	yǒngqì	courage	105
用作	yòngzuò	be used for	81
油	yóu	oil	4
优点	yōudiǎn	merit	6
优点	yōudiǎn	advantage	75
优厚待遇	yōuhòudàiyù	excellent pay and benefits	87
优惠	yōuhuì	discount	11
有教无类	yǒujiàowúlèi	to provide education for all people without discrimination	34
有进取心	yǒujìnqǔxīn	with enterprising spirit	87
游客	yóukè	tourist	23
有苦有乐	yǒukǔyǒulè	pain and happiness	98
游览	yóulǎn	to go sightseeing	18
有利和不利	yǒulìhébùlì	pros and cons	89
又流利又清楚	yòuliúlìyòuqīngchǔ	fluently and clearly	39
有利于	yǒulìyú	advantageous to; favourable to	63
忧虑	yōulù	worrying	109

Character	Pinyin	English	Page
优美	yōuměi	graceful	50
幽默	yōumò	humour; humorous	101
油腻	yóunì	greasy; oily	6
尤其	yóuqí	especially	66
有起有落	yǒuqǐyǒuluò	ups and downs	98
有趣	yǒuqù	interesting	46
由人陪伴	yóurénpéibàn	to chaperone	45
优势	yōushì	advantage	34
油条	yóutiáo	deep-fried twisted dough sticks	8
有威望的	yǒuwēiwàngde	prestigious	104
有效	yǒuxiào	effective; (-ly)	63
有效率的	yǒuxiàolǜde	efficient	31
优秀	yōuxiù	excellent	109
有压力的	yǒuyālìde	stressed	30
有意义的	yǒuyìyìde	meaningful	32
有意者	yǒuyìzhě	people who are interested in a position/job	97
由于	yóuyú	because; due to	6
有争议的	yǒuzhēngyìde	controversial	104
有志者事竟成	yǒuzhìzhěshìjìng chéng	'Where there's a will, there's a way'	39
有助于	yǒuzhùyú	to contribute to	32
有滋有味地	yǒuzīyǒuwèide	enthusiastically	95
与… 相处	yǔ...xiāngchǔ	to get along with somebody	95
园林	yuánlín	gardens	18
院落	yuànluò	courtyard	81
愿望	yuànwàng	wish; aspiration; desire	48
原先	yuánxiān	original	95
元宵	yuánxiāo	dumplings made of glutinous rice flour stuffed with different fillings	44
元宵节	yuánxiāojié	Lantern Festival; Yuan Xiao Festival	45
愿意	yuànyì	willing to	105
原因	yuányīn	reason	11
源远流长	yuányuǎnliúcháng	long standing	44
原汁原味	yuánzhīyuánwèi	original taste	6
语调	yǔdiào	intonation	39
乐队	yuèduì	band	101
约会博弈	yuēhuìbóyì	dating game	101
乐迷	yuèmí	fan of a singer, musician, etc.	107
乐器	yuèqì	musical instrument	50
预防	yùfáng	to prevent	66
玉佛寺	yùfósì	Jade Buddha Temple	18
愉快	yúkuài	happy; pleasant	18
玉米	yùmǐ	maize	66
匀	yún	evenly	4
运程	yùnchéng	fate; luck	105
允许	yǔnxǔ	to allow; to let	112
运用	yùnyòng	use	113
鱼尾狮塔	yúwěishītǎ	Merlion	79
鱼香肉丝	yúxiāngròusī	fish flavoured shredded pork	10
寓意	yùyì	implied meaning	23
在家办公族	zàijiābàngōngzú	people who work at home	95
在线	zàixiàn	online	107
赞成	zànchéng	to agree	40
枣	zǎo	jujube; Chinese date	48
早恋	zǎoliàn	romantic relationship at a young age	70
早期	zǎoqī	early stage; early period	53
增加	zēngjiā	to add; to increase	50
增进	zēngjìn	to increase	68
择你所爱	zénǐsuǒài	to choose what you love	93
窄	zhǎi	narrow	81
栅栏	zhàlán	fence	21
沾… 边	zhān... biān	relevant; close to	111
丈	zhàng	unit of length, approximately 3.33 metres	50
账单	zhàngdān	bill	25
占据	zhànjù	to occupy	95
展览	zhǎnlǎn	exhibition	32
展露	zhǎnlù	to display; to show	93
展示	zhǎnshì	to show	70
着急	zháojí	anxious	72
朝九晚五	zhāojiǔwǎnwǔ	nine to five	95
招聘	zhāopìn	recruitment	97
朝气	zhāoqì	vitality	95
招手	zhāoshǒu	to wave	20
炸鱼和炸土豆条	zháyúhézhátǔdòu tiáo	fish and chips	3
浙江	zhèjiāng	Zhejiang Province	6
针	zhēn	needle	68
珍宝海鲜舫	zhēnbǎohǎixiān fǎng	Jumbo Seafood Restaurant	77
针对	zhēnduì	be aimed at	12
政策	zhèngcè	policy	76
正房	zhèngfáng	principal room (in a courtyard, usually facing south)	81
政府	zhèngfǔ	government	36
正好	zhènghǎo	as it happens	20
整洁	zhěngjié	clean and tidy	84
证明	zhèngmíng	to prove	68
正确	zhèngquè	correct	29
正月	zhēngyuè	the first month of the lunar calendar	44
正直	zhèngzhí	upright	105
镇静	zhènjìng	to calm down; to cool down	68
针灸	zhēnjiǔ	acupuncture and moxibustion	68
侦探	zhēntàn	detective	40
直播	zhíbō	live broadcast	112
支持	zhīchí	to support	70
值得	zhídé	worthwhile	101
制定	zhìdìng	to draw up	112
脂肪	zhīfáng	fat	63
智慧	zhìhuì	wisdom	105
直接	zhíjiē	directly	15
智力	zhìlì	intelligence	111
治疗	zhìliáo	treatment	68
智力问答	zhìlìwèndá	quiz	50
制片人	zhìpiànrén	film producer	107
纸上谈兵	zhǐshàngtánbīng	to engage in idle theorising	40
指示牌	zhǐshìpái	signpost	20
职位	zhíwèi	post; job	99
职业	zhíyè	occupation	89
…之一	... zhīyī	one of ...	53
制造	zhìzào	to make; to produce	40
职责	zhízé	(job) duties	87
重	zhòng	heavy; heavily seasoned	7
中等教育普通证书	zhōngděngjiàoyù pǔtōngzhèngshū	GCSE examination	29
中国足球协会	zhōngguózúqiú xiéhuì	Chinese Football Association	109
钟楼	zhōnglóu	bell tower; clock tower	18
重视	zhòngshì	to pay attention to; to take something seriously	8
中小学生	zhōngxiǎoxué shēng	(abbreviation for) middle school and primary school students	70
中旬	zhōngxún	the middle ten days of a month	50
重要	zhòngyào	important	1
种子	zhǒngzi	seed	66
粥	zhōu	porridge; congee	8
周游	zhōuyóu	to travel around	87
抓紧	zhuājǐn	to grasp	101
专长	zhuāncháng	expertise	97
转发	zhuǎnfā	to forward to	101
装有	zhuāngyǒu	to install	20
状元	zhuàngyuán	Number One Scholar; the very best	34

Character	Pinyin	English	Page
转化	zhuǎnhuà	to transform	107
专辑	zhuānjí	album	101
专家	zhuānjiā	specialist	36
专门	zhuānmén	special	20
专心	zhuānxīn	undivided attention; concentration	34
转型	zhuǎnxíng	transformation	95
专业	zhuānyè	profession	38
专业人士	zhuānyèrénshì	professional	107
主办	zhǔbàn	to host (an event)	99
珠宝首饰	zhūbǎoshǒushì	jewellery	17
注册	zhùcè	register	107
竹竿	zhúgān	bamboo pole	50
追求完美	zhuīqiúwánměi	to pursue perfection	91
追星族	zhuīxīngzú	fan	101
追忆	zhuīyì	to recollect	107
追逐时尚	zhuīzhúshíshàng	to keep up with fashion	107
逐渐	zhújiàn	gradually	68
注明	zhùmíng	to note	99
准备	zhǔnbèi	preparation	4
助人为乐	zhùrénwéilè	helpful	87
诸圣日前夕	zhūshèngrìqiánxī	Halloween	45
住宿	zhùsù	accommodation	79
主席	zhǔxí	chairperson	87
主要	zhǔyào	major; main	6
主意	zhǔyi	idea	26
茱萸叶	zhūyúyè	leaf of a cornel plant	55
住在大城市的人	zhùzàidàchéngshìderén	people living in the big cities	76

Character	Pinyin	English	Page
住宅	zhùzhái	residence	81
自…至…	zì... zhì	from ... to ...	83
资格	zīgé	qualification	109
自豪	zìháo	to be proud of	40
自来水	zìláishuǐ	tap water	15
资料	zīliào	material	90
姊妹学校	zǐmèixuéxiào	partner school	36
自始至终	zìshǐzhìzhōng	right from the beginning	31
自信	zìxìn	self-confident	87
自行车王国	zìxíngchēwángguó	bicycle kingdom	76
咨询	zīxún	consultation	90
自由	zìyóu	freedom	26
资源	zīyuán	resource	29
走开	zǒukāi	to walk away	17
钻石珠宝	zuànshízhūbǎo	diamonds and jewellery	84
足够	zúgòu	enough	8
最佳的	zuìjiāde	best	66
最环保的交通工具	zuìhuánbǎodejiāotōnggōngjù	greenest mode of transport	76
最新动态	zuìxīndòngtài	update	107
最终	zuìzhōng	ultimate	53
尊敬	zūnjìng	respectable	90
做客	zuòkè	be a guest	1
作为	zuòwéi	as; be regarded as	6
左右	zuǒyòu	about; roughly	20
组织	zǔzhī	organise/organisation	31

汉字检索

Character glossary – looking up characters by radical and residual stroke count

Chinese *characters* (字) can be grouped according to *radical*. One system of organising radicals is shown in the table; the radical often gives a hint as to the meaning of the 字.

So in 语 you can see the radical 讠; without any more hints, you can guess that this 字's core meaning has something to do with 'words' (see rad. 149).

Some radicals have different forms, depending on

- whether the 字 is being written in traditional or simplified form
- where the radical appears in the 字 (e.g. rad. 61 (心, *heart*) appears as 忄 on the left, but 小 on the bottom of a 字. It is worth familiarising yourself with the radicals' appearance in all their forms; it can be useful to know that the rad. 147 (见, *see*) was traditionally written as 見. This is why it is grouped under '7 strokes' in many dictionaries.

Radical table

1 stroke

No.	Radical	Meaning
1	一	one
2	丨	down
3	丶	dot
4	丿	left
5	乙	twist
6	亅	hook

2 strokes

No.	Radical	Meaning
7	二	two
8	亠	lid
9	人 亻	man
10	儿	legs
11	入	enter
12	八	eight
13	冂	borders
14	冖	crown
15	冫	ice
16	几	table
17	凵	bowl
18	刀 刂	knife
19	力	strength
20	勹	wrap
21	匕	ladle
22	匚	basket
23	匸	box
24	十	ten
25	卜	foretell
26	卩	seal
27	厂	living place
28	厶	private
29	又	repeat

3 strokes

No.	Radical	Meaning
30	口	mouth
31	囗	surround
32	土	earth
33	士	knight
34	夂	follow
35	夊	slow
36	夕	dusk
37	大	big
38	女	woman
39	子	child
40	宀	roof
41	寸	inch
42	小	small
43	尢 尤 尣	lame
44	尸	corpse
45	屮	sprout
46	山	mountain
47	川 巛	river
48	工	work
49	己	self
50	巾	cloth
51	干	shield
52	幺	youngest
53	广	house near a hill
54	廴	march
55	廾	clasp
56	弋	dart
57	弓	bow
58	彐 彑	pig's head
59	彡	streaks
60	彳	step

4 strokes

No.	Radical	Meaning
61	心 忄 小	heart
62	戈	lance
63	户	door
64	手 扌	hand
65	支	branch
66	攴 攵	knock
67	文	language
68	斗	peck[1]
69	斤	weight
70	方	square
71	无	nil
72	日	sun
73	曰	say
74	月	moon
75	木	tree
76	欠	owe
77	止	stop
78	歹	bad
79	殳	weapon
80	毋 母	don't
81	比	compare
82	毛	fur
83	氏	clan
84	气	breath
85	水 氵 氺	water
86	火 灬	fire
87	爪 爫	claws
88	父	father
89	爻	criss-cross
90	爿 丬	piece of wood
91	片	slice
92	牙	tooth
93	牛	cow
94	犬 犭	dog

5 strokes

No.	Radical	Meaning
95	玄	dark
96	玉 王	jade
97	瓜	melon
98	瓦	tile
99	甘	sweet
100	生	birth
101	用	use
102	田	field
103	疋	bolt[2]
104	疒	sick
105	癶	back
106	白	white
107	皮	skin
108	皿	dish
109	目	eye
110	矛	spear
111	矢	arrow
112	石	rock
113	示 礻	show
114	禸	track
115	禾	grain
116	穴	cave
117	立	stand

6 strokes

No.	Radical	Meaning
118	竹 ⺮	bamboo
119	米	rice
120	糸 纟	silk
121	缶	crock
122	网 罒	net
123	羊	sheep
124	羽	feather
125	老	old
126	而	conj. meaning varies
127	耒	plough
128	耳	ear
129	聿	brush
130	肉 月	meat
131	臣	bureau-crat
132	自	self
133	至	reach
134	臼	mortar
135	舌	tongue
136	舛	discord
137	舟	boat
138	艮	blunt
139	色	colour
140	草 艹	grass
141	虍	tiger

7 strokes

No.	Radical	Meaning
142	虫	bug
143	血	blood
144	行	go
145	衣 衤	gown
146	西 覀	cover
147	見 见	see
148	角	horn
149	言 讠 訁	words
150	谷	valley
151	豆	bean
152	豕	pig
153	豸	insect
154	貝 贝	cowrie shell
155	赤	red
156	走	walk
157	足 ⻊	foot
158	身	torso
159	車 车	car
160	辛	bitter
161	辰	time

8 strokes

No.	Radical	Meaning
162	辶	halt
163	邑 阝	city
164	酉	wine
165	采	distin-guish
166	里	village
167	金 钅 釒	gold
168	長 长	long
169	門 门	gate
170	阜 阝	mound
171	隶	catch
172	隹	dove
173	雨	rain
174	青	green
175	非	wrong

9 strokes

No.	Radical	Meaning
176	面	face
177	革	leather
178	韋 韦	leather
179	韭	leek
180	音	tone
181	頁 页	page
182	風 风	wind
183	飛	fly
184	食 饣 飠	food
185	首	chief
186	香	scent

10 strokes

No.	Radical	Meaning
187	馬 马	horse
188	骨	bone
189	高	tall
190	髟	hair
191	鬥	fight
192	鬯	mixed wine
193	鬲	cauldron
194	鬼	ghost

11 strokes

No.	Radical	Meaning
195	魚 鱼	fish
196	鳥 鸟	bird
197	鹵	stew
198	鹿	deer
199	麦	wheat

12 strokes

No.	Radical	Meaning
200	麻	hemp
201	黄	yellow
202	黍	millet
203	黑	black
204	黹	embroider

13 strokes

No.	Radical	Meaning
205	黽	toad
206	鼎	cauldron
207	鼓	drum
208	鼠	mouse

14 strokes

No.	Radical	Meaning
209	鼻	nose
210	齊 齐	all

15 strokes

No.	Radical	Meaning
211	齒 齿	teeth

16 strokes

No.	Radical	Meaning
212	龍 龙	dragon
213	龜 龟	tortoise

17 strokes

No.	Radical	Meaning
214	龠	flute

The main glossary lists all new words introduced in this book. If you want to look up the Chinese for an English word, or vice versa, you can go straight there and look up the English or *pinyin*, which are in alphabetical order.

However, if your word includes a 字 whose pinyin you *don't* know, you can find it in this character glossary by:

1) finding the 字's radical in the above table (some 字 hide their radicals quite well! Familiarity helps, so don't despair if it seems tricky at first);
2) *(disregarding the radical)* counting how many strokes are needed to write the *remainder* of the 字 (the 'residual stroke count');
3) turning to the heading for the radical in this lookup list;
4) looking for the residual stroke count in the left column under this heading – your 字 (if you've identified the correct radical!) should be one of those listed alongside;
5) making a note of this 字's *pinyin* readings (some have more than one); and
6) using these pinyin readings to look up the word in the 生词 from page 133 to 144 (of this book) (you might have a few possible combinations from 字 with multiple readings, but one combination should be there).

NB:

(i) By its nature, this brief list cannot hope to compete with a good dictionary. Good dictionaries offer a range of methods to look up words and/or 字, whereas these lists are restricted to *pinyin* or radical/residual stroke count.

(ii) 字 met at GCSE level[3] are not glossed in this list – even 字 which are needed to make words introduced in this book.

---

1 An old unit of measure. If you've never wondered how much pickled pepper is in a 'peck of pickled pepper', now would be the perfect time to find out!

2 Not a 'nuts and bolts' bolt, but a *bolt* of cloth.

3 See Edexcel specification for GCSE Chinese, published March 2001, for examinations from 2003.

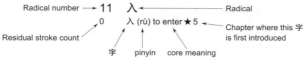

Radical number → **11 入** ← Radical
0 入 (rù) to enter ★ 5 ← Chapter where this 字 is first introduced
Residual stroke count
字   pinyin   core meaning

---

1 一
1　丁 (dīng) man ★ 1
2　与 (yú, yǔ, yù) and; with; to give ★ 3
3　专 (zhuān) to monopolise; expert ★ 2
4　且 (qiě) also; just ★ 1
　　世 (shì) generation; world ★ 4
　　丝 (sī) silk ★ 1
5　丢 (diū) to discard ★ 8
6　严 (yán) strict ★ 5

2 丨
3　丰 (fēng) bountiful ★ 1
8　临 (lín) to approach ★ 8

3 、
1　之 (zhī) it, him, her, them; to go to ★ 4
4　主 (zhǔ) master ★ 1
8　举 (jǔ) to lift up; to recommend ★ 6

4 丿
2　久 (jiǔ) long time (ago) ★ 1
　　义 (yì) justice; meaning ★ 1
3　乏 (fá) lack ★ 8
9　乘 (chéng, shèng) to take; war chariot ★ 1

5 乙
7　乳 (rǔ) breast; milk ★ 5

6 亅
1　了 (le, liǎo) to finish ★ 1
3　予 (yú, yǔ) I, me; to give ★ 3
5　争 (zhēng) dispute; fight ★ 8
7　事 (shì) matter; incident; to serve ★ 1

7 二
1　于 (yú) in; on; at ★ 1

8 亠
4　交 (jiāo) to hand out; to join ★ 1
6　享 (xiǎng) to enjoy ★ 5
15　赢 (yíng) to win ★ 3

9 人 (亻)
2　从 (cōng, cóng) from; by; since ★ 3
　　介 (jiè) to lie between; to mind ★ 6
　　今 (jīn) now ★ 6
　　仅 (jǐn) only ★ 4
　　仁 (rén) kindness ★ 4
　　仍 (réng) still ★ 1
3　代 (dài) replacement; era; generation ★ 1
　　付 (fù) to give; to pay ★ 1
　　令 (lǐng, lìng) ream; order; to cause ★ 3
　　仙 (xiān) immortal ★ 4
　　仪 (yí) ceremony ★ 1
4　传 (chuán, zhuàn) to pass; biography ★ 1
　　仿 (fǎng) to imitate; as if ★ 8
　　份 (fèn) part ★ 5
　　价 (jià, jie) price; value ★ 1

企 (qǐ) to stand on tiptoe; to look forward to ★ 7
任 (rén, rèn) to appoint; to let; duty ★ 2
似 (sì, shì) resemble ★ 1
伟 (wěi) great ★ 7
伪 (wěi) false ★ 1
优 (yōu) superior; excellent ★ 1
众 (zhòng) crowd ★ 7
5　伴 (bàn) partner; to accompany ★ 5
但 (dàn) only; however ★ 1
佛 (fó, fú) Buddha ★ 2
估 (gū) to estimate ★ 3
何 (hé) what; why; where; which; how ★ 8
伶 (líng) actor; lonely ★ 8
伸 (shēn) to extend ★ 8
位 (wèi) throne; status; seat ★ 3
余 (yú) I; surplus; beyond ★ 7
6　佳 (jiā) auspicious; delightful; good ★ 1
侍 (shì) to serve ★ 7
供 (gōng, gòng) to provide; offerings ★ 1
依 (yī) to rely on ★ 6
侦 (zhēn) to investigate; to scout ★ 3
7　保 (bǎo) protect, defend ★ 1
便 (biàn, pián) convenient; cheap ★ 6
促 (cù) to urge ★ 4
例 (lì) clever ★ 8
俑 (yǒng) wooden figure buried with dead ★ 2
8　倒 (dǎo, dào) to fall; to pour; upside down ★ 1
候 (hòu) to wait; time; condition ★ 1
借 (jiè) to borrow; to lend ★ 7
俱 (jù) all; complete ★ 1
修 (xiū) to study; to repair; to build ★ 2
值 (zhí) value; be worth ★ 8
9　健 (jiàn) healthy ★ 5
倦 (juàn) be tired of ★ 5
偶 (ǒu) idol; even; coincidently ★ 8
10　傣 (dǎi) Dai minority ★ 4
11　傲 (ào) proud ★ 8

10 儿
2　元 (yuán) first; dollar; basic ★ 3
允 (yǔn) to allow ★ 8
4　充 (chōng) full; to fill, to act as ★ 1
光 (guāng) light; bare; only ★ 5
免 (miǎn) to avoid; to evade ★ 2

11 入
0　入 (rù) to enter ★ 5

12 八
4　关 (guān) to close; to involve ★ 2
5　兵 (bīng) soldier; troops ★ 2
6　典 (diǎn) law; standard work of scholarship; ceremony ★ 2
其 (qí) his, her, its, their; that ★ 1

7　养 (yǎng) to support; to raise ★ 1
总 (zǒng) to collect; overall ★ 7

13 冂
3　册 (cè) book; volume; list ★ 8
4　再 (zài) again ★ 7

14 冖
4　农 (nóng) agriculture ★ 4
8　冥 (míng) the underworld ★ 4

15 冫
4　冲 (chōng) to rinse; to charge ★ 7
　　决 (jué) to decide ★ 5
6　净 (jìng) clean ★ 1
8　凉 (liáng, liàng) cool ★ 1
9　减 (jiǎn) to decrease ★ 3
　　凑 (còu) to assemble ★ 2

16 几
1　凡 (fán) any, every; ordinary ★ 7

17 凵
3　击 (jī) to attack ★ 5

18 刀 (刂)
0　刀 (dāo) knife ★ 4
2　分 (fēn, fèn) to divide; component ★ 3
切 (qiē, qiè) to cut; slice; be close to ★ 1
4　创 (chuāng, chuàng) wound; to achieve ★ 7
划 (huá, huà) to row; to scratch; plan ★ 4
列 (liè) a line; to list ★ 1
5　初 (chū) initial; primary ★ 2
利 (lì) advantage; profit ★ 1
判 (pàn) to judge ★ 7
6　刺 (cī, cì) splinter; to prick; to prod ★ 5
制 (zhì) system; to make ★ 2
7　剑 (jiàn) sword, dagger ★ 4
9　剪 (jiǎn) scissors; to cut ★ 4

19 力
0　力 (lì) power ★ 3
2　办 (bàn) to manage ★ 3
3　功 (gōng) achievement; merit; skill ★ 4
5　劲 (jìn, jìng) energy; strong ★ 3
劳 (láo) labour ★ 1
励 (lì) to encourage ★ 6
努 (nǔ) to exert effort ★ 3
助 (zhù) to help; to assist ★ 3
6　势 (shì) force; tendency ★ 3
7　勇 (yǒng) brave ★ 8
10　勤 (qín) diligent ★ 3

20 勹
2　勾 (gōu, gòu) to cancel; hook; to connect ★ 8
匀 (yún) evenly ★ 1

21 匕
2　化 (huā, huà) to spend; to convert; -ise ★ 1

24 十
2　升 (shēng) to rise; to promote ★ 3
3　半 (bàn) half ★ 8
4　华 (huá, huà) splendid; best part; China ★ 3
协 (xié) to cooperate ★ 7

25 卜
3　占 (zhān, zhàn) to practise divination; to occupy ★ 7

26 卩
5　即 (jí) that is ★ 4
6　卷 (juǎn, juàn) to roll up; book ★ 1

27 厂
4　压 (yā, yà) to press; pressure ★ 3
厌 (yàn) to detest, be fed up with ★ 7
6　质 (zhì) quality; substance ★ 1
7　厚 (hòu) thick; profound ★ 4
8　原 (yuán) origin ★ 1
9　厢 (xiāng) wing; carriage ★ 1
10　厦 (shà, xià) tall building ★ 6

28 厶
6　参 (cān, cēn, shēn) to take part in; ginseng ★ 2

29 又
0　又 (yòu) again; in addition ★ 3
2　反 (fǎn) in reverse; contrary to ★ 1
双 (shuāng) pair; both ★ 3
6　变 (biàn) to change ★ 8
取 (qǔ) to obtain; to select ★ 7
受 (shòu) to receive; to accept ★ 1

30 口
2　古 (gǔ) ancient ★ 1
另 (lìng) the other ★ 2
叶 (yè) leaf ★ 4
3　各 (gè) every ★ 1
合 (hé, gě) to combine; whole ★ 1
吉 (jí) lucky ★ 1
同 (tóng, tòng) same; similar; with ★ 1
向 (xiàng) toward; direction ★ 7
4　吹 (chuī) to blow; to play ★ 4
吨 (dūn) ton ★ 4
否 (fǒu, pǐ) to deny; not ★ 2
含 (hán) to contain ★ 5
听 (tīng) to hear ★ 3
5　和 (hé, hè, huó, huò) and; harmony; peace ★ 5
呼 (hū) to breathe out; to call ★ 4
命 (mìng) life; destiny; order ★ 3
味 (wèi) taste ★ 1
周 (zhōu) circumference; all around ★ 7
6　哈 (hā, hǎ, hà) sound of laughter ★ 2
咸 (xián) salty ★ 1
咨 (zī) to consult ★ 7

9
喷 (pēn, pèn) to blow out ★ 1
善 (shàn) virtuous; kind; be good at; be apt to ★ 4
10 嗓 (sǎng) voice; throat ★ 5
13 器 (qì) vessel; instrument ★ 3

31 口
3 团 (tuán) round; group ★ 4
4 围 (wéi) to surround; around ★ 4
5 固 (gù) to become solid; resolutely ★ 5
8 圈 (quān, juàn) to encircle; ring; group ★ 5

32 土
4 坟 (fén) grave ★ 4
坏 (huài) rotten; bad ★ 7
坚 (jiān) hard; resolute ★ 1
均 (jūn) equal; all ★ 3
6 型 (xíng) pattern; model ★ 5
7 埋 (mái, mán) to bury; to complain ★ 5
8 堵 (dǔ) wall; to block ★ 6
基 (jī) foundation ★ 2
培 (péi) to cultivate ★ 8
9 塔 (tǎ) tower ★ 2
10 墓 (mù) grave; tomb ★ 4
11 境 (jìng) boundary; region ★ 7
墙 (qiáng) wall ★ 2
12 增 (zēng) to add; to increase ★ 4

33 士
3 壮 (zhuàng) grand; robust ★ 5
4 声 (shēng) sound; voice ★ 3
7 壶 (hú) jar; pot ★ 1

35 夂
6 复 (fù) to duplicate; to return; to repeat; to recover ★ 2

36 夕
0 夕 (xī) evening ★ 4
5 夜 (yè) night ★ 3
8 够 (gòu) enough ★ 1

37 大
5 奋 (fèn) to strive ★ 3
奇 (jī, qí) odd; strange ★ 1
6 奖 (jiǎng) award; prize ★ 8
类 (lèi) kind; type ★ 1
奏 (zòu) to play music; to report ★ 7
7 套 (tào) set ★ 5
9 奥 (ào) profound; mysterious ★ 8

38 女
3 如 (rú) if; such as ★ 3
4 妒 (dù) jealous ★ 8
妨 (fáng) to obstruct ★ 8
妙 (miào) wonderful, subtle ★ 7
妖 (yāo) evil spirit; bewitching ★ 4
5 始 (shǐ) begin ★ 3
姊 (zǐ) elder sister ★ 3
6 姜 (jiāng) ginger ★ 1
姿 (zī) one's manner ★ 5
7 娱 (yú) pleasure ★ 8
8 婴 (yīng) infant ★ 7
10 嫉 (jí) jealous ★ 8
11 嫩 (nèn) delicate; young ★ 1

39 子
1 孔 (kǒng) opening; surname ★ 3
3 存 (cún) to exist; to survive ★ 2
4 孝 (xiào) filial devotion ★ 8

40 宀
2 宁 (níng, nìng) peaceful; would rather ★ 6
3 守 (shǒu) to defend; to keep watch ★ 4
宅 (zhái) residence ★ 6
4 宋 (sòng) Song dynasty ★ 2
完 (wán) complete; be over ★ 2
5 宝 (bǎo) treasure; precious ★ 2
定 (dìng) to decide ★ 2
官 (guān) official ★ 5
实 (shí) solid; real; fact ★ 3
宜 (yí) suitable ★ 6
6 宫 (gōng) palace ★ 1
宣 (xuān) announce ★ 8
7 害 (hài) harm; to feel ★ 3
宽 (kuān) wide ★ 8
容 (róng) to hold; to tolerate; appearance ★ 3
宵 (xiāo) night ★ 4
宴 (yàn) banquet; feast ★ 2
8 密 (mì) dense; intimate; secret ★ 4
宿 (sù, xiǔ, xiù) to sleep; constellation ★ 1
9 富 (fù) rich; be full of ★ 4
寒 (hán) chilly ★ 3
寓 (yù) to dwell; to imply ★ 2

41 寸
0 寸 (cùn) inch ★ 5
3 导 (dǎo) to lead; to instruct ★ 3
寺 (sì) temple ★ 2
4 寿 (shòu) longevity ★ 4
9 尊 (zūn) to respect ★ 7

42 小
3 当 (dāng, dàng) to undertake; just; proper ★ 1
5 尚 (shàng) still; to value ★ 8
6 尝 (cháng) to taste ★ 6

43 尢 (兀, 尣)
1 尤 (yóu) especially ★ 5
4 尬 (gà) limp; embarrassing; embarrassed ★ 8
10 尴 (gān) embarrassing; embarrassed ★ 8

44 尸
2 尼 (ní) Buddhist nun ★ 4
3 尽 (jìn) exhausted; to the utmost ★ 6
尾 (wěi, yǐ) tail; end ★ 3
9 属 (shǔ, zhǔ) category; to belong to; to combine ★ 1

46 山
3 岁 (suì) age; year ★ 4
屿 (yǔ) island ★ 6
4 岛 (dǎo) island ★ 6
8 崇 (chóng) high; to revere ★ 7

47 川 (巛)
0 川 (chuān) river ★ 1

48 工
3 巧 (qiǎo) skillful ★ 2
7 差 (chā, chà, chāi, cī) to differ ★ 1

49 己
1 巴 (bā) greatly desire ★ 2

50 巾
2 布 (bù) cloth; to announce ★ 5
4 帐 (zhàng) tent; account ★ 1
6 带 (dài) belt; zone; to take; to bring ★ 4
帝 (dì) emperor; god ★ 2
席 (xí) seat ★ 7

51 干
0 干 (gān, gàn) dry; to do ★ 1
2 平 (píng) flat; level; fair; peaceful ★ 1
5 幸 (xìng) fortunately ★ 3

52 幺
0 乡 (xiāng) rural area; village ★ 2
6 幽 (yōu) quiet; dark ★ 8

53 广
3 庆 (qìng) to congratulate, to celebrate ★ 1
4 序 (xù) sequence ★ 3
应 (yīng, yìng) should; to answer ★ 1
5 底 (dǐ) at the end of ★ 2
府 (fǔ) government; prefecture ★ 3
6 废 (fèi) to give up; to discard ★ 8
8 康 (kāng) healthy ★ 5
10 廉 (lián) honorable; cheap ★ 6

54 廴
4 延 (yán) to delay; to prolong ★ 5
6 建 (jiàn) to build; to establish; to propose ★ 1

55 廾
3 异 (yì) different ★ 1
4 弄 (nòng, lòng) to do; alley ★ 7
弃 (qì) to discard ★ 8
6 弈 (yì) to play chess ★ 8

56 弋
3 式 (shì) style ★ 5

57 弓
1 引 (yǐn) to pull, to attract ★ 4
2 弘 (hóng) great; to expand ★ 4
4 张 (zhāng) to stretch; sheet ★ 3
5 弦 (xián) string ★ 3
8 弹 (dàn, tán) to play; bullet ★ 7
9 强 (jiàng, qiáng, qiǎng) strong ★ 3

58 彐 (彐, 彑)
2 归 (guī) to return; to converge ★ 6
3 寻 (xún, xín) to seek ★ 7
4 灵 (líng) clever; spirit ★ 5
15 彝 (yí) Yi nationality; wine vessel ★ 4

59 彡
4 形 (xíng) appearance; form ★ 1
6 须 (xū) must; have to ★ 1
8 彬 (bīn) well-bred ★ 3
彩 (cǎi) colour ★ 4

60 彳
5 彼 (bǐ) that; there; those ★ 3
径 (jìng) path; directly ★ 8
往 (wǎng, wàng) go; formerly; toward ★ 2
征 (zhēng) to invade; sign ★ 1
6 待 (dāi, dài) to treat, to entertain; to wait; to stay ★ 4
律 (lǜ) regulation ★ 5
8 得 (dé, de, děi) to acquire; have to ★ 1
14 徽 (huī) badge ★ 1

61 心 (忄, 小)
1 必 (bì) surely; must ★ 2
忆 (yì) to reflect upon; memory ★ 8
3 忍 (rěn) to endure ★ 8
忘 (wáng, wàng) to forget; to omit ★ 8
志 (zhì) determination; annals ★ 3
4 忽 (hū) suddenly; to neglect ★ 6
态 (tài) form; appearance; condition ★ 8
忧 (yōu) grief ★ 5
5 怪 (guài) peculiar ★ 1
急 (jí) quick; urgent ★ 3
思 (sī) to consider; thought ★ 2
6 恒 (héng) persistent ★ 4
恢 (huī) immense; to restore ★ 5
恋 (liàn) love; to long for ★ 5
虑 (lǜ) concern ★ 8
恼 (nǎo) angry; irritated ★ 4
恰 (qià) be in harmony; to consult ★ 8
7 患 (huàn) to suffer from ★ 5
悉 (xī) entirely; to learn ★ 8
悠 (yōu) distant; leisurely ★ 8
8 悲 (bēi) sorrow ★ 4
惯 (guàn) habit ★ 1
惠 (huì) favour ★ 1
情 (qíng) affection; condition ★ 3
惜 (xī) to cherish; to have pity on ★ 2
9 慈 (cí) kind; loving ★ 8
慨 (kǎi) indignant; generous ★ 8
愉 (yú) joyful; pleased ★ 1
10 慕 (mù) to yearn for; to admire ★ 4
愿 (yuàn) hope; wish; willing ★ 4
11 慧 (huì) intelligent ★ 8
慷 (kāng) generous ★ 8
12 懂 (dǒng) to understand ★ 8
13 懒 (lǎn) lazy ★ 8

62 戈
3 戒 (jiè) to warn; to give up ★ 5
5 战 (zhàn) war; battle ★ 5
6 载 (zǎi, zài) to record; to carry ★ 4
7 戛 (jiá) to tap lightly ★ 8

64 手 (扌)
0 才 (cái) talent; only then ★ 8
1 扎 (zhā, zhá, zā) to tie; to prick; to pitch ★ 7
3 扩 (kuò) to expand ★ 3
扫 (sǎo, sào) to sweep ★ 4
扬 (yáng) to scatter; to raise; to spread ★ 4
执 (zhí) to keep; to carry out ★ 8
4 把 (bǎ, bà) to hold; to guard; to regard as ★ 4
承 (chéng) to hold; to undertake; to continue ★ 8
抗 (kàng) to resist ★ 5
批 (pī) to criticise ★ 8
折 (shé, zhē, zhé) to break off; to bend ★ 1
投 (tóu) to throw; to send ★ 8
找 (zhǎo) to look for; to find ★ 7
抓 (zhuā) to scratch; to clutch ★ 8
5 拜 (bài) to bow ★ 7
拌 (bàn) to mix ★ 1
拨 (bō) to move; to set aside ★ 3

担 (dān, dàn) to carry on a shoulder pole, to undertake ★ 5
拘 (jū) to restrain; to detain ★ 8
拉 (lā, lá) to pull, to drag; to lengthen ★ 4
拥 (yōng) to embrace; crowd ★ 2
择 (zé, zhái) to select ★ 6
招 (zhāo) to beckon; to recruit ★ 2

6 按 (àn) in accordance with ★ 2
持 (chí) to support; to grasp ★ 1
挂 (guà) to hang; to put up ★ 4
挥 (huī) to wave; to wipe away ★ 8
挤 (jǐ) crowd, to squeeze ★ 2
括 (kuò) to include ★ 1
拿 (ná) to grasp; to bring ★ 8
拳 (quán) fist; boxing ★ 5
挑 (tiāo, tiǎo) to select; to carry; to poke ★ 6
指 (zhǐ) finger; to point to ★ 2

7 捅 (tǒng) to poke ★ 8

8 搭 (dā) to add to; to go by ★ 1
掉 (diào) to turn; to drop ★ 1
接 (jiē) to connect ★ 2
捷 (jié) victory; prompt ★ 6
据 (jū, jù) to occupy; to rely on ★ 4
控 (kòng) to accuse; to control ★ 5
描 (miáo) to copy, to sketch ★ 8
排 (pái, pǎi) to arrange; row; line ★ 2
探 (tàn) to search; to visit ★ 3
推 (tuī) to push ★ 7

9 插 (chā) stick into ★ 1

10 搏 (bó) to fight; beat ★ 5
摄 (shè) to absorb ★ 7
摇 (yáo) to shake ★ 8

11 摔 (shuāi) to tumble ★ 4

12 播 (bō) to sow; to broadcast ★ 1

66 攴(攵)
3 改 (gǎi) to change; to improve ★ 5
4 放 (fàng) to put, to release ★ 1
5 故 (gù) ancient; reason ★ 2
政 (zhèng) political affairs ★ 3
6 效 (xiào) effect ★ 3
7 敏 (mǐn) clever; sensitive ★ 5
救 (jiù) to save; to help ★ 5
8 敬 (jìng) to respect ★ 7
10 敲 (qiāo) to tap; to knock ★ 1
12 整 (zhěng) neat; whole ★ 2

68 斗
0 斗 (dǒu, dòu) Chinese peck; to struggle against ★ 3
6 料 (liào) to expect; material, ingredient ★ 1

69 斤
7 断 (duàn) to sever; to interrupt ★ 3
8 斯 (sī) this; then; thus ★ 4

70 方
5 施 (shī) to grant; to carry out ★ 3
7 旋 (xuán, xuàn) to revolve; to return; whirl ★ 6
族 (zú) nationality; group ★ 2
10 旗 (qí) banner; flag ★ 4

71 无
0 无 (wú) none; no; not ★ 3
5 既 (jì) already; since ★ 1

72 日
2 旬 (xún) ten-day period ★ 4
3 旱 (hàn) drought; dry ★ 4
4 昂 (áng) to hold one's head high; soaring ★ 8
旺 (wàng) prosperous ★ 8
易 (yì) to change; easy ★ 4
5 显 (xiǎn) to display ★ 5
映 (yìng) to project; to reflect light ★ 1
6 晕 (yūn, yùn) dizzy ★ 5
8 普 (pǔ) universal; general ★ 2
智 (zhì) wisdom ★ 4
9 暗 (àn) dark; in secret ★ 8

73 曰
2 曲 (qū, qǔ) crooked; wrong; song ★ 7
8 曾 (céng, zēng) once ★ 7
替 (tì) to substitute for ★ 7
最 (zuì) most ★ 4

74 月
7 朗 (lǎng) bright ★ 7
望 (wàng) to hope; to look over ★ 4
8 朝 (cháo, zhāo) facing; dynasty; morning ★ 6

75 木
1 未 (wèi) not yet ★ 4
2 杂 (zá) mixed ★ 7
3 材 (cái) material; ability ★ 1
杆 (gān, gǎn) pole ★ 8
极 (jí) extreme ★ 3
束 (shù) to control; bundle ★ 2
杏 (xìng) apricot ★ 4
4 板 (bǎn) board ★ 7
杭 (háng) short for Hangzhou ★ 2
杰 (jié) hero; outstanding ★ 7
松 (sōng) pine tree; loose; to loosen ★ 2
枣 (zǎo) jujube; Chinese date ★ 4
5 标 (biāo) mark; symbol ★ 6
查 (chá, zhā) to investigate ★ 3
柳 (liǔ) willow ★ 4
某 (mǒu) certain thing or person ★ 7
柔 (róu) soft; gentle ★ 8
柿 (shì) persimmon ★ 1
6 档 (dàng) shelf; frame ★ 7
根 (gēn) root; unit for long thin objects ★ 1
桂 (guì) laurel ★ 2
样 (yàng) pattern; style ★ 1
7 梯 (tī) ladder; stairs ★ 2
桶 (tǒng) bucket ★ 4
8 棒 (bàng) excellent; stick ★ 6
椒 (jiāo) hot spice plant ★ 1
9 楚 (chǔ) clear ★ 3
概 (gài) general; approximate ★ 1
楼 (lóu) building; floor ★ 2
10 模 (mó, mú) standard, pattern; to copy ★ 2
榨 (zhà) to extract juice ★ 1
11 横 (héng, hèng) horizontal; across; harsh and unreasonable ★ 2

76 欠
4 欣 (xīn) delighted ★ 4
8 欺 (qī) to deceive ★ 8
9 歇 (xiē) to have a rest ★ 6

77 止
0 止 (zhǐ) to stop ★ 3
2 此 (cǐ) this; these; in this case ★ 1
4 武 (wǔ) military ★ 3

78 歹
2 死 (sǐ) to die; death ★ 1
6 殊 (shū) special ★ 5
11 毅 (yì) resolute ★ 5

80 毋(母)
3 每 (měi) every; each ★ 1

83 氏
1 民 (mín) people; civilian ★ 2

84 气
4 氛 (fēn) atmosphere ★ 3

85 水(氵,水)
2 汉 (hàn) Chinese people ★ 3
汇 (huì) to gather together ★ 4
求 (qiú) to seek; to request ★ 1
4 泛 (fàn) to float; extensive ★ 1
沟 (gōu) ditch, drain ★ 3
沛 (pèi) abundant ★ 7
沙 (shā) sand ★ 6
汰 (tài) to eliminate ★ 8
5 泪 (lèi) tear ★ 4
泼 (pō) to splash ★ 4
泉 (quán) fountain ★ 6
沿 (yán, yàn) to go along; water's edge ★ 2
油 (yóu) oil; paints ★ 1
沾 (zhān) moisten; to touch ★ 8
治 (zhì) to govern; to regulate; to cure ★ 5
注 (zhù) to focus ★ 3
6 济 (jì) to help; to cross a river ★ 3
浆 (jiāng, jiàng) thick fluid; to starch ★ 1
洁 (jié) clean ★ 6
浏 (liú) clear; swift ★ 8
浓 (nóng) thick; strong ★ 1
洋 (yáng) ocean; foreign; western ★ 3
7 浪 (làng) wave; unrestrained ★ 8
流 (liú) to flow; class ★ 3
消 (xiāo) to die out; to melt away ★ 1
浙 (zhè) short for Zhejiang province ★ 1
8 淡 (dàn) weak; light ★ 1
淀 (diàn) shallow water; precipitate ★ 5
渐 (jiān, jiàn) gradually; to soak ★ 4
清 (qīng) clear; distinct; Qing dynasty ★ 1
深 (shēn) deep; difficult ★ 1
淘 (táo) to wash in sieve; to weed out ★ 6
添 (tiān) to add ★ 1
涯 (yá) shore ★ 4
9 渡 (dù) to cross; to ferry ★ 4
湖 (hú) lake ★ 1
滋 (zī) multiply; to burst ★ 7
10 滨 (bīn) sea coast; river bank ★ 2
滚 (gǔn) to roll; to get away ★ 8
滑 (huá) to slide; slippery ★ 1
溜 (liū, liù) to slide ★ 8
满 (mǎn) to fill; full ★ 6
滩 (tān) beach; shoal ★ 2

11 源 (yuán) source ★ 3
滴 (dī) drip; drop of ★ 1
漏 (lòu) to leak; hourglass ★ 8
漫 (màn) to overflow; everywhere ★ 7
漂 (piāo, piǎo) to float; to breach ★ 4
12 潮 (cháo) tide; damp ★ 3
潜 (qián) to hide; secretly ★ 8
13 激 (jī) to excite; sharp ★ 5

86 火(灬)
3 灸 (jiǔ) moxibustion ★ 5
灾 (zāi) disaster ★ 4
4 炎 (yán) hot; inflammation ★ 5
炼 (liàn) to smelt; to refine ★ 5
6 烦 (fán) trouble ★ 8
烤 (kǎo) to bake; to roast ★ 1
烈 (liè) fiery; violent ★ 6
11 熬 (āo, áo) to boil; to endure ★ 3
熟 (shú) ripe; familiar; skilled ★ 3

89 爻
7 爽 (shuǎng) refreshing ★ 1

90 爿[丬]
6 将 (jiāng, jiàng) will; be going to; general ★ 8

91 片
8 牌 (pái) placard; brand ★ 2

93 牛
4 牧 (mù) to herd ★ 4
特 (tè) special; unique ★ 1

94 犬(犭)
3 状 (zhuàng) shape; certificate ★ 3
6 独 (dú) solitary ★ 1
狱 (yù) prison; case; lawsuit ★ 7
8 猜 (cāi) to guess ★ 4
猎 (liè) to hunt ★ 4
猛 (měng) violent; suddenly ★ 8
9 猴 (hóu) monkey ★ 6
献 (xiàn) to offer; to show ★ 5

96 玉(王)
0 玉 (yù) jade ★ 2
4 玩 (wán) to play with ★ 2
现 (xiàn) to appear; existing ★ 1
5 珍 (zhēn) precious; rare ★ 6
6 班 (bān) class; job ★ 2
珠 (zhū) pearl; bead ★ 2
7 琅 (láng) the sound of reading aloud ★ 6
8 琳 (lín) gem ★ 6
琴 (qín) a general name for certain musical instruments ★ 7

97 瓜
0 瓜 (guā) melon ★ 1
14 瓣 (bàn) clove of ★ 1

99 甘
6 甜 (tián) sweet ★ 1

102 田
0 由 (yóu) reason; from; by ★ 1
4 界 (jiè) boundary; domain ★ 4

103 疋
9 疑 (yí) doubt ★ 8

104 疒

1 瘟 (wēn) epidemic ★ 4
2 疗 (liáo) to cure ★ 5
5 疲 (pí) exhausted ★ 5
　 症 (zhēng, zhèng) disease; illness ★ 5
11 瘾 (yǐn) addiction ★ 8
12 癌 (ái) cancer ★ 5

105 癶

7 登 (dēng) to rise; to climb ★ 4

106 白

0 白 (bái) white; pure ★ 1
4 皆 (jiē) all ★ 6
　 皇 (huáng) imperial; emperor ★ 2

107 皮

0 皮 (pí) skin; fur ★ 1

108 皿

4 盆 (pén) basin ★ 4
5 盐 (yán) salt ★ 1
　 益 (yì) profit; benefit; advantage ★ 3
6 盛 (chéng, shèng) flourishing; to contain; to fill ★ 1
　 盖 (gài) lid; cover ★ 1
　 盘 (pán) dish; to examine; to coil ★ 1
8 盟 (méng) alliance; to take an oath ★ 8

109 目

4 盼 (pàn) to gaze; hope for ★ 4
　 省 (shěng, xǐng) province; to save ★ 2
5 真 (zhēn) real ★ 1
6 着 (zhāo, zháo, zhe, zhuó) to feel ★ 5
12 瞰 (kàn) to overlook ★ 6

111 矢

3 知 (zhī) to know ★ 2
7 短 (duǎn) short; brief ★ 6

112 石

3 矿 (kuàng) mine; ore ★ 5
4 研 (yán) to grind; to research ★ 3
5 础 (chǔ) foundation stone ★ 3
6 硕 (shuò) great; large ★ 3
7 确 (què) certain; real ★ 7
　 硬 (yìng) hard ★ 2
8 碑 (bēi) stone tablet ★ 7
　 碎 (suì) to smash; broken ★ 1
10 磅 (bàng, páng) pound; to weigh ★ 5
11 磨 (mó, mò) to polish; to wear out; mill ★ 8

113 示 (礻)

0 示 (shì) to show ★ 1
3 祀 (sì) to offer sacrifices to gods or the dead ★ 4
4 祈 (qí) to pray ★ 4
5 神 (shén) spirit; god ★ 5
　 祝 (zhù) to express good wishes ★ 1
6 祭 (jì) to offer sacrifices to gods or ancestors ★ 4
　 祥 (xiáng) good luck; happiness ★ 1
7 祸 (huò) misfortune ★ 4
8 禁 (jīn, jìn) to forbid; to prohibit; to ban ★ 4

---

9 福 (fú) happiness; good fortune ★ 1

115 禾

2 私 (sī) private; personal ★ 3
　 秀 (xiù) elegant; excellent ★ 8
4 种 (zhǒng, zhòng) seed; to plant ★ 5
5 秘 (bì, mì) secret; mysterious ★ 5
　 称 (chèn, chēng) be called; to match ★ 1
　 租 (zū) to rent; rent ★ 2
7 稍 (shāo) a little bit ★ 2
9 稳 (wěn) stable; steady ★ 8

116 穴

0 穴 (xué) cave; hole ★ 5
2 究 (jiū) to investigate ★ 3
　 穷 (qióng) poor; limit ★ 7
4 突 (tū) abrupt; to stick out ★ 8
5 窄 (zhǎi) narrow ★ 6

117 立

0 立 (lì) to stand; to establish ★ 4
1 产 (chǎn) to produce; product ★ 1
4 亲 (qīn, qìng) relative; parent ★ 2
　 竖 (shù) vertical; to erect ★ 1
　 竞 (jìng) to compete ★ 4
6 竟 (jìng) eventually; unexpectedly ★ 3
7 童 (tóng) child; virgin ★ 2

118 竹 (⺮)

0 竹 (zhú) bamboo ★ 4
3 竿 (gān) bamboo pole ★ 4
4 笑 (xiào) to smile; to laugh ★ 3
5 符 (fú) symbol; to tally with ★ 8
　 笼 (lóng, lǒng) cage; basket ★ 4
　 笙 (shēng) reed pipe wind instrument ★ 4
6 策 (cè) scheme ★ 6
　 筝 (zhēng) a 21- or 25-stringed plucked instrument ★ 4
　 筑 (zhú, zhù) to build ★ 6
7 筹 (chóu) chip; to plan ★ 7
　 简 (jiǎn) simple ★ 1
　 筷 (kuài) chopsticks ★ 1
8 管 (guǎn) pipe; tube; to manage ★ 5
10 篝 (gōu) bamboo cage ★ 4

119 米

4 粉 (fěn) powder; plaster ★ 5
6 粥 (zhōu) porridge; congee ★ 1
8 精 (jīng) essence; spirit ★ 1
10 糖 (táng) sugar; sweets ★ 1

120 糸 (纟)

1 系 (jì, xì) system; to link ★ 1
3 纤 (xiān, qiàn) delicate; tow line ★ 5
　 约 (yuē) agreement; to invite; about ★ 3
4 纷 (fēn) in disorder ★ 7
　 紧 (jǐn) tense ★ 2
　 纳 (nà) to accept ★ 4
　 素 (sù) plain; element ★ 3
　 纸 (zhǐ) paper ★ 3
5 经 (jīng) to engage in ★ 3
　 累 (léi, lěi, lèi) tired; weary ★ 6
　 细 (xì) tiny ★ 2
　 线 (xiàn) line; thread; string ★ 4
　 绎 (yì) to unravel; to sort out ★ 6

　 织 (zhī) to knit ★ 2
　 终 (zhōng) end; in the end ★ 3
　 组 (zǔ) to organise; group ★ 2
6 给 (gěi, jǐ) to give; for ★ 3
　 绝 (jué) to terminate ★ 6
　 络 (luò) network; to twine ★ 6
　 统 (tǒng) interconnected system; to unite ★ 1
8 绷 (bēng, běng, bèng) to stretch tight; to crack ★ 3
　 维 (wéi) to maintain; thought ★ 5
　 绪 (xù) end of thread; mental or emotional statue ★ 5
　 续 (xù) to continue; to succeed ★ 3
9 编 (biān) to weave; to arrange; to compile ★ 7
　 缓 (huǎn) leisurely; to postpone ★ 3
11 繁 (fán) complicated ★ 7

121 缶

4 缺 (quē) to lack; gap; imperfect ★ 4

122 网 (罒, ⺳)

3 罕 (hǎn) scarce; rare ★ 6
8 置 (zhì) to place; to set up ★ 8

123 羊

5 羞 (xiū) shame; shy ★ 3
7 群 (qún) group; crowd ★ 8

124 羽

11 翼 (yì) wing ★ 7
12 翻 (fān) to turn over; to translate ★ 1

125 老 (耂)

4 者 (zhě) person ★ 3

126 而

0 而 (ér) and then; and yet ★ 1
3 耐 (nài) be able to endure ★ 8

128 耳

5 聊 (liáo) to chat; slightly ★ 6
7 聘 (pìn) to employ ★ 7
8 聚 (jù) to assemble; to collect ★ 4

130 肉 (月)

2 肌 (jī) muscle; flesh ★ 5
3 肠 (cháng) intestines; sausage ★ 5
　 肝 (gān) liver ★ 5
　 肖 (xiāo, xiào) to resemble ★ 8
4 肪 (fáng) animal fat ★ 5
　 肥 (féi) fat; obese; fertile ★ 5
　 肤 (fū) skin ★ 5
5 胆 (dǎn) courage; gall bladder ★ 8
　 胡 (hú) recklessly ★ 6
　 胜 (shèng) victory; wonderful ★ 2
　 胃 (wèi) stomach ★ 1
6 脉 (mài, mò) vein; pulse ★ 5
　 能 (néng) be able to; ability ★ 1
　 脏 (zāng, zàng) organ; dirty ★ 5
　 脂 (zhī) fat; grease ★ 5
7 脸 (liǎn) face ★ 4
　 脱 (tuō) to take off ★ 8
8 腐 (fǔ) to decay; bean curd ★ 1
　 腔 (qiāng) cavity; accent ★ 3
9 腻 (nì) greasy; oily; tired of ★ 1

---

133 至

0 至 (zhì) to reach; extremely ★ 2
4 致 (zhì) to send, to deliver; to cause ★ 5

135 舌

6 舒 (shū) unfold; comfortable ★ 5
7 辞 (cí) to take leave ★ 4

137 舟

4 般 (bān) kind; category ★ 1
　 舫 (fǎng) boat ★ 6
　 航 (háng) boat; to navigate ★ 2
　 舵 (duò) rudder; helm ★ 4
6 艇 (tǐng) small boat ★ 6

139 色

0 色 (sè, shǎi) colour; quality; scene ★ 1

140 艸 (艹)

5 苦 (kǔ) bitter; hardship ★ 3
　 苗 (miáo) young plant; Miao nationality ★ 4
6 荡 (dàng) to swing; pond; to cleanse ★ 4
　 荐 (jiàn) to recommend ★ 7
　 荣 (róng) glory; to prosper ★ 8
　 茱 (zhū) cornel plant ★ 3
7 获 (huò) to obtain; to seize ★ 3
8 菊 (jú) chrysanthemum ★ 4
　 营 (yíng) camp; to operate ★ 1
9 葱 (cōng) spring onion ★ 1
　 落 (là, lào, luò) to fall behind; to lower ★ 3
　 萸 (yú) cornel plant ★ 4
10 蒙 (mēng, méng, měng) to cover; ignorant; Mongolia ★ 4
　 蒜 (suàn) garlic ★ 1
13 薪 (xīn) fuel; salary ★ 7
14 藏 (cáng, zàng) to conceal; to hoard ★ 5

141 虍

2 虎 (hǔ) tiger; vigorous ★ 5
5 虚 (xū) false; in vain ★ 1

142 虫

10 融 (róng) to melt; to fuse; to blend ★ 1

143 血

0 血 (xiě, xuè) blood ★ 5

144 行

10 衡 (héng) to measure; to weigh; to judge ★ 7

145 衣 (衤)

2 补 (bǔ) to mend; to supplement ★ 1
4 衰 (shuāi) to decline; to decrease; to weaken ★ 3
5 被 (bèi) by; bedding ★ 4
　 袖 (xiù) sleeve ★ 8
6 裁 (cái) cut out; to decrease; to check ★ 7
　 装 (zhuāng) clothes; to install ★ 2

146 西 (覀)

3 要 (yāo, yào) to ask; important ★ 1

147 見 [见]

0 见 (jiàn, xiàn) to see ★ 3
2 观 (guān, guàn) to view; appearance ★ 2
4 规 (guī) rule; custom; law ★ 2

---

148 角
0 角 (jiǎo, jué) horn; angle; corner ★4
6 触 (chù) to touch ★5
解 (jiě, jiè, xiè) to loosen; to explain ★1

149 言 [讠] (言)
0 言 (yán) word; to say ★8
2 认 (rèn) to recognise ★2
3 记 (jì) to record; to remember ★1
讨 (tǎo) to discuss; to beg for ★2
议 (yì) opinion; to discuss ★2
4 诀 (jué) to bid farewell; knack ★5
论 (lún, lùn) to discuss; opinion ★1
设 (shè) to set up; to work out ★2
许 (xǔ) permit; to promise ★2
5 评 (píng) to criticise; to evaluate ★3
识 (shí, zhì) to recognise; to remember ★2
诉 (sù) to accuse; to sue; to inform ★3
译 (yì) to translate ★4
证 (zhèng) to confirm; proof ★3
6 诚 (chéng) honest ★7
诗 (shī) poetry; poem ★4
询 (xún) to inquire into; to consult ★7
7 说 (shuì, shuō) to speak; to try to persuade ★4
诱 (yòu) to guide; to entice ★8
8 谈 (tán) to talk; conversation ★3
9 谋 (móu) plan; scheme; to seek ★7
谍 (dié) to spy ★8
谐 (xié) to agree; humorous ★2
谜 (mí) riddle; puzzle ★4
12 谱 (pǔ) chart; to compose ★1

150 谷
0 谷 (gǔ) valley; grain ★4

151 豆
0 豆 (dòu) bean; pea ★1

152 豕
5 象 (xiàng) elephant; image; to resemble ★1
7 豪 (háo) brave; unrestrained ★6

153 豸
7 貌 (mào) appearance ★1

154 貝 [贝]
2 负 (fù) to load; to carry ★6
3 贡 (gòng) tribute ★7
4 败 (bài) be defeated; to fail ★8
责 (zé) responsibility; duty ★7
5 费 (fèi) expenses; to spend; wasteful ★2
贵 (guì) expensive ★8
贸 (mào) trade ★3
贴 (tiē) to stick; to glue ★4
8 赋 (fù) to bestow on; tax ★8
赏 (shǎng) reward; to appreciate ★4
9 赖 (lài) to depend on; to accuse falsely ★8
12 赞 (zàn) to help; to support; praise ★3

156 走
2 赴 (fù) to go to ★8
3 赶 (gǎn) to rush; to pursue; to drive away ★1
起 (qǐ) to stand up; to begin ★2
8 趣 (qù) what attracts one's attention ★4

157 足 (⻊)
4 跃 (yuè) to skip; to jump ★7
5 践 (jiàn) to trample ★7
6 跤 (jiāo) to stumble; to wrestle ★4
8 踏 (tā, tà) to step on ★4
踢 (tī) kick ★5
踪 (zōng) footprints, tracks ★8
12 蹴 (cù) kick; leap; solemn ★4

159 車 [车]
4 轰 (hōng) boom; to blast ★8
软 (ruǎn) soft; flexible ★1
转 (zhuǎn, zhuàn) to shift; to pass on; to rotate ★7
7 辅 (fǔ) to assist ★7
9 辑 (jí) to edit; to compile; volume ★7

160 辛
0 辛 (xīn) bitter; laborious ★5
7 辣 (là) hot; spicy ★1

162 辶
3 迅 (xùn) quick ★3
4 迟 (chí) late; slow ★8
返 (fǎn) to return ★2
还 (hái, huán) still; yet; also; to return ★2
进 (jìn) to make progress, to enter ★1
连 (lián) to join; continuous; even ★1
5 迪 (dí) to enlighten; to guide ★6
述 (shù) to narrate; to state ★3
6 逅 (hòu) to meet by chance ★8
迹 (jī) trace, remains ★2
迷 (mí) to enchant; fan ★8
逆 (nì) contrary; traitor ★8
适 (shì) to pursue; appropriate ★1
退 (tuì) to retreat; to withdraw ★7
选 (xuǎn) to choose; selections ★6
追 (zhuī) to pursue; to recall ★4
7 逛 (guàng) to stroll ★4
逝 (shì) to die ★4
速 (sù) quick; prompt ★3
通 (tōng, tòng) to pass through; common; to communicate ★2
途 (tú) path; journey; course ★1
造 (zào) to create ★3
逐 (zhú) to chase; one by one ★4
9 遍 (biàn) everywhere ★2
遗 (wèi, yí) to lose; to omit; to leave behind ★2
遇 (yù) to encounter ★7
13 避 (bì) to avoid ★2
邂 (xiè) to meet by chance ★8
邀 (yāo) to invite; to intercept ★8

163 邑 (⻏)
4 邪 (xié) evil; perverse ★4

164 酉
3 配 (pèi) to go with; match ★1
6 酬 (chóu) to toast; to reward ★7
酱 (jiàng) jam; sauce ★1
7 酷 (kù) cool ★8
8 酸 (suān) sour; acid ★1
醋 (cù) vinegar; jealousy ★1
9 醒 (xǐng) to wake up ★7

165 采
1 采 (cǎi, cài) to adopt; to pick ★4

166 里
2 重 (chóng, zhòng) heavy; to repeat ★1
4 野 (yě) wilderness; wild ★6
5 量 (liáng, liàng) to measure, quantity ★1

167 金 [钅] (釒)
0 金 (jīn) gold; metals in general ★8
2 针 (zhēn) needle; acupuncture ★1
钉 (dīng, dìng) nail; to sew on ★2
4 钙 (gài) calcium ★1
钢 (gāng, gàng) steel; to sharpen ★7
锋 (fēng) sharp point of a sword ★8
锅 (guō) pan; wok ★1
铺 (pū, pù) shop; bed; to pave ★2
锐 (ruì) sharp ★7
销 (xiāo) to fuse; to sell ★7
8 锣 (luó) gong ★4
9 锻 (duàn) to forge metal ★5
10 镇 (zhèn) town; calm; to suppress ★1

169 門 (门)
2 闪 (shǎn) to flash; to evade ★4
4 闲 (xián) idle time ★5
5 闹 (nào) noisy; to make ★3

170 阜 (⻖)
4 防 (fáng) to defend; to prevent ★5
阴 (yīn) 'female' principle; dark; secret ★3
5 阿 (ā, ē) (used for vowel sound in foreign words) ★6
陈 (chén) to exhibit; to plead ★6
附 (fù) to adhere to; near to ★7
陆 (liù, lù) continental ★8
6 降 (jiàng, xiáng) to descend; to subdue ★4
陌 (mò) footpath between rice fields ★8
限 (xiàn) boundary; limit ★8
7 除 (chú) to eliminate; except ★2
险 (xiǎn) narrow pass; danger ★8
8 陶 (táo) ceramics ★3
9 隆 (lōng, lóng) plentiful; grand ★4
随 (suí) to follow ★3
隐 (yǐn) to hide; secret ★3
10 隔 (gé) to separate; to partition ★2

172 隹
3 雀 (qiǎo, què) sparrow ★6
4 雇 (gù) to employ ★7
集 (jí) to gather together ★3
雄 (xióng) male; grand; powerful ★4
雁 (yàn) wild goose ★2

173 雨
6 需 (xū) need; requirement ★4
13 露 (lòu, lù) dew; to reveal ★6

174 青
6 静 (jìng) quiet ★5

175 非
7 靠 (kào) to depend on; near ★5

177 革
8 鞠 (jū) rear; to bring up ★4

181 頁 (页)
3 顺 (shùn) in sequence; along ★3
项 (xiàng) neck; sum ★7
4 顾 (gù) to look back; to look after ★1
5 领 (lǐng) collar; to guide; to lead ★3
7 频 (pín) frequently ★8
颖 (yǐng) sharp point; clever ★8
9 题 (tí) title; to inscribe ★5

184 食 [饣] (飠)
0 食 (shí, sì) to eat; food ★1
4 饮 (yǐn, yìn) to drink ★1
5 饰 (shì) to decorate ★2
饱 (bǎo) to eat one's fill ★1
6 饺 (jiǎo) dumpling ★1
11 馒 (mán) steamed bread ★1

185 首
0 首 (shǒu) head; first; leader ★1

187 馬 [马]
4 驱 (qū) to drive away; to expel ★4
6 骄 (jiāo) haughty ★8
7 验 (yàn) to examine ★5
9 骗 (piàn) to swindle ★5
14 骤 (zhòu) to trot; sudden ★1

194 鬼
0 鬼 (guǐ) ghost ★4
5 魅 (mèi) evil spirit; demon ★8
11 魔 (mó) devil; magic power ★4

196 鳥 [鸟]
0 鸟 (niǎo) bird ★6

199 麦
0 麦 (mài) wheat; barley ★1

200 麻
0 麻 (má) hemp; sesame; to numb ★1

201 黄
0 黄 (huáng) yellow ★1

202 黍
3 黎 (lí) numerous; Li nationality ★4

203 黑
4 默 (mò) silent ★8

207 鼓
0 鼓 (gǔ) drum; to rouse ★4

录音目录

The recordings on the Audio CD are indicated in the Student's Book with the following listening symbol: 🔊